Venturing Abroad
International
Business Expansion
Via Joint Ventures

Jack Enen, Jr.

LIBERTY HALL
PRESS™

LIBERTY HALL PRESS books are published by LIBERTY HALL PRESS, an imprint of McGraw-Hill, Inc. Its trademark, consisting of the words "LIBERTY HALL PRESS" and the portrayal of Benjamin Franklin, is registered in the United States Patent and Trademark Office.

FIRST EDITION
FIRST PRINTING

© 1991 by LIBERTY HALL PRESS, an imprint of McGraw-Hill, Inc.

Library of Congress Cataloging-in-Publication Data

Enen, Jack.
Venturing abroad : international business expansion via joint ventures / by Jack Enen, Jr.
p.   cm.
ISBN 0-8306-8653-3
1. Joint ventures—Handbooks, manuals, etc.   2. Export credit--United States—Handbooks, manuals, etc.   3. Small business--Management—United States—Handbooks, manuals, etc.   I. Title.
HD62.47.E54   1990
658'.049—dc20   90-36761
                                                                CIP

For information about other McGraw-Hill materials, call 1-800-2-McGraw in the U.S. In other countries, call your nearest McGraw-Hill office.

Questions regarding the content of this book should be addressed to:

Reader Inquiry Branch
LIBERTY HALL PRESS
Blue Ridge Summit, PA 17294-0850

Vice President and Editorial Director: David J. Conti
Book Editor: Susan L. Rockwell
Production: Katherine G. Brown
Book Design: Jaclyn J. Boone

Contents

Introduction

The new borderless global economy presents many exciting challenges and opportunities for businesses. Business expansion in the competitive world of the 1990s will require increased opportunity recognition, creative marketing, countertrade, and joint venturing. We must implement these skills in overseas business development to sustain and improve our standard of living.

Virtually all small-to-medium-size businesses in the United States manufacture products or offer services that are exportable, yet only about 15–20% are estimated to be involved in international trade. It is believed that for each one percent increase in exports multitudes of new quality jobs are produced in the United States.

Venturing Abroad was written to encourage and show businesses how to take advantage of overseas expansion opportunities. The book focuses on the joint venture as the essential vehicle for international growth in the 1990s.

Strategic international business planning and implementation begins with overseas selling. With joint ventures, selling leads into assembling and manufacturing operations. For decades, export and overseas strategic alliances have been considered gravy on domestic sales, but in this new global economy alliances are vital for United States companies to survive in the 21st century.

The first three chapters address the changing world, its effect on future global business strategy, and profitable business competition. This is a decade of sharing, and joint venturing will be a tool for international business expansion that employs SAM (sell-assembly-manufacture) strategy.

Chapters 3, 4, and 5 look into important aspects of overseas business development such as the selection of your partner, international joint venture management, control, return on your investment, and the structure and checkpoints of an agreement.

The next group of chapters—6, 7, and 8—detail an overseas joint venture with a list of factors to consider including antitrust information. This section also offers insight and guidance to financing overseas trade and joint ventures.

Politics and economics are inseparable in international trade. Chapters 9, 10, and 11 examine how the United States government through foreign aid administration can help small-to-medium-size business to establish joint ventures abroad. What you should do when dealing with foreign corrupt practices will also be discussed. The dynamic European 1992 alliance and its incentives for locating inside of Europe are examined.

The final chapters—12, 13, and 14—focus on Eastern Europe as a new home for joint ventures. Fast-paced events in the development of these new, free economies, including the Soviet Union, provide exciting overseas business opportunities.

The world is your oyster. United States businesses are armed with technology and know-how and are ready to begin waging an international commercial war. This new conflict should not be fought with barriers to free trade, but with a head-on competitive spirit that is a part of American heritage and tradition. Manufacturing and service industries in America have the leading edge to win the battles in the globalized economy.

There are many vital issues before the United States Congress, the president, and the American people. The national deficit, the foreign trade deficit, educational reform, drug prevention and cure, medical services, and environmental protection are major problems that need immediate attention. Solutions require tremendous financial resources that can only be generated by increasing the wealth of America and raising the output of gross national product. Our manufacturing base, currently in decline, must be increased. We must venture abroad with the Yankee trader spirit in search of new alliances to improve market share, expand businesses, and raise standards of living for all peoples around the globe.

The ideas, principles, and experiences outlined in *Venturing Abroad* will motivate and assist you in meeting the urgent challenge. If these overseas alliances are neglected, the United States could suffer a serious decline in world economic and political status by the end of this decade. *Venturing Abroad* can define the immediate challenge of expansion and offer clear solutions, but only you can implement international business development principles.

1

A World Economy

CHANGES THROUGHOUT THE WORLD ARE OPENING NEW OPPORTUNITIES FOR business expansion. How can you participate and profit from these new and exciting world events? Learn to improve market share, to increase jobs in America by forming international strategic alliances, and to secure your economic future by effectively competing in the globalized economy.

MEETING AND RECOGNIZING THE OPPORTUNITY

International business development considerations must be as dynamic and flexible as our rapidly changing world. Managers of small-to-mid-sized businesses must be able to understand, and more importantly, recognize new opportunities and employ flexible approaches to the global market. Consumers in overseas client markets have the same needs as those in the United States. In the 1990s, there will be more demands upon business to include local content in products supplied in client nations. America is no longer the only place in the world to do business. You must think about the rest of the world if you are to survive and profit.

The foreign trade deficit continues to be a drain on the United States. For the first eight months of 1989, the deficit averaged $9.2 billion. Of that amount, imports of foreign oil amounted to 43 percent (or approximately $4 billion). Our appetite for foreign-made products and overseas oil continues to place a burden on the United States economy. If the American public would encourage congress and the president to pass legislation favorable to domestic oil production it would have a major impact on reducing the foreign trade deficit. The recent invasion by Iraq into Kuwait has greatly amplified this problem. Increasing oil prices take needed capital out of the United States economy as we increase our foreign trade deficit by importing more and more expensive foreign oil. In addition, small-to-medium-size companies should enter international markets to keep America's economy healthy.

THE EFFECT OF COMMUNICATION

High-tech transportation and modern communications have altered the way goods and services are marketed in our borderless economy. The minicam and satellite communications have changed economic and political policies in the world by visually alerting people to the wonders of freedom and democracy. New technology from western democracies has had a profound effect on economic reform. Television images of democratic protests in China, Poland, and East Germany had a powerful effect on the changes that have occurred in Czechoslovakia, Romania, Bulgaria, and elsewhere. Romania, in its futile efforts to crush the reform movement, closed its borders to the media in an attempt to conceal its brutality, but underestimated the quest of its people.

Information, as a product, will have a significant effect on world commerce in the last decade of this century. Today, via satellite, information for courses can be transmitted to teachers in remote villages. Tapping into databases via satellite has made information-sharing possible between developed and undeveloped countries. In the future, competition will be among global companies; not among countries.

IMPORTANT CHANGES IN WEST AND EAST EUROPE

Political reform is dynamic in Eastern Europe. Movement toward more political freedom must be in concert with economic freedom. Marxist and Leninist philosophies have failed in the marketplace. Shortages of food and consumer goods abound in Soviet-dominated countries of Eastern Europe and in less developed countries of the world. As the quest for political freedom intensifies, opportunities to establish free economies are born.

Events since the middle of 1989 in Eastern Europe have rapidly transformed politics and economics of the region. The United States government and Eastern European countries are encouraging economic development by joint ventures. The transformation from 40 years of communistic thinking and state planning will not be accomplished easily. The people will have to make great personal sacrifices.

MERGING RESOURCES

Population increases accelerate the demand for more and more quality jobs. Developing countries around the world have important natural resources such as labor, raw materials, and expanding markets. They need the resources of technology, know-how, marketing, and management expertise that abounds in American companies. Somehow, these resources need to be merged to maximize business opportunity, develop resources, expand exports, and create more quality jobs—in the United States and other countries. The joint venture is an excellent way to merge these resources and to accelerate economic development in each country.

In support of their overseas partners, many United States companies retain a meaningful market share by manufacturing a substantial percentage of the parts needed to finish their products at overseas locations. It is common for a company who has exported finished products to ship United States parts to the host country for the assembly and start-up technology that needs local labor. This type of manufacturing increases the labor and raw materials for the host country and, thereby, improves local market share to approximately 40% for the United States and 60% local.

CREATIVE COMPETITION

Our able competitors, the industrialized European economic community and Japan, are formidable marketing foes in the global economy. They have been trading for centuries using *countertrade* or *barter*, a marketing technique where something is exchanged for something else of value that ultimately can be sold. Financing joint ventures with countertrade will become more common in the coming decade, especially in dealings with Eastern Europe and the Soviet Union. If we are to retain a dominant trading position in the new global economy, the United States must become more proficient in employing this strategy.

With rising nationalism and unstable economies, traditional markets will strive even more to employ their resources in combination with industrialized know-how. They have the brawn, and America has the brains. This new decade will test our ability to think for a living and to recognize and develop opportunities.

THE SAM STRATEGY AND OTHER CONSIDERATIONS

The overseas sales-to-assembly-to-manufacture (SAM) strategy is an essential step to gain sales experience in international markets.

Choosing an overseas business associate, representative, or partner is the most significant decision that you might make in overseas trade. Each individual's expectations are analyzed with clear, initial understandings, in writing, to avoid future conflicts and dissolutions.

The written agreement is the road map of the joint venture. It provides the objectives of each partner and the means to achieve them within the expectations of all the partners. A United States Department of Commerce checklist can be used by counsel to prepare these important documents for both the joint venture and the licensing of technology.

Conducting profitable international operations today depends on the availability of competitive financing. The trade merchant bank can offer diversified financial support in the form of pre-shipment working capital. Other sources include letters of credit and countertrade.

The Foreign Corrupt Practices Act says, in terms that everyone can understand, that bribing a foreign government official can result in a serious United States federal penalty.

NATIONS ARE MERGED

America is ceasing to exist as a system of production and exchange separate from the rest of the world. The United States has become an economic unit where technologies, investments, and savings move effortlessly across borders without individual nations controlling their destinies. Each of the 186 nations in the world possess resources that are fundamental to each nation's economic well being. In some cases, the resource is labor only. In other countries its resources might include raw materials and various specified skills. Whatever the resource, in a free-market economy, capital will move in the direction of its most efficient employment. Multinational corporations abide by this principle.

HOW SECURE IS YOUR JOB?

You might ask how important is it that all Americans understand this new world economy? American jobs are at stake. You might feel that only the large multinational corporations are involved in international trade. Consider the proprietor of a small, single family-owned drugstore around the corner. The owner is equally involved in the new global economy, and yet, might not be aware of it. The drug store might sell Hamilton—American-made wrist watches. His competitor down the street or in the shopping mall sells Seiko—Japanese-made watches. Therefore, the price the Hamilton owner can charge, and subsequently, the gross profit he can earn is challenged by the imported model sold by his competitor. While the druggist might not be aware of his situation, he is in the center of global economics.

The days of simply exporting to overseas markets from American shores is disappearing in light of the substantial trading blocs that are developing in East and West Europe and the Pacific Rim. The Berlin Wall is down. Brandenburg Gate in the center of Berlin was opened late December of 1989. Poland, Hungary, East Germany, Bulgaria, Czechoslovakia, and Romania are reforming their political systems. The message from Eastern Europe is a call for assistance from the West. As the Solidarity leader of Poland, Lech Walesa, pointed out during his November 1989 trip to the United States, Poland is not asking for charity but partnerships with investors. This means joint ventures will create jobs both in the East and the West.

CAPITAL WILL FOLLOW OPPORTUNITY

New technologies of worldwide communication and information transfers and transportation have reconstructed world markets. American industries based in the United States can no longer simply rely on a long-term strategy of exporting products abroad to compete with Japanese or European companies. The MultiNational Corporation (MNC), headquartered in the United States, which has production facilities in Trinidad and a sales and marketing force in London and Rio de Janeiro, now competes with other similar globalized corporations that are in search of large economies, reduced labor costs, and high productivity.

Due to the integration of the American worker into the global economy, that includes Eastern Europe, Asia, Western Europe, and Africa, corporations can relocate their production facilities. Many apparel companies prepare patterns in the United States but fly the pieces to Pacific Rim, Mexico, or the Caribbean Basin for sewing. World politics, as well as economics, has a dynamic effect on the global economy. For example, many firms in the Pacific Rim are shifting locations from Taiwan to the Caribbean Basin. They are concerned about the ramifications of Hong Kong in 1997 as a result of the events in June 1989 at Tiananmen Square in Beijing. These companies are also concerned about rising prices and the appreciation of currencies in the Orient. Alternatives to the Pacific Rim are being sought. In addition to apparent political considerations, there are economic reasons also. For example, labor rates in Trinidad and Tobago are the equivalent to $1.00 to $1.50 per hour in the U.S. Rising costs in Asia, tightening American quotas for Asian imports, and gaining access to United States markets through the Caribbean Basin Initiative provide stimulus for Taiwan industrial relocation.

The global competitiveness of workers does not necessarily depend on the success of a corporation or industry, but rather on what job function they perform within the global economy. The services of a Chrysler executive are more highly valued in the world market than the Chrysler production worker. The welder in Detroit at Ford competes with a welder in Korea for his wage scale, not his counterpart at GM. As new markets open, especially in Eastern Europe, these wage differentials will have an effect on worldwide living standards. United States small-to-medium-size business, through joint venture in global markets, may offset this disturbing trend.

SYMBOLIC-ANALYTIC JOBS GROWING

Symbolic-analytic jobs are based on the manipulation of information: data, words, and visual symbols. People such as management consultants, lawyers, writers, real estate developers, investment bankers, scientists, trade merchant bankers, public-relations executives, teachers, stock brokers, merger and acquisition specialists, leveraged buyout brokers, engineers, marketing managers, advertising executives, painters, artists, television directors and producers, editors, etc. are engaged in symbolic analysis. Some of the functions they perform focus on discovering ways to efficiently employ resources and placing financial assets for highest efficiency. The main thrust is in saving time and energy. In the performance of analytical, design, or strategic planning functions, they work independently or in small meetings. As an example, the man using his cellular car phone while driving his car, is probably a symbolic analyst, who is making a deal or giving advice to someone about how to do something more efficiently, or maybe, he is simply closing a transaction. Symbolic analysts in the United States are the most skilled, and therefore, the most effective in the world at this moment in time. This category of America's work force is thinking for a living by creating opportunities.

In a world of instant communication and high technology, symbolic analysts of the United States work force will be invaluable in providing the knowledge and skills for small- to medium-size business desiring to enter the global economy. Symbolic analysis is estimated by many to account for more than 40% of the gross national product, and almost 20% of the jobs in the United States. Symbolic analytic jobs have been increasing at three times the rate of total employment in manufacturing.

When you read employment statistics, note the increases or decreases by category to develop an understanding of where wealth is being created in America. You will notice a gradual decline in basic manufacturing and construction. Manufacturing and high per-unit productivity are the primary contributors to the gross national product or wealth in America. A constant decline of employment of Americans should be considered an alarming statistic, if it persists over a long period of time. This statistic is a red flag signaling the need for all United States businesses to improve market share, hence corporate growth by entering the global marketplace.

ROUTINE PRODUCTION JOBS IN TROUBLE

This category of United States employment involves jobs with repetitive tasks, such as one of many steps in a process leading up to a finished product. Manufacturing jobs in auto plants, bakeries, and computer assembly lines are traditional examples of this category. With high-tech computer software and information storage systems, repetitive production jobs are now found in banks, retailing, wholesaling, health care, telephone operations, bill collecting, etc. These industries employ people who spend all day in front of CRTs processing information. In the global economy, American employees that earn their living in this sector of the economy have found that immigrants and foreign workers that are in the

United States often are willing to do the same repetitive work for a much reduced pay scale.

This segment of our work force will be the most mobile in the 1990s decade. Regeneration of opportunities such as international joint venturing and new start-ups will provide most new jobs in production. America's flexible and adaptable free enterprise system, if it continues to operate without government interference, will provide new and exciting opportunities as superfluous activities and jobs expire.

ROUTINE PERSONAL JOBS ARE HOLDING

Unlike routine production services, skillful personal services focus on working with other people as opposed to working with raw materials or computer terminals. Categories of this type of American worker may include paralegals, home health aids, medical assistants, financial services salespeople, day care workers, medical secretaries, beauticians, travel agencies, receptionists, food counterhelp, cab drivers, therapy assistants, consultants, travel agents, and sales professionals in department stores. These three categories—symbolic analysis, routine production services, and routine personal services—account for about 75 percent of the work force in America. The other 25 percent of the nation's work force consists of mainly government employees. These would include teachers, utility workers, defense system engineers, mayors, city council members, post office personnel, etc. With the exception of the defense contractor, most of these jobs are not affected by the global economy. Each worker in the three main job categories, however, is in a unique and competitive position in the new world economic order, and significant employment of the American labor force in global terms is a must for positive growth in the United States economy. Maintaining current high employment rates in the face of growing foreign competition will mandate that the small- to medium-size businesses need to focus more on international growth opportunities.

INTEGRATION INTO THE GLOBAL ECONOMY

Market changes the past few years have virtually placed all United States businesses in the global economy by competing with foreign-made products and services. Even the smallest American merchant is in international trade if he sells a product. American-made cookies in one shop may compete with the Danish-made cookies in a shop down the street or around the corner. It is critical to have an understanding of the globalized, borderless economy and its impact on American jobs. Newspapers weekly report layoffs around the country. The loss of a single American job should be dramatic enough for serious concern. But it's not one job that you often read about, it is hundreds, and in some cases thousands. It's not all happening in one day, it is creeping up slowly on America's conscience.

America's work force is competing with productivity, quality, and price of foreign products produced by overseas labor. The Bureau of Labor statistics projects that the rate of increase of United States jobs in the 1990s will be about 15 percent; half the rate for the 1980s. Restructuring of the economy is dividing the labor force between the service industries and knowledge industries. Integration into the world economy through joint venturing is essential for the coming decade.

The Texas Department of Commerce says that of the eligible companies in Texas with exportable products, only 20 percent are engaged in international trade. The positive note is that an increase of just 5 percent in these statistics means 50,000 new quality jobs in the state. Many say the national statistic is more devastating than in Texas. The cited percentage increase relates only to exports that could be dramatically increased by using the principles set forth in this book.

In the 1950s and through much of the 1970s, American products and services were somewhat proprietary in world markets. Today, and more so in the decade leading into the 21st century, America has formidable and competent marketing foes. United States business must be creative, flexible, and adaptable to meet the challenge of this overseas competition.

If the joint venture option is included in your international marketing kit, it will be useful when you hear an Indonesian buyer say, "Well, your Japanese competitor assembles a product similar to yours in Palambang and the import duty for your product into our country is now 400 percent." With the joint venture option researched and close at hand, you can confidently respond, "It is our corporate philosophy to have a local partner to assist us to involve local resources, such as Indonesian labor and raw materials, in the production of goods in the country where we market our products. We were considering setting up our production facility in Djakarta."

THE NEED TO BE ADAPTABLE AND FLEXIBLE

With this understanding of the merger of the United States economy with the global economy and market, and the competitive position of the three functional job categories in international terms, formation of joint ventures can be a dramatically successful tool in integrating economies, and thus, increasing employment of the work force. Developing countries including Eastern Europe, represent a growing industrial and consumer market. Unlimited opportunity exists for United States business to expand into these geographic areas with joint ventures that will expand United States market share and thereby create quality jobs in all the earlier categories.

The trend toward joint ventures is illustrated in the Soviet Union. The number of concluded joint ventures with noncommunist nations as of January 1987, were 23; as of February 1989, 256; as of August 1989, 722; and as of October 1989, 936, even though only 33 percent were in operation.

IF WE DON'T SELL, THEY WILL

It was distressing in the late 1970s and early 1980s to observe the economic damage that politicians and trade embargos can do to the United States economy. The Russians were getting bids for equipment to construct a natural gas pipeline from Eastern into Western Europe. Caterpillar Tractor Company was close to being awarded the contract to furnish much of the heavy machinery for the project. For political reasons, the President of the United States halted the sale. Capital and American jobs went to Komatsu Heavy Duty Machinery Division in Japan, a company, strangely enough, licensed by Caterpillar to produce comparable equipment. Caterpillar in the United States had to lay off American workers due to the loss of the sale to their competent, foreign licensee with a comparable product. About this same time, a Saudi prince commented in Abqaig that America should focus on exporting its products, not its morals.

In today's world and in the coming new century, the United States now finds that it is no longer the sole or proprietary supplier of a majority of needed goods in the world economy. America is in a very competitive world economy. Any product, other than those that directly affect national security, should be exportable. Anytime we deny United States industry the right to export through sanctions or embargos in this and future decades, that void will be quickly filled by international competition. The government must be certain that such action will be beneficial to the security interests of the country because there will be a cost to the United States of wealth and jobs.

TOO MUCH EMPHASIS ON QUARTERLY RESULTS

Americans can learn overseas marketing and joint venturing from each other and from capable foreign competition. There is much to be learned from the Japanese since their rise from the ashes of WWII. What they have achieved has occurred through an understanding and implementation of strategic planning. An alarming trend is apparent in the United States. Corporate concentration focuses on profits today, or in the next quarter. Mr. Akio Morita, Chairman of the SONY Corporation, said in the fall of 1989 on a United States morning news program, "American business is shortsighted and focusing too much on the bottom line. They need to invest more for the future through market expansion and research and development. And sometimes, it seems the American worker is treated as a tool to be used for profits." While these statements accurately reflect a noticeable trend in United States, think about this point. What could American industries achieve in product development and overseas business expansion if long-term capital costs in the United States were equal to the 3 percent capital cost in Japan?

In January 1990, the National Science Foundation announced that corporate funding for basic research in America is down for the first time in 14 years. Spending on applied research, the effort to bring new products to market, was slightly up, but investment in basic research, the essence of innovation, was down. They cite many reasons such as debt service created in leveraged buy-outs, interest rates, and the need to make short term profits to keep investors happy. If this is the beginning of a trend, it could spell long-term trouble in the United States. Innovation would become the province of other nations. Technology has been America's leading edge in the global economy.

The best way to encourage research is to provide long term tax incentives and to lower costs of capital and debt. Lower interest rates and higher savings rates require taking serious steps to reduce the national deficit. American industry must continue with basic research if this nation is to support the present-day standard of living for every American.

United States workers and industry are, after all, competing for markets and customers with other nations that almost invariably save more and invest more than we do. One reason for their doing so is that many countries are far more patient than we Americans about investing for the future. They adhere to long-term investment horizons. In the U.S., especially, the managers of large institutional pools of capital, such as pension funds, are goaded continually to produce short-term performance goals.

United States senate hearings during 1989 suggested some managers of such funds are addicted to short-term profits and quarterly performance gains. Often the fund managers are appraised on—and compensated for—their alacrity in cashing in for a quick buck rather than holding on for the long pull. Quite obviously, such a strategy can discourage publicly held companies from major financial commitments to enhance long-term productivity and innovation. Research and development investments rarely, if ever, pay off in the following quarter, but in today's competitive world economy, we must treat such an investment as a fault and not a virtue. Investment in export sales and joint venture development must be for the long haul; there are no quick bucks in exports or joint venture formulations.

Most recent estimates of return on investments from joint venturing in the Soviet Union is two to ten years. American small- to medium-size business must consider long-term international partnerships and/or joint ventures as vital to increasing market share for American product. However, sales of completed goods overseas from your United States location should precede consideration of joint venture in international locations. Due to the importance of this fact, about a third of this book is devoted to selling in international markets. The message in this book is: open your eyes to the new and dynamic international opportunities in a world that is experiencing exciting democratic revolutions and change; if you are not in export, get involved in selling in the globalized economy; if you are exporting, seriously consider the overseas joint venture as an option to expand market share, and to create the need for more production—the requisite for hiring more employees.

2

International
Joint Venture

THE J. PAUL GETTY PHILOSOPHY

MR. J. PAUL GETTY, WHO FOUNDED THE GETTY OIL COMPANY, AMASSED A GREAT fortune in his lifetime abiding by many sound principles, one among which we may apply to our consideration of joint ventures. Getty said as follows, "I'd rather have a 1 percent interest in each of 100 producing oilwells than 100 percent interest in a single dry hole." He recognized that risks should be spread to provide insulation from a single misfortune. Another geologist put it another way, "Don't fall in love with a single prospect, always spread your risks." What is true in searching for hydrocarbons, a truly high-risk business, is also true in developing international trade. Don't bet the farm on a single prospect, a sale, or venture.

Lee of General Dynamics also recognizes—even though his 40 percent interest in a proposed Japanese joint venture will provide as much cash flow as the off-the-shelf sales—that a real possibility existed for the Japanese to turn to Israel, Italy, France, or the United Kingdom for similar technology in a joint venture. Precluding that event, 40 percent of something is infinitely more valuable than 100 percent of nothing. Embargos that have haunted United States commercial enterprises in the past are now, thankfully, ineffectual and should remain in the past. The joint venture permits business development opportunity through partnerships in which each can meet the needs of his or her country as well as the needs of the enterprise.

The joint venture may be premature for your business at this time, but it should be in your tool box of international business development options. A competitor might catch you asleep at the switch and capture a significant market by closing a border if you are not aware of his actions and your options. Retention and probable expansion of market share is desirable from a minority interest position where the possibility of compensating volume increases are real. And, you want to avoid, if at all possible, the market shut-out by the more aggressive competitor who instigates joint venture manufacturing inside a country where you are currently trading. Keep the joint venture option open and ready to use when periodic market analysis or competitive forces dictate. In fact, there is considerable mileage to be gained from offering joint ventures well in advance of waiting until they become mandatory.

RETAIN AND EXPAND PRESENT MARKET SHARE

As we enter the 1990s and beyond, the economic and political climates in less developed nations will be under seige from continued population growth. This expansion will place increased demand on the marketplace for food, jobs, consumer goods, and services. Foreign exchange, needed for imports, will continue to be in short supply as overseas debt remains. A renewed spirit of nationalism will emerge as leaders look for industries to locate in their countries to convert indigenous labor and other natural resources into products for exports to generate foreign exchange, and for goods and services for local consumption.

Countries with natural resources and labor see their future prosperity as the development of their industrial, agricultural, and service sectors within their country with outside assistance and technology from developed nations. They must attract this technology, know-how, and industry to employ their resources to survive the next century. It is evident that most, if not all countries have recognized this important fact. Everchanging laws and increasingly nationalistic feelings in the developing countries and other nations make it more difficult to simply sell the finished product into these countries. Many small- to medium-size United States companies today export a considerable volume of business into most of these countries. Market share, in some cases has long been established. However, as conditions change and competition from other developed countries arrives on the scene, United States companies increasingly will be advised to consider joint ventures with their domestic counterparts to preserve and increase market share. Adding local content to imported components increases market acceptability and overall sales volume.

As a minimum gain from your new partnership, you eliminate the possibility of a market shut-out caused by competitive forces setting up shop in your marketplace. Countries that have locally assembled or manufactured goods will place such items on a prohibited import list or subject them to unreasonable tariff protection. Changing competitive market strategies will make it imperative that you remain alert to this possibility.

If you are doing business in a country from your United States facility, you will certainly enhance your potential for future growth and expansion of market share with a joint venture in the host country. Present markets will be protected and a firm basis for long-term expansion will have been defined. Some individually owned and managed small- to mid-sized companies feel that an overseas joint venture is a give-away of their work and will cause job loss in their community. This thinking must give way to a deeper understanding of the new, integrated global economy. Experience, facts, arguments, and actual cases set out in this text will provide a greater understanding of the need to partner-to-win in international markets in this decade and beyond.

In some markets such as in Europe, by 1992, it will be a necessity, not an option, that you have a physical presence in the common market for product certification on European soil.

OPEN NEW SALES OPPORTUNITIES

While it is relatively uncommon, a joint venture can be used to open new markets. For example, a specific market can be closed to imports due to local manufacture of a product competitive to yours. The only solution to tap this market is to install your assembly or manufacturing operation inside the country to compete for market share. This decision is dictated by many factors to be discussed later in this book, but essentially the size of the market and income potential govern this consideration.

New technology or business diversification can lend itself to a joint venture arrangement when earlier such considerations were impractical. Breakthroughs in manufacturing procedures can open new potential for opening an untapped market. Growing, expanding businesses are dynamic in nature and should retain the joint venture strategy as a tool to open new markets when circumstances and timing are right. The more you improve market share, the greater the opportunity for new jobs.

CREATE JOBS AT HOME AND ABROAD

When new markets are opened or expanded new jobs are always created. The recent FS-X fighter plane proposed joint venture with Japan is an example. Dr. Vernon Lee, Vice President of General Dynamics, Japan, in General Dynamic's corporate magazine, *CODE ONE*, in an article entitled, "FS-X Partnership for the Future," July 1989, said their share of the development program will be worth about $375 million, representing three-quarters of the United States industry's 40 percent work share.

General Dynamics is the F–16 licensor and principal subcontractor to Mitsubishi Heavy Industries, the Japanese prime contractor for the FS-X. U.S. companies will also receive 40 percent of future work if the FS-X goes into production at the end of the current development phase. Lee estimated that

United States production share for 130 aircraft would total $2–2.5 billion, with General Dynamics likely to receive about half.

"In terms of contract value and employment, General Dynamics will get at least as much work from this program as we would have if Japan had made an off-the-shelf purchase of the same number of aircraft, which was never an option anyway," Lee said. In addition, Lee said, General Dynamics and other United States firms stand to gain more than the direct dollar value for their participation since the FS-X agreement provides for technology transfer from Japan to the United States, as well as from the United States to Japan.

Joint ventures benefit United States industry by retention and/or expansion of market share. This retention or expansion is completed by manufacturing a substantial percentage of the key components required to finish the end products at overseas locations. Usually, the end result, as with General Dynamics, over a long period, approximates 40 percent U.S. and 60 percent local content. These numbers can vary from situation to situation according to laws, customs, or the business transaction.

Even though General Dynamics is a huge, multinational corporation as opposed to small- to medium-size business, the same basic principles and considerations for international business development apply regardless of the size of the enterprise.

How does a joint venture increase jobs at home and overseas? You are presently selling, for example, 100 things per year into a given country. These, of course, are manufactured 100 percent in your United States facility. One day, you are advised that the laws in the host country that imports your product have changed, and they now insist on some local content in the manufacture of the product. You can turn this lemon into a lemon pie.

First, negotiate a joint venture with your present representative, if you have one, or with a new partner and write an agreement to comply with the new laws. Next, ship the parts needed and assemble your products with local labor from the host country. As a result of local input, sales of your products increase from 100 per year to over 500 per year. You profit from the sale of the parts manufactured in your United States plant, and you own 40 percent of the profits of the joint venture operation that just dramatically increased market share. When your exports jumped from 100 completed units to 500 disassembled units, you created new employment opportunities at home as well as in the host country. You own 100 percent of the increased production at home as well as a substantial interest in the new joint venture.

Under the terms of your joint venture agreement, you will eventually be required to shift a portion of your manufacturing to the host country for a greater share of local content. With greater local content, your market share for the products may increase to 2,000 per year or more inside the host country. Employ the Getty principle by accepting lesser ownership in an international joint venture in exchange for greater market share and business expansion at home.

Your historical sales were 100 products per year. Admitting local content through a joint venture formation contributed to an increase in market share, first to 500, then to 2,000. You traded in 100 percent ownership of the profits from the questionable continued export sales of 100 assembled products, for 100 percent profits on the parts required to make the overseas joint venture. In return, you also own a substantial interest in the joint venture producing 2,000 assembled products. Together, the parts supplied and interest in the new venture have substantially contributed to your corporate expansion, job creation, and profit picture. A problem has turned into a dramatic new business, both in the United States and in the overseas joint venture. These opportunities are available for virtually every small- to medium-size United States business. The first step is to begin exporting now, and as your level of experience grows, look to joint venturing to expand your market share.

You should be pleased with the job creation effect of this strategic and tactical move. Maybe you employed 10 people to make 100 assembled products per year. When parts were required for 500 products, you increased your payroll by 20 workers. The United States content required to support local production of 2,000 products per year increased the need for an additional ten employees at home. In this example, the joint venture was an intelligent decision. Jobs were created in both countries. This simplified illustration accurately portrays how jobs are created in successful joint ventures. Many executives in small- to medium-size American companies feel that the joint venture gives away the farm. They say you lose the competitive edge, sacrifice technology, and in essence, control of the market. In fact, partnering through joint ventures into the 21st century might be the only option to preserve markets, and hence jobs. Consuming nations in the global economy will demand their share of the process. Developing nations can contribute labor, materials, and services, but require technological management, and marketing skills available in American business. By the way, you shouldn't wait for laws or competitors to compel you to exercise the joint venture option. Early deployment can be an effective marketing strategy.

POLITICS MAY IMPACT JOINT VENTURE DECISIONS

Recognizing that economic and political freedoms must be linked for the other to exist and thrive, the joint venture lends itself to supporting and preserving democracy. The presidential trip to Poland and Hungary early in the summer of 1989, and subsequent congressional support for developing free market economies in Eastern Europe, are examples of how joint ventures can be effective political tools in support of democratic reforms in Eastern Europe. The President called for economic assistance to raise the standards of living in the countries receiving United States foreign aid.

This could mean a window of opportunity for United States businesses to enter closed markets with technology and know-how. Joint enterprises, funded with United States foreign aid, would be geared to the development of a new, free economy in the receiving country. This start-up aid for the initiation and expansion of commercial activity in Poland, for example, will open doors for United States business. It is doubtful that aid directed into the general system can survive indigenous bureaucratic mishandling, which leads to funds that are earmarked for free enterprise somehow falling through the cracks.

This new approach is unique because it attempts to open free markets in an otherwise closed economy. It reinforces the necessity to develop free markets concurrent with free elections. Poland and many other developing countries have extensive unemployment, inadequate standards of living, excessive inflation, insufficient food production, and hunger for consumer goods. The United States must also create jobs and work on reducing the foreign trade deficit.

If this political approach to a developing country, namely Poland or Hungary, is proposing to trade foreign-aid dollars for jobs in both countries through joint ventures, it must be acclaimed as a milestone in United States foreign policy. The new plan that embraces Democratic reform in developing countries with financial subsidy has unlimited growth potential in support of both the United States and less developed economies.

The Japanese embarked on a similar economic policy toward less developed countries many years ago. Financial aid is linked to internal Japanese economic and industrial development. They have long recognized the value of the developing country as an industrial and consumer market. Government-financed joint venture projects have always been keyed to using Japanese industry. Their public financing underwrites the efforts of private business to form cooperative economic relationships in developing countries with low interest loans for technology transfers, resource development, and mutual job creation. There are, of course, many forms of United States overseas financial aid. In fairness to United States foreign policy, many United States aid programs, especially involving the Pentagon and the military are linked to spending in this country.

The small- to medium-size business in the United States is better situated and more free than Japan to develop joint ventures in less-developed countries. Most of Japan's small business entry has been through multinational corporations. These huge corporations use trading companies that market products and services of the smaller segments of Japanese industry.

Political changes are occurring rapidly in the world, and you as an entrepreneur should stay abreast of these changes that will affect your global business strategy. Who would have imagined at the beginning of 1989 that from August to December, the nations of Poland, Hungary, Czechoslovakia, Romania, and East Germany would make such strides in shedding communism. This political reform movement has signaled that these countries need help from the West. This opens up a new arena of opportunity that before was absent from two- to five-year business plans of small- to medium-size business in America.

It is essential to your joint venture investment that you maintain a keen awareness of the internal politics of the host country. An understanding of local feelings towards the joint enterprise and the effect of cultural differences will be invaluable to you when planning corporate strategy for this and other joint ventures. Each enterprise that you formulate will arm you for the next international challenge. Political and cultural sensitivity are attributes of a seasoned international business development executive.

In Chapter 10 of this text, the government's role and how it can impact funding international joint ventures in developing nations is explored. The political systems in Eastern Europe (and the Soviet Union) are changing dramatically, but multitudes of incompetent party officials that have caused these economic woes remain entrenched in bureaucratic roles. It will take supreme effort on the part of the indigenous population to unseat these party loyalists. Finding suitable and educated management to run the new privately owned enterprises will present challenges, and hence, opportunities. The directing of United States foreign aid through joint ventures seems infinitely more feasible than simply feeding a hungry, bureaucratic elephant.

3

The Sell-Assembly-
Manufacture Strategy

THE INTERNATIONAL CHALLENGE

IN THE COMING DECADES, THE VALUE OF SAM STRATEGY FOR UNITED STATES small- to medium-size business in the joint venture will increase dramatically. The initials stand for three important stages of international business development—sell, assembly, and manufacture. Consideration of these steps leading into joint ventures is deemed essential for American companies to increase market share in the new globalized economy. This section of the text will address the three steps beginning with selling finished goods in international markets, assembling of United States goods overseas in joint venture arrangements for local content, and manufacturing under license and/or joint venture agreements for increased local content in the host country. The sale, assembly, and manufacturing joint venture strategy introduces local content to improve market share in the host country.

This book is intended to guide you through the stages leading into the formulation and operation of joint ventures and foreign partnerships. The Japanese have employed the joint venture strategy for many decades to maintain and improve market share on a global basis. Changing market forces and increasing global competition dictate that American business must look to international partnerships to increase sales and create new, quality jobs in America.

The small- to medium-size business in America is innovative, flexible, technologically advanced, quality conscious, profitable, and productive. In fact, this sector of our industrial economy was responsible for creating nearly half of all the new jobs in the United States in the 1980s. However, despite its high level of innovation and export potential, this segment of American business exports very little. Some studies suggest that only 10 percent of United States firms export, and just 250 companies account for nearly 80 percent of the total dollar value of exports. Other data suggests that some 30,000 United States small- to medium-size businesses have the capability to be exporting. While they have exciting products and services, most of these tend to be too domestically focused for new markets. The new realities of the global marketplace make review of these marketing strategies imperative, but many small- to medium-size companies don't know where or how to start. This chapter describes the logical steps to enter overseas markets from both a tactical and strategic standpoint.

SELLING IN INTERNATIONAL MARKETS

Sales techniques used to sell in domestic markets include fundamental principles that are transferable into the international arena. Selling from Austin to Boston isn't that much different than selling from Los Angeles to Malaysia. Both situations require hard work and tenacity. There are, however, differences to consider if you are to be successful in selling United States finished goods overseas. Early recognition of business development opportunity, adaptability and flexibility in meeting market demand, and creativity in sales presentations are three invaluable attributes for success in international markets.

The history of United States small- to medium-size businesses is just over 214 years old; many formidable overseas competitors originate from cultures that have engaged in international trade for generations. The American pioneering spirit is determinate and resourceful—attributes that are fundamental to overseas trading. Study the long-developed marketing and selling skills of overseas traders, and where applicable, combine this knowledge garnered from winners with your American ingenuity. This combination will serve you well as you enter into the new globalized market as many opportunities develop for your products and services.

An example of Chinese sales creativity surfaced one Sunday morning a few years ago in Hong Kong while shopping for an inexpensive wrist watch. The intent was to find an unattractive watch that could be sent to an employee in the United States as a joke. Therefore, the budgeted, top-end price we were willing to pay was the U.S. equivalent of $2.00. The shopkeeper just opened and as we walked inside he started his sales pitch by saying, "The first customer of the day gets a ten percent discount." An atrocious model was selected and priced at $2. After some haggling, we got the price down to $1.50. After that, the shopkeeper wouldn't budge. When asked why, he retorted, "Because that's a semi-automatic watch." When asked, "What is a semi-automatic watch?" he replied, "You don't have to wind it all the time." Of course, he then sold us the watch. That young

Chinese man was a professional salesman, and his sales talent was as much inherited as acquired.

CHILI'S INC. SETS A FINE EXAMPLE

It was possible to visit with the top management of Chili's Inc. in Dallas, Texas, recently. They are just beginning to explore international franchising opportunities as an extension to their businesses in the United States. Their mission and company philosophy as explained by Mr. John C. Miller, Vice President, JV/Franchise, summarizes an effective business development strategy in meeting the challenges of overseas trade.

Chili's Mission Statement

- To be a premier and progressive growth company with a balanced approach toward people, quality, and profitability;
- To cultivate customer loyalty by listening to, caring about, and providing our customers with a quality dining experience;
- To enhance a high level of excellence, innovation, integrity, and ethics;
- To attract, develop, and retain a superior team;
- To be focused, sensitive, and responsive to our employees and our environment;
- To enhance long-term shareholder wealth

Chili's company philosophy would travel well in international circles, and adoption of this philosophy would enhance cultural and business acceptance of United States businesses throughout the entire global economy. Chili's believes that employees are their best asset, and they set high standards for their managers. The following are the basic principles of conduct and business from which Chili's operates. Remember these points when venturing abroad.

CHILI'S COMPANY PHILOSOPHY

Live by the highest level of integrity and ethics. This is the essential backbone of our company. Without this there is no trust or credibility.

Encourage people to set and develop priorities. Your health comes first, without that you have nothing. The family comes second. Business comes third. Recognizing and organizing the first two is vital so you can take care of the third.

Face tough problems. Do not sidestep or procrastinate by delegating tough problems. It is neither fair nor good business practice to let the person below you bear the brunt of making a hard decision.

Set and demand standards of excellence. Anybody who accepts mediocrity in school, at Chili's, or in life is a person who compromises. No organization or department will perform better than the established standards or levels of expectation.

Do what is best for the business. Evaluate alternatives and implement only those that will have the most positive impact on the company by meeting or exceeding the set standards.

Potential rewards must be worth the risk. Risks are inherent in business. However, success in business is a result of analyzing risks and taking only those that have substantial upside potential.

Provide clear direction. Establish definite goals so that all support services can be focused on attaining them.

Keep it simple and direct. Minimize confusion. Execute the fundamentals and cut for the goal line.

Have a sense of urgency. Once you have determined the right thing to do, do it now. Be impatient for results.

Do not waste time worrying about things you cannot do anything about. Do not try to fix things that are impossible. Concentrate on the possibles.

Maintain the ability to fail. We cannot innovate unless we are willing to accept some mistakes.

Be tough but fair with people. Being tough means setting standards and demanding excellence. Rewards and penalties should be consistent and reflect job performance. Listening and people sensitivity skills should be utilized to provide a sound base for evaluations and reviews.

Commit to a quality working environment. A company is only as strong as its people. Develop and support the whole person approach to individual growth. By providing an outstanding work environment, the corporation and the individual can achieve great heights.

Believe in corporate citizenship. Each individual has a social obligation to the community to devote time, energy, and resources to enrich the American way of life.

You cannot accomplish anything unless you are having fun. A sense of humor helps relieve tensions and create a more enjoyable working environment.

Chili's management philosophy regarding employees would prepare anyone to deal with cultural sensitivites while venturing abroad. Chili's philosophy says, "We treat employees as we would like to be treated, with respect, courtesy, and fairness. Everyone deserves to know what to expect in their working environment. Therefore, consistency in our performance and attitude is required."

It continues, "Employees are human beings with the same needs and feelings that management has. Chili's has a moral obligation to develop them as total individuals, not just workers. Our ability to empathize has always set us apart from the crowd in developing employee loyalty."

MAKING THE EXPORT DECISION

Is exporting right for you and your company? World trade is increasingly important to the health of the American economy and to the growth of small- to medium-size companies. Exporting not only creates jobs, but provides firms with new growth, new markets, and additional profits. There has never been a better time, especially for small business, to begin to export. As the global economy becomes more interdependent, opportunities for small- to medium-size businesses to compete in the world marketplace become more attractive.

Exporters can play a significant role in improving the United States balance of trade and at the same time improve their competitiveness and profit picture. The many benefits of entering into international trade include:

- increased corporate growth
- additional markets
- improved profit picture
- expansion of the client base
- tax advantages
- new products and services
- awareness of the competition
- favorable recognition
- expansion of market share with joint ventures

Many thousands of small firms are already in the global marketplace, but this segment of American business still represents the largest potential of exporters. Of all the companies who export, 52 percent are businesses with fewer than 100 employees. This fact alone should encourage you to become an exporter.

It is not difficult to enter export markets. The decision involves a commitment from the top, hard work, perseverance, and allocation of resources. You need to plan, do your market research, and pay close attention to detail. You need to find your nitch in the market. Follow these basic steps in making the export decision:

- Know the capabilities of your business
- Know the export potential of your product or service

- Identify market needs
- Determine which overseas markets are right for you
- Study market entry strategies, emulate winners, and learn export procedure
- Learn how to process exports

There are two basic ways to enter the overseas market, directly or indirectly. Direct selling involves sending your own personnel overseas to create sales with end-user customers. Indirect selling may involve the use of export management (EMCs) or trading companies (ETCs), sales to domestic firms that export your product, and sales through representatives or brokers. As a selling technique, you can appoint commissioned sales representatives or agents in countries with on-the-spot marketing experience and follow-up capability to improve your share of the market. These same appointees might be the nucleus of your joint venture network to be employed later in your SAM program.

CHECKLIST FOR THE EXPORT DECISION

I. Level of Experience

1. Have you already done business in a country or countries? (or from which countries have you received inquiries?)

   Market knowledge of your products and services become known through many business channels such as word-of-mouth, domestic trade journal advertising, competitors, friends, associates, and, yes, from satisfied customers who have international operations. You may be destined to export in spite of your present intentions. Your products and services could be in demand and your decision to begin exporting could be market driven.

2. If you received inquiries, which of your product lines were most frequently mentioned?

   This analysis is easily compiled and should focus on the product and country of origin of the inquiry. International sales opportunities exist in 186 countries. This study should identify your best opportunities by country and by product to enable you to select your prime export markets.

3. Make a list of each potential buyer by product, country-by-country from the inquiries.

   This analysis will also involve categorizing of inquiries, i.e., is the inquiry from: a government office, an end user such as a retailer, or a middleman such as a stocking wholesaler, distributor, importer, or sales representative? Include classifications by country in this analysis. If a viable commercial pattern develops in this analysis, you should determine the seriousness of these inquiries. This can be done through international banks, Dun and Bradstreet type services, the United States and Foreign Commercial Service office of The United States Department of Commerce, other American firms with whom the inquirer has done business, your suppliers, your competitors, and complementary businesses that may have a trading history with this potential customer.

4. Is there a trend in the number of sales inquiries?

Your answer should be influenced by the amount of time and effort that you have expended in obtaining these inquiries. Have you solicited this overseas business interest in your product or service? If these inquiries have come to you unsolicited, you should ask if you truly want to enter the export market? If so, are you capitalizing on each inquiry? What is the overseas reception to your responses? If inquiries are constant, your product is in demand and you should consider exporting. Once you determine and implement your marketing strategy, you will see an increase in the frequency of inquiries from many sources.

5. Who are your main competitors, domestic and foreign?

This is an important analysis. If your competition is foreign, you must determine if they have pricing advantages, and if so, from what standpoint. Are they in close proximity to the market? Have they established joint ventures for local content? If so, what are the host country import restrictions, if any? What are the import tariffs as a result of competitive local content? If your competitor is domestic, you need to know his market position in the targeted country, pricing, deliveries, and after-the-sale service capability. Is your domestic counterpart involved in host-country assembly or manufacture? If so, how has this fact affected your competitive position? What can you do to reverse the situation?

6. What lessons have you learned from past export experiences, if any?

This is important to consider, because exporting errors, if not repeated, can be vast sources of experience. A collection of miscues over the past three decades provides much of the information for this text. Sharing of learning experiences, some of which were not only painful, but expensive, can help you to avoid similar mistakes. In any business activity, you have a learning curve. There is also a price to pay in learning international business development. Obviously, experience that you already have will be helpful. And, you must guard against letting previous unfortunate experiences in international trade diminish your enthusiasm for the challenges of the coming decades, especially in light of the many opportunities in the new, globalized economy.

II. MANAGEMENT AND PERSONNEL

1. Who will be responsible for the export department and its organization and staff?

The decision to enter into the international trade arena, once thought to be bonus business is today a requirement for corporate survival into the 21st century. Development of overseas trade requires a serious commitment from the top of the organization. You need full-time marketing, management, and support services to solicit business, issue quotations, and process international sales. In the beginning, you can hire an export management company (EMC) or an export trading company (ETC), but and if you do, you will need someone on a full-time basis to supervise their activities on your behalf. You can use a consultant with hands-on international business development experience to guide you through the initial periods of establishing an in-house export department. Always ensure that you have a competent employee to understudy with the consultant to learn about overseas trade and later assume the consultant's duties after he or she departs.

Alternatively, you can employ a full-time manager who has proven international business development credentials. Such a person might have been in overseas trade for years, but be short on experience in your product or service area. It will be far more cost effective to train a person with an international background in your business, product, and service philosophy than to try to replicate his or her international experience from scratch.

2. How much senior management time should or could be allocated after the decision is made?

The answer to this question, as in the previous one, involves commitment. Experience has shown that you must have full and complete support from the very top of the organization. This backing must be communicated throughout the organization in order that everyone, including the credit manager, production superintendant, quality control manager, design engineers, etc., understands the seriousness of management or owner's commitment. Once you enter the field of international marketing, you must convey to everyone that you are a long-term player.

3. What will management expect from this effort?

This is a reasonable question and must be understood before undertaking an export effort. Consultants should always ask prospective clients, "What do you want to accomplish, in what time frame, with how much capital?" If client expectations are near-term, in the interest of mutual harmony, you should pass on the assignment. Many businesses harbour the misconception that exporting is instant wealth. International trade and joint venture formulations can be extremely rewarding and profitable. Building personal and commercial relationships over time in which mutual trust and respect develops between trading partners is often essential before the first purchase order for a product or service is received. Will top management adopt an overseas marketing strategy that involves a significant commitment to time and money for its success? Joint ventures, for example, can take years to produce the anticipated return on investment.

4. What organization structure is required to ensure that export sales are adequately serviced?

This is an important consideration. After-the-sale servicing of a product is as essential to international success as it is with domestic sales success. You will need a structure, be it your own staff, an EMC group, a foreign representative, or a local distributor to provide overseas service for your product. If independent sales and service representatives are employed in the United States operation, this expertise may be transferable to your international strategy. Also, if you subcontract service in the United States, that can be an overseas option. It is reasonable to believe that your domestic-styled servicing network can work in some international locations.

5. Who will follow through after planning is accomplished?

A designated international manager should be appointed for the follow-through activity. He or she should also have a full-time secretary or administrative assistant dedicated to learning the export process including the new paperwork that will flow across the exporter's desk. While the business principles of overseas trade are basically the same as domestic, steps, procedures, services, and logistics are vastly different in each host country. If you have decided to sell directly into your export market, a designated sales or marketing person must be appointed to work in the targeted areas. Continuity is essential in building relationships with selected clients. To begin this process, always send the same marketing or sales personnel when possible. The client base will develop a sense of anticipation of the next visit as your marketing plan unfurls.

III. PRODUCTION CAPABILITY

1. How is present plant capacity being used?

Business trends are cyclical in nature. If domestic business is lagging, it is tempting to look to outside markets to employ excess production capacity. International sales represent new markets. Considering overseas markets as simply a fill-in for domestic production capacity is short-term thinking. While it may address current need, it could have long-range effects on your corporate international future. You should delay the export decision until you can make the long-term commitment to accepting overseas orders. Once you establish your company in the global economy, you will be expected to remain in service of that market.

2. Will filling of new export orders negatively impact domestic sales?

This is another question that must be answered before accepting your first overseas purchase order. It also involves commitment. Will the company set aside a portion of manufacturing capacity commensurate with your overseas sales forecast? Will this capacity be reserved to produce overseas orders sold on a timely basis? An international salesman cannot make delivery promises if he is selling from an empty sack. Will international orders command equal respect with established domestic sales at the shop floor level? They will, if the export commitment is communicated from the top of the firm. Effective planning and coordination between domestic and international marketing managers, engineers, and production planners will be required.

3. What new costs are encountered in additional production?

Production questions involve cost analysis. Will new machines be needed? What will be the profit margin of international sales versus domestic markets? In Turkey in 1967, a requirement for a huge amount of steel bars for the government was opened to public bidding. Each of these steel bars required threading on each end. The quantity was enormous and the dollar value of the sale was staggering. After the field salesman worked for the order for several months, the company, to his surprise, issued a noncompetitive quotation so as not to receive the order. The rationale was as follows: the company realized that the bid had to be highly competitive. A high-profit margin item would be sacrificed in exchange for a high-volume sale. Demand outside of Turkey exceeded the supply at the time of the request for tender. If they received the contract, machines normally used to produce high-margin sales items would be tied up manufacturing this one-off, high-volume, low-profit sale. The threading operation added little value, and the company was, in reality, acting as an unlicensed steel broker. Management decided not to incumber production with a low-profit sale, regardless of the origin or size of the order to continue to meet deliveries for established, long-standing international clients.

4. Are there fluctuations in the annual workload? When? Why?

Planning for these interruptions in workload must be provided on a quarterly basis. If a significant trend in available plant capacity becomes obvious, it may indicate that export sales activity should be encouraged. However, overseas sales must not be solicited simply to take-up-the-slack in domestic production.

5. Are minimum-order quantities required for export sales?

This could be considered in the early going, but should not be significant in your long-term objectives and plans for developing an export strategy. You can accept lesser gross sales margins in the start-up mode, but these will more than be compensated over the long term. Like most business decisions, there is a price to be paid on the front end for market entry.

6. Do export sales require any special designing, packaging, or labeling?

This depends on marketing research in each geographical area where you intend to sell your products, but if sold in a country with a language other than English, the answer is yes. You would need translations in the host country language for brochures, package markings, machinery tags, operating instructions, wording for service contracts, safety messages, shipping containers, and for anything else that needed clarification. It will be a significant cost to be considered in the market-entry strategy.

IV. FINANCIAL CAPACITY

1. How much capital can be tied up in exports?

This question, as with many of the previous ones, refers to top management commitment. In addition to corporate will and desire to enter the export arena, there must be an allocation of operating funds for at least two, if not more, years for market entry. Answers to this question can also be found in the analysis of capital and cash flows. Exporting in the coming decades will extend beyond the shipment of goods from the United States against irrevocable and confirmed letters of credit. The export commitment in the global economy will include an understanding of the cost and value of international joint venturing for the mutual benefit of the United States small- to medium-size firm and the counterpart in the host country. Long-term capital commitments must not end with the sale of finished goods overseas, it must provide for the eventual assembly and manufacturing of goods overseas, which means putting capital back into the strategy for long-term growth.

2. What level of export operating costs can be supported?

There will be new and unusual operating expenses on the company's books after entry into export. Communication costs will rise dramatically through implementation of international phone calls, fax transmissions, telexes, courier services, and other communicating essentials in your operating budget. Overseas trips will involve costs that are double or triple that of domestic travel. Planning will be essential to realize the maximum efficiency from each travel dollar expended. Round figures United States $400 to $500/day, in addition to airfare, is a good rule-of-thumb for budgeting purposes. The amount varies, of course, from country to country, and hotel to hotel. For example, a taxi ride from Tokyo airport to downtown costs today approximately $150. The bus service is approximately $40. You can use that figure as a realistic expense to visualize how international travel could conceivably cost $350 per day, or more.

3. How are the initial expenses of export efforts to be allocated? In-house? Consultants? EMCs? ETCs?

Answer this question with corporate objectives. In-house allocations will need to be based on your strategy. You will need an export manager, even if you employ consultants, EMCs or EMTs. In addition to keeping tabs on a third party hired to develop and run your export business, you probably will want to simultaneously develop your own, in-house expertise and capability for future export corporate strategy such as joint venturing. Consultants are invaluable sources of assistance if they have had practical, in-the-trenches experience.

4. Are there any new corporate development plans that may compete for capital with export plans?

This question has to do with allocation of resources. Entering the international marketplace will require a substantial capital commitment if you are to be successful. It is recognized that domestic corporate development plans may compete with your international business development plans. If resources are committed to export, it will be detrimental to your reputation to change direction in the middle of an international business development activity. It is difficult enough to "break-in" to the market. To enter export markets and represent that certain activities will occur, and then suddenly withdraw because of a lack of capital due to a competing domestic activity, would spell the end of a brief overseas career.

5. By what date must export pay for itself? Are you prepared to make the 2–5 year commitment to develop excellence in exports? in joint ventures?

The answer to this question must come from the top of the organization, preferably the chairman, president, or CEO. There is no "quick fix" in exports. Small- to medium-size companies considering entry into Europe by midnight on December 31, 1992, are ahead of the game if planning was initiated five years ago. Participation in the globalized economy does not seem to be simply a question of whether export will pay for itself, but rather can the small- to medium-size business survive without an international strategy. This strategy that includes joint ventures and partnerships can create new jobs in America and the host country. Granted, this may be a long-term objective for the new exporter, but it must be considered now if we, in the United States, are to sustain our dominant position in living standards, technology, world commerce, and politics for generations to follow.

ELEMENTS OF AN INTERNATIONAL BUSINESS PLAN

Once you have made the export decision, you will need an export business plan. The future comes whether you are ready for it or not, and it has been said, that life is what is happening while you are making plans. An international business plan helps you anticipate the future and make well-informed decisions. Planning is a continuous process in the management of business. It involves the plan, the action, the evaluation, and the control of the events according to the plan. The plan should be revised as needed, but at a minimum of at least once a year.

DEFINE LONG TERM GOALS

To begin the business plan, define your long-term goals in international business. You should ask yourself what are your personal goals for the next 25 years? What are your ten-year goals for the business? How does entering international trade help you reach your goals? What are your one-, three-, and five-year goals for the business? Answers to these questions are fundamental to your understanding the purpose of entering overseas trade.

THE PURPOSE OF ENTERING EXPORT

Outline and study your purpose of entering international business. Who will use the business plan and for what purpose? Identify specific goals such as sales volume anticipated, profit before taxes, compensation for your effort, the amount of time you can commit, your goals for personal growth and education, and any other objectives or goals that apply.

INDUSTRY BACKGROUND

Describe the background of your industry. How was it developed? What has been its growth? How competitive has it been in international markets? What is its future internationally? Next, list sources of industry information. What industry trade associations exist? Are there any government studies or compiled export statistics? Define the role of small- to medium-size business. How well do small businesses fit? How well will your business fit? And finally, describe the background of your business. Why have you been successful in the domestic market? What is your pattern of growth? What external factors contributed? Has growth been seasonal? What competitive advantages do you feel that your firm has over other domestic or international firms?

EXPORTING METHODS

Decide on your method of exporting. You should select between the two basic options: direct and indirect. Indirect methods include appointing an EMC to represent you overseas, selling to United States buying offices of large foreign firms or foreign government buying offices, or selling to large United States firms for export through their own overseas distribution networks. For direct methods, you can establish responsibility within your own organization for exporting using the services of an export consultant to identify markets and develop promotional material. Or, you can establish complete responsibility for export trade within your own organization to include market research, establishment of distribution networks, performance of exporting functions, and aftermarket servicing.

AVAILABLE INTERNATIONAL SKILLS

Identify and analyze international skills that are available to you and your company. Which owners have international experience? Which employees? Who is your accountant? Your lawyer? Your banker? Do they have access to international expertise? Who is your international freight forwarder? Who is your export consultant? Who are your other key advisors? Who is your advisor at the United States & Foreign Commercial Office of the United States Department of Commerce?

KEY EMPLOYEES

Identify essential key employees for your export team. To expand your business successfully into international trade, it is important to have trained, qualified employees performing important tasks. Have you identified needed employees? Have you identified outside resources required? Have you determined when to write policy?

IDENTIFY PRODUCTS AND SERVICES

Identify products and/or services to be offered internationally. You should probably consider products that have been selling well domestically with the understanding that products or services must meet a need. In the foreign market, need is satisfied with regard to function, price, and esthetic value. Also evaluate the products you intend to offer internationally. What makes them unique? How good is the quality? Why will foreign buyers purchase from you? And finally, what levels of inventory will be required?

TARGET MARKETS AND CUSTOMERS

Determine which markets offer the best prospects for export sales. Which countries were the largest purchasers of like products the last three years? Which represents the best market considering freight rates? Which has a projected growth rate? Which three countries offer the most potential? How soon are you likely to begin assembly and/or manufacturing? Is it essential for market entry? Will it lead to market expansion? If so, how will this affect sales projections and how quickly?

Determining projected sales levels is difficult, but necessary. What is your current percentage of the United States market? What do you anticipate in overseas volume? First year? Following? What is the projected sales for similar products? What can you project for sales in your targeted markets? Identify your customers in a chosen market. What companies, agents, or distributors have purchased like or similar products? Of this same group, which have made inquiries or asked for information? If needed, will your distributor or manufacturer's representative make a good joint-venture partner? If so, how soon can he or she gear up to assemble or partially manufacture your products? Will you provide for this option in your long-term strategic plan?

Which group represents the best customer for you? Determine your method of distribution. How do other firms sell in your chosen market? Will you sell direct? Who will represent your company? Who will provide after-the-sale service? Will you appoint an exclusive agent or a nonexclusive distributor? What type of facilities will he need? What type of client should he be familiar with? What is his territory? His financial strength? What other competitive or noncompetitive lines does he carry? How many salesmen should they have and how often should they cover the territory? Will you use an export management company to do your marketing and distribution for you? If so, have you developed a reasonable sales and marketing plan with realistic goals that can be agreed upon?

SUPPORT FUNCTIONS

Identify product concerns. Can the potential buyer see a sample of your product in his foreign location? What product labeling standards must be met? What spare parts should a customer have on hand? Can the product be delivered on time? If an export license is required, will it be granted? Identify literature concerns. If required, do you have literature in another language other than English? Is sales literature sufficiently technical? Do they ensure quality and informative representatation of your product? How frequently are technical manuals updated? Identify customer relations concerns. What is delivery time and method of shipment? What are payment terms? What are warranty terms? Who will service the product, if needed? How will you communicate with your customer, if needed? How often will you visit the territory to see the end users and provide sales support to your third party distributor or representative? Are you prepared to give the same order and delivery preference to your international customers that you give to domestic customers?

COMPETITIVE ANALYSIS

Identify one major international competitor in each market targeted. Compare your international business to the competition. Elements to compare include advertising, location, products, service, sales methods, pricing, frequency of travel, sales results, and image.

MARKETING STRATEGY

In international sales, the chosen terms of sale are very important. Should you make the product available at your plant, at the port of exit, landed at the port of importation, or delivered free and clear to the customer's door? The answer considers market requirements and the amount of risk you are prepared to take. Define pricing strategy. How do you calculate the price for each product? What factors have you considered in setting pricing? Upon review of inco terms with an international freight forwarder, which terms of sale are suited for your product? Which products' sales are sensitive to pricing? How important is pricing in the overall strategy? What are discount policies? Define promotional strategy. What advertising materials will you use? What trade shows will you participate in, if any? What time of year and how often will you travel to foreign customer markets? Define customer services. What special customer services do you offer? What type of payment options do you offer? How do you handle return of merchandise?

SALES FORECAST

Forecasting sales is the starting point for financial projections. Since the sales forecast is extremely important, it is essential that you use realistic figures. Remember, the sales forecast shows the expected time that the sale is made. Actual cash flow is impacted by delivery dates and payment terms.

COST OF GOODS SOLD

Costs of goods in international sales are determined by pricing strategies and terms of sale. In order to ascertain the costs associated with different terms of sale, you should consult with a freight forwarder. A typical costing worksheet would include many of the following factors:

- export packing
- documentation
- dispatch
- forwarding
- bank documentation
- handling
- terminal charges
- ocean freight
- bunker surcharge

- container loading
- inland freight
- consular legalization
- truck/rail unloading
- wharfage
- bank collection fees
- cargo insurance
- other miscellaneous
- courier mail/fax/telex

INTERNATIONAL OVERHEAD EXPENSES

In determining overhead costs for export activities, avoid including costs that pertain to domestic sales. These expenses could include legal fees, accounting fees, promotional material, travel, communication equipment (fax/telex/telephone), advertising allowances, promotional expenses (trade shows, etc.) and others.

FINANCIAL STRATEGY

What sources are available to investigate the credit of the buyer? What payment terms will you quote? Will you insist on a letter of credit? Will you investigate export credit insurance? Will you need to consult a trade merchant bank for preshipment working capital? Can extension of terms be considered? Does your bank have in-depth knowledge of international finance transactions?

MISTAKES COMMON TO NEW EXPORTERS

There are several common mistakes made by potential exporters when entering the international marketplace.

Failure to obtain qualified export counseling and to develop a master international marketing plan before starting an export business. To be successful, a firm must first clearly define goals, objectives, and problems encountered. Secondly, it must develop a definitive plan to accomplish an objective despite the problems involved. Unless the firm is fortunate enough to possess a staff with considerable export experience, it may not be able to take this first crucial step without qualified outside guidance.

Insufficient commitment by top management to overcome the initial difficulties and financial requirements of exporting. It may take more time and effort to establish a firm in a foreign market than in a domestic one. Although the early delays and costs involved in exporting may seem difficult to justify when compared to established domestic trade, the exporter should take a long-range view of this process and carefully monitor international marketing efforts through these early difficulties. If a good foundation is laid for export business, the benefits derived should eventually outweigh the investment.

Insufficient care in selecting overseas distributors. The selection of each foreign representative or distributor is critical. The complications involved in overseas communications and transportation require international distributors to act with greater independence than domestic counterparts. Also, since a new exporter's history, trademarks, and reputation are usually unknown in a foreign market, foreign customers might buy on the strength of a distributor's reputation. A firm should therefore conduct a personal evaluation of the personnel handling its account, the distributor's facilities, and the management methods employed.

Chasing orders from around the world instead of establishing a basis for profitable operations and orderly growth. If exporters expect distributors to actively promote their accounts, the distributors must be trained, assisted, and their performance must be continually monitored. This might require a company marketing executive to be permanently located in the distributor's geographical region. New exporters should concentrate their efforts in one or two areas until there is sufficient business to support a company representative. Then, while this initial core is expanded, the exporter can move into the next selected area.

Neglecting export business when U.S. market booms. Too many companies turn to exporting when business falls off in the United States. When domestic business starts to boom again, they neglect their export trade or relegate it to second place. Such neglect can seriously harm the business and motivation of their overseas representatives, strangle the U.S. company's own export trade, and leave the firm without recourse when domestic business falls off once more. Even if domestic business remains strong, the company might eventually realize that they have only succeeded in shutting off a valuable source of additional profits.

Failure to treat international distributors on an equal basis with domestic counterparts. Often, companies carry out institutional advertising campaigns, special discount offers, sales incentive programs, special credit-term programs, and warranty offers in the United States market, but fail to make similar assistance available to their international distributors. This mistake can undermine the enthusiasm and morale of overseas marketing representatives.

Assumption that a given market technique and product will automatically be successful in all countries. What works in one market may not work in others. Each market has to be treated separately to ensure maximum success.

Unwillingness to modify products to meet regulations or cultural preferences of other countries. Local safety and security codes, as well as import restrictions, cannot be ignored by foreign distributors. If necessary modifications are not made at the factory, the distributor must do them—usually at greater cost and, perhaps, not as well. It should also be noted that the resulting smaller profit margin makes your account less attractive for the representative.

Failure to print service, sale, and warranty messages in locally understood languages. Although a distributor's top management may speak English, it is unlikely that all sales personnel (let alone service personnel) have this capability. Without a clear understanding of sales messages and service instructions, these persons may be less effective in performing their functions.

Failure to consider the use of an export management company. If a firm decides it cannot afford its own export department (or has tried one unsuccessfully), it should consider the possibility of appointing an appropriate export management company (EMC).

Failure to provide readily available servicing for the product. A product without the necessary service support can acquire a bad reputation in a short period, potentially preventing further sales.

Failure to consider joint venturing or licensing agreements. Import restrictions in some countries, insufficient personnel/financial resources, or too limited a product line cause many companies to dismiss international marketing as unfeasible. Yet, many products that can compete on a national basis in the United States can be successfully sold in many markets of the world. A licensing or joint venture agreement might be the simple, profitable answer to many reservations. In general, all that is needed for success is flexibility in using the proper combination of marketing techniques.

HAVE A SALES PLAN IN MIND

Your sales plan should have both strategic and tactical objectives. Strategic may involve the ultimate joint venture or alliance; tactical may be the export sale. The Japanese have 100-year plans. Your long-term plan may be a series of short-term plans, but at least know your objectives when entering the overseas market. The Japanese have been successful for years by finding out exactly what the market wants to buy, then providing that product. The key is to identify needs or market nitches. In prior decades, Americans have tended to make the product first and then try to force it upon the marketplace. This approach adversely effects market share development. The realities of the global economy and its competitive considerations have caused American businessmen in more recent years to correct this approach by adapting to new market forces.

Entry into export markets can be a long and painful process. You must be prepared for a minimum commitment of two years, but more often than not, your objectives will only be realized in the third or fourth year. There is gold at the end of the rainbow, but the journey can be tedious as in any learning curve. Don't expect instant acceptance or instant profits. Identify your market, do your homework, solicit your overseas agents, distributors, or representatives, train them in your product line, support your network, and visit your markets frequently on a regular basis to ensure market coverage. In short, follow your business plan and remain alert to your corporate objectives.

Study your business plan frequently and modify as needed. Do this to ensure you are going ahead with your original objective. It is easy in international trade to get deviated from the original purpose. If you decide to be a manufacturer's representative, stay the course, don't diversify activity to such a degree that you fail in your original purpose. Remind yourself, by looking over your original business plan frequently, exactly which goals you had in mind when starting your exporting business and what you wanted to achieve. Are you still on course?

IMPLEMENT THE PLAN

With a strategy, sufficient time, and corporate resources, the West African market was penetrated within one year by exhibiting reliability and dependability. A one-year travel itinerary was prepared that included four visits to each city and field location during that year. While having lunch in Luanda, Angola, with a client, say, on March 1st, we would schedule the next luncheon in Angola on May 7, and write that into our diary. Fortunately, each appointment was kept on schedule throughout the entire year. Due to dependability, long-standing relationships and trust were developed with our clients, and purchase orders began to be issued on a grand scale. During this one-year period, we were also able to identify, evaluate, and appoint many effective sales representatives. Due to their sales and service effectiveness with our new, mutual clients, the requirement for sales support in the region was reduced by fifty percent. This allowed new market development in other regions such as Eastern Europe.

There are many ways to implement your overseas business plan. Initially, you might have your personnel travel from your domestic plant location to various qualified overseas markets. It is important in building trust in international business, that you maintain continuity by sending the same individual to the same market on a regular basis. You must demonstrate confidence in this person and provide home office support when needed. Once your overseas clients and representatives have the same confidence in your personnel, significant business will develop.

Depending on your business plan, you may at some sales level transfer an employee to a central location in the region to be more geographically situated near your customers and representatives. Your decision to do this must be based on an expense analysis that considers foreign taxes, United States taxes, cost of schooling for dependents, transportation costs, housing and food costs, political climate, and market demands. Although some tax exemption is allowed up to a certain amount, we are the only country in the world that taxes its citizens that work overseas. All benefits such as housing allowances, airfare for vacations, and other benefits are included in the tax base. This tax is a disincentive for Americans to reside in markets where they could more effectively influence sales of American goods abroad. This contributes directly to our foreign trade deficit and gives our overseas competitors a tremendous advantage.

TRAVELING OVERSEAS AND TECHNIQUE SELLING

When you begin selling and shipping products overseas, you'll need to make periodic trips to visit your customers and overseas distributors, franchises, and representatives. These visits will be expensive, but viewed by your clients and marketing team as an indication of your commitment to your international market. Export sales that lead into long-term relationships are anything but get-rich-quick scenarios. They require an expensive and lengthy commitment from you, your company, and your shareholders. The rewards are out there in the global economy, but you must develop the relationships required for long-term players.

One tool to take along to use in sales and after-the-sale service is a camera. We always tried to have a picture taken with a customer or his field personnel and their families, especially in such remote areas as the jungles of Brazil or Indonesia. Once back in the states, we would have the film developed, write a personal note, include a picture or pictures, and mail the package directly to the employee. This effort made a lasting impression in every country we traveled because of the extra effort we put into the personal nature of the thank-you note.

Another useful selling tool is a slide presentation program or other teaching aid such as a video tape that covers the latest technology in your company and in your industry. In remote areas, overseas nationals and United States expatriates are starved for knowledge in the latest technology in their specific field or area of interest. A good rule is teach technique first, then offer your product as a means to employ that technique.

In the global economy, technique selling works because in most remote areas in developing countries especially, operations are often held together with a ball of twine and a coat hanger. Whereas in the United States, you have access to the yellow pages and overnight delivery of almost anything you need. International marketing and overseas operations teach business development executives and managers how to be creative and resourceful. Technique selling instructs your client on how to do something more effectively and efficiently. In overseas markets, improving efficiency is always an operational priority of your clients.

As a final comment on technique selling, a company in West Texas that we worked for constructed a little red school house on the grounds of the home office, next to the plant, but separate from the office buildings. In this red school house, the company housed all of its educational programs, tools, and examples of product performance experiences for the periodic arrival of its overseas customers and prospective clients. The focus was on education and technique selling at its best. It was so effective that wherever you traveled in the world on a business trip within that industry, you met someone who had been schooled in that little wooden red building.

FIVE PROVEN CHARACTERISTICS FOR EXPORT SUCCESS

Mr. John Endean, director of policy analysis, American Business Conference, sums up exporting sales of completed goods in the following observations. Success in exporting is not the preserve of huge multinational corporations. Consider, for example, the experience of the member firms of the American Business Conference (ABC). ABC consists of (in 1987) 100 fast growing firms with revenues between $10 million and $2 billion. ABC companies have enjoyed unusual success in the world market. Between 1984 and 1986, their exports grew at a compounded annual growth rate of 21 percent—ten times the rate of other publicly held companies of the same size.

Although no two companies took the same route to international success, certain common characteristics did emerge during a study that helped to explain why ABC firms are flourishing abroad. The characteristics might be called the ABC's of export success. Five were especially notable.

1. Product Excellence. As the Chairman of the American Business Conference, Arthur Levitt, Jr. has observed, "Excellence travels well. Undergirding any successful export strategy is a determination to sell a product that people want to buy." The Japanese have been masters at producing quality products since WWII. Dedication to serving international markets with the best possible product characterizes ABC firms—from Cray supercomputers to Cross pens to Stryker medical products. ABC manufacturers offer what the world demands at a standard of quality second to none.

2. Marketing Excellence. Products will not sell if poorly marketed. Recognizing Japan's fascination with American pop culture, Brown–Forman cracked the Japanese market by identifying its California Coolers and Jack Daniels bourbon as classic Americana. Locite, a manufacturer of industrial and household adhesives, charmed French customers with its super glue when an advertisement showing a beautiful young woman repairing a rip in her miniskirt appeared. Less provocatively, ABC's high-tech firms pay close attention to changing engineering standards in dozens of foreign markets and modify their products accordingly.

3. Getting Started Early. A distinctive feature of ABC companies is how early they went international. Millipore, a manufacturer of filtration systems, began exporting when its total sales were less than $10 million. Analog Devices, a manufacturer of linear integrated circuits, found foreign customers before the entire company reached the $1 million revenue mark. These and other ABC companies recognized early they wanted to be players in an international market.

4. Incremental Expansion. A company need not bet the ranch on exporting. ABC companies typically expanded their international business incrementally. They began by entering markets most nearly compatible to our own, such as Canada and the United Kingdom. Penetration of more challenging markets followed. At no one time did they take too great a financial risk. By keeping their investments modest and their companies lean and flexible, they nurtured their efforts carefully. It is no accident that 64 percent of the international ventures of ABC companies were profitable within one year, and 76 percent within two years.

5. Organizational Management. Companies must want to win internationally. A commitment to that goal begins at the top. Virtually, without exception, the chief executive officers of ABC firms led their companies into the world market. These CEOs had the vision and persistence to tap opportunities abroad, find the appropriate foreign distribution channels, and cut through the red tape to get their product to market. This takes time: nearly one-half of all ABC chief executives spend more than 20 percent of their working hours on international business matters; for one out of ten, the proportion exceeds 40 percent.

Managerial commitment, prudent risk taking, incremental growth, excellence in product and marketing—none of the ABC's of exporting are surprising or counterintuitive. They are the components of business success everywhere. To a great extent what works in Peoria works in Paris as well. American ingenuity is leaps and bounds ahead of our foreign competition. Often, the only missing ingredient for small- to medium-size business is the willingness to try. Now, in the coming decade, more than at any other time in recent memory, conditions are just right for fledgling exporters. As Arthur Levitt has said, "With the dollar at reasonably competitive levels and with government programs such as EXPORT NOW in place to provide advice, America's entrepreneurial companies can be competitive internationally. As the example of ABC firms demonstrates, there are profits to be made abroad and, from the standpoint of the economy as a whole, a real opportunity to put a dent in the trade deficit."

SELLING BY THE EXPORT NOW PROGRAM

EXPORT NOW encourages small- to medium-size businesses to enter international trade through the many agencies of the United States Department of Commerce, the Small Business Administration, and international small business development centers. These government agencies offer seminars, counseling, programs, services, and publications to assist exporters. Exporting is practical and profitable, and not just for giant corporations, but also for the smaller business. In fact, almost any American firm with a good product or service to sell may have real export potential. However, many firms that are successful in the United States market are uncertain where to begin when it comes to trading with other countries. Some overestimate the problems involved in exporting while others make it unnecessarily complicated. EXPORT NOW stresses five steps to make a company's first venture into exporting as smooth as possible.

1. Assess your market potential.

2. Get expert counseling and assistance immediately.

3. Select one or two markets from the hundreds available.

4. Formulate an export strategy.

5. Select a selling technique.

The United States Department of Commerce publishes a magazine entitled *Business America* which focuses on promotion of international trade for America's smaller businesses. Successful exporters in many varied industries and services from all 50 states on a regular basis furnish the magazine with a goldmine of information about the success of their selling techniques in a variety of markets. These true stories are regularly published in the "Exporting Pays Off" section of the magazine and can be very useful information for the new exporter as well as the seasoned trader. It is helpful to catalog a cross-section of experiences of companies that implement the five steps in the EXPORT NOW program.

Step 1: Assess Your Export Potential. Since exporting requires an extension of your firm's resources, it is important you first assess your export potential. This assessment should include a look at industry trends, the firm's domestic position in the industry, the effects exporting will have on your present operations, the status of resources, including cash, and the anticipated export potential of the product.

J-Tec Associates of Cedar Rapids, Iowa, sent executives on several trips to Europe to appraise demand for its precision flow-measuring equipment. They also sounded out possible customers at United States Department of Commerce activities, such as trade shows and the matchmaker program, and tested the market reaction by advertising in *Commercial News USA*, the department's magazine, which is distributed to over 110,000 overseas agents, distributors, government officials, and end-users.

Check Technology Corporation of Eagan, Minnesota, did some research and discovered that checking-account customers of banks in foreign countries receive only 25 to 75 checks per order, compared to 200 to 800 checks per order in the United States. Check Technology recognized that its computer-controlled electronic printing systems could fill a need overseas for producing personal checks at low cost; its system avoids the costly set-up expense of traditional technologies and therefore saves when small orders are printed. They went after the market and now export accounts for more than half of its total sales.

California Biological Supply Company of Burlington, North Carolina, had an unorthodox way of sizing up its overseas market potential for its educational supplies for science: sending foreign teachers mail-order catalogs. "Many people told us that mail order would not work overseas," the firm's export manager said, "but we have gotten an astonishing response rate—about double the rate of domestic mailings."

I-O Corporation of Salt Lake City, Utah, makes computer equipment and accessories. Some United States firms get their first inklings that they have an exportable product from scattered unsolicited foreign inquiries. "We really had not thought of exporting," said the international sales manager, "but we knew all along that we had a product that was used everywhere. It took us a while to realize that our particular products were sought after overseas." The firm thought initially that 25 percent of its total production might be sold overseas, today it's 50 percent.

Step 2: Get Expert Counseling. Once a company has assessed its export potential and made a firm decision to commit time and resources, the next step is to get expert counseling and assistance immediately. The nearest district office of the International Trade Administration within the United States Department of Commerce is a logical starting point for any company that needs international marketing assistance or technical product information. Export management companies, export trading companies, state development agencies, state departments of commerce, and other departments within state government entities often provide additional assistance to exporters. Many other groups and consultants, both in government and the private sector, stand ready to lend experienced, expert guidance to companies beginning in export trade.

Industry trade associations provide companies with numerous special services including the opportunity to meet experienced exporters. Experienced firms, and yes, sometimes even direct competitors, can be among the most valuable sources of information for new exporters. Finally, private sector consulting firms with experienced personnel and the business departments within major universities that specialize in international programs should also be considered as a source of additional information.

Eagle-Pitcher Minerals, of Reno, Nevada advises, "Check with the Department of Commerce to gain your initial knowledge about foreign marketing. Join export councils and international trade groups. Talk with other company executives involved in selling overseas; even if their product line is different from yours, they can help you learn the mechanics of exporting."

Southwest Hide Company's (Boise, Idaho) managing partner noticed that beginning exporters fear the logistics of exporting, such as letters of credit and overseas shipping. "Just find a company that has an active export operation and ask them questions." He said he is willing to talk to inexperienced exporters and give them pointers, and he believes other seasoned exporters feel the same way.

Victor Stanley's (Dunkirk, Maryland) president says don't overlook the value of state government. He has received valuable assistance from the Maryland Office of International Trade and from its offices in Brussels and Hong Kong.

Osprey Corporation, of Atlanta, Georgia found that a reliable freight forwarding agent can take away many of the headaches to exporting. This company makes air filtration and dust equipment for textile industries. The freight for-warder easily handled export paperwork and translations and was familiar with government regulations. Osprey also found that the practice of having sales rep-resentatives and/or business connections in other countries helped smooth the way to exporting.

Step 3: Select Markets. After a firm is armed with expert counseling, it must select one or two ideal markets from hundreds that are available. Language and cultural differences, special trade regulations, local competition, economic conditions, and other vital factors must be evaluated to maximize success over-seas. Once again, the United States Department of Commerce's district offices are an excellent place to begin. The commerce department offers a wide range of research programs. In addition, the department employs a global network of United States and foreign commercial service officers and other international trade specialists who conduct overseas market research and gather commercial data of broad interest to exporters. The commerce department also offers a variety of trade promotion programs that help exporters test foreign markets and evaluate export potential within a specific geographic area.

Nordson Corporation's (Westlake, Ohio) president advises beginning ex-porters: "Pick your countries carefully in accordance with your overall market-ing strategy, so you can use your resources most productively. Concentrate your efforts. Don't dissipate your time and energy."

A trade association representing your products can help you figure out which countries are promising markets. For example, the American Hardware Manufacturers Association of Schaumburg, Illinois, promotes exports of mem-bers' products and services through a series of programs, activities, and events. It has a policy of assisting members in all areas of export marketing. Each year, it hosts a national hardware show, attended by a substantial number of foreign visitors.

The Menlo Tool Company, of Warren Michigan, lacking the resources for extensive foreign travel, found the Department of Commerce could lead the way to overseas customers. The company, which manufactures carbide cutting tools, has made effective use of the department's Trade Opportunities Program (TOP), which provides current sales leads from overseas firms seeking to pur-chase or represent the company's products; these leads are available electroni-cally from the commerce department and are redistributed by the private sector in printed or electronic form.

Lec Corporation, of Minnetonka, Minnesota, decided where to concentrate its export push by placing notices about its medical products in overseas trade journals. It also located foreign customers and business partners by using the export services of the United States Department of Commerce through the Min-neapolis District Office of the International Trade Administration and also the services of the Minnesota Trade Office.

Sandco, Inc.'s (Tulsa, Oklahoma) president, who took over the management over 20 years ago, felt certain that large export markets must exist for Sandco's printing supplies and equipment, and she decided to go after the business. She started traveling to international trade shows around the world where she met dealers interested in Sandco's products. Today, attending trade shows remains one of Sandco's most effective ways of locating foreign business.

Step 4: Formulate An Export Strategy. In general, a successful export marketing strategy identifies and correlates at least four factors that jointly determine the most suitable kind of export operation: the firm's export objectives, both immediate and long range; specific tactics the firm will use; scheduling of activities, deadlines, etc. that reflect chosen objectives and tactics; and allocation of resources among scheduled activities. The marketing plan and schedule of activities should cover a two–five-year period, depending on the kind of product exported, the strength of competitors, conditions in the target markets, and other factors.

Elliott–Williams Company, of Indianapolis, Indiana shaped their export strategy around the developing countries, upon learning that 50 to 80 percent of the perishable commodities produced there go to waste. They recognized a perfect opportunity to sell their prefabricated refrigerated buildings.

Fulghum Industries, Inc., of Wadley, Georgia, in July of 1987 looked at the international situation and decided it was the right time to start building an export marketing program for its woodyard equipment for the pulp and paper industry. An important factor in the decision was the low level of the dollar, which made American products more competitive. Then, too, the firm knew there was a lot of activity in building woodyard mills and modernizing woodyard equipment. The company is moving very deliberately—one or two countries at a time—in building its foreign marketing program. It started in Chile and is now looking to Australia and New Zealand.

Several companies told *Business America*, any firm's export strategy must have the support of the people at the top. The president of Econocorp, of Randolf, Massachusetts, said, "A company must have an export mentality, and it must start with the person at the top. The company has to be committed to export to make it really go, and the commitment must go right down to the employees in shipping and receiving." The director of international sales for the Elliott–Williams Company, Inc., of Indianapolis, concurred: "It is crucial to have commitment to export by a top-level executive. No small company should attempt to go after exports without having the support of the president of the company."

A successful export strategy involves commitment, long-range planning, and continuity. According to a number of business executives interviewed by *Business America*, "You have to devote full attention to exporting. It's not something you can do part time. You need a full commitment."

Involve nationals. Many United States companies recommended involving natives of each country in sales operations, whether as representatives, agents, or employees. The president of Universal Data Systems (Huntsville, Alabama), whose firm has a network of overseas distributors, said, "You have to work through nationals. If you send United States folks into a foreign country, you have to expect that it will take a couple of years for them to find their way around. Instead, you have to find people that are embedded in the local economy." Universal Data Systems carefully selected distributors that helped the company cope with trade barriers, special requirements of highly mobilized postal and telegraph companies, and preferences for local products.

Step 5: Select A Selling Technique. After investigating and selecting foreign markets for your products, the fifth step in an export venture is to select a selling technique. There are two basic selling techniques in exporting: direct and indirect selling. The decision to market products directly to use the services of an intermediary should be made on the basis of several important factors: the size of the firm, the nature of its products, previous export experience and expertise, and business conditions in selected overseas markets.

In direct selling, the United States firm deals with a foreign importer, and the U.S. firm is usually responsible for shipping the product overseas. However, direct selling might include using the services of foreign sales representatives or agents. In selecting this method, the product involved and the way it is marketed in the United States will provide a clue as to how it can be marketed internationally. The customary business methods and established channels of distribution in targeted foreign countries can also have a bearing on the marketing channel selected.

A good number of companies interviewed by *Business America* place high priority on developing a network of overseas agents and distributors. Conap, Inc. (Olean, N.Y.), manufacturer of epoxy and polyurethane resin systems, is one of many firms that use the agent or distributor service of the United States Department of Commerce to obtain names of potential agents.

Mark Andy Inc., of Chesterfield, Missouri, opened a sales and service office in 1987 in Switzerland "to get closer to our European distributors and customers." The office is staffed by European sales people and technicians who speak to customers in their own languages, and they also stock spare parts. The decision to open the office in Switzerland was based on projections that Europe might prove to be an even stronger market for Mark Andy products than the United States market.

Heyco Inc., of Kenilworth, New Jersey, makes transactions easy for its foreign users who can avoid such complications as letters of credit and customs duties; they simply go to native distributors and buy Heyco products as they would buy local products. Heyco requires that local distributors carry a full service inventory and maintain a technically trained sales force.

Artmor Plastics Corporation, of Cumberland, Maryland, does not use overseas agents or representatives; it sells directly to customers. The company's founder has visited more than 50 countries as a one-man band; he makes many friends in his travels to whom he sends a chatty newsletter—a large number of them give him repeat business.

Other compaies have written to *Business America* and offered marketing or international business suggestions based on their personal experiences. Five excellent suggestions included this advice.

Learn about foreign credit and collections. The vice president-export for Allen Testproducts Division of Kalamazoo, Michigan, says that skill in managing foreign credit and collections is critical for export success. "We have become adept in credit/collections management," he said. "We have developed an almost foolproof method for keeping losses in this area close to zero." One way the firm keeps its risks low is to buy insurance from the Foreign Credit Insurance Association (FCIA), an agency of the Export-Import Bank of the United States. The president of Artmor Plastics Corporation, who sells directly to overseas end-users, said, "I've never lost one penny in foreign orders—and I sell mostly on open credit."

Use the fax. To carry on overseas dialogue, Conap, Inc., of Olean, N.Y., uses the telephone, the fax, and the telex exclusively. The marketing director of Belco Industries, Inc., of Carrizozo, New Mexico, advises new exporters, "Get yourself a fax machine to simplify your communication with overseas customers." When a foreign inquiry comes in, Parr Instrument Co., of Moline, Illinois, uses the telephone, telex, fax, and courier services to respond quickly. It ships most export orders by airfreight. Also, the fax machine permits exchange of pictures, drawings, sketches, and other illustrations that can be useful to clarify inquiries.

Support your overseas distributors. Allen Testproducts Division manufactures automobile diagnostic and testing equipment and provides strong support for overseas distributors in 70 countries. The home office sends out executives to visit them often. It also sends out technicians to train distributors on how to use and service the equipment and how to sell it. The company's goal is to make foreign distributors as knowledgeable and effective as the Allen salespeople in the United States.

Adapt to foreign requirements. The vice president for production of the Rich Lumber Company, of Beardstown, Illinois, said the company had gone to considerable expense to fill a trial order for hardwood strips for a flooring company in Finland. They converted to the metric system and adjusted to container shipping. "It was very disappointing to find that we had actually lost money on the first container." Now three years later—having increased productivity about 150 percent—the company is doing much better on its foreign shipments. "We learned how to do it faster and more efficiently," the vice president said.

Learn how to sell in Japan. Beauty Products International, of Malibu, California, a two-man export trading company founded only three years ago, arranged a 30-day pilot project in 1988 to sell nail enamel and lipstick in 50 outlets of a major Japanese retailer. The trial run was so successful that now products are being sold in 1,200 retail stores. By year's end, that will increase to 3,000 stores nationwide. For Quality Control Instruments, of Oak Ridge, Tennessee, a four-employee firm, Japan is the largest of its 26 foreign markets. Nippon Steel responded to the Tennessee firm's advertisement in a trade journal, then sent three executives to talk to the president of Quality Control. The result: regular orders, running at the scale of $5,000 per month. The president of Quality Control says he likes doing business with the Japanese because they pay promptly and place more orders.

4

Additional Tips For Selling Overseas

ENTRY INTO EXPORT BEGINS WITH THE SALE OF THE FINISHED PRODUCT. YOU MIGHT at some stage require advertising in the country in which you are selling a product. You should employ local agencies, where possible, that are sensitive to their own country and markets. It is doubtful that an agency in the United States would be as close to the Korean market as an agency in Seoul, Korea.

You should employ corporate counsel before entering the export market. When selecting counsel, it might be wise to choose a law firm that has correspondents in overseas locations that are of interest to you in your marketing plan. Contract law will be different in each country, and correspondent firms will simplify the gathering and evaluation of essential and pertinent information.

BE FLEXIBLE AND ADAPTABLE IN MARKET APPROACH

Be flexible in your approach to international sales. Do not make the mistake of forcing your American-made product on an overseas market. Studies have shown repeatedly that companies that were market driven in international sales, were successful over 70 percent of the time. You must respond to the needs of your local market. The Japanese employed this concept successfuly to introduce automobiles into United States markets. Once they asked American consumers what car they wanted, in approximately three years, that specific car was on the market ready for the very consumer that contributed to the design.

Quaker Oats, after establishing an international plant facility, usually produced 70 percent of indigenous products and 30 percent of foreign products that before had been imported. They did not attempt to sell American products to a

Venezuelan consumer. They produced Venezuelan products already acceptable in the marketplace.

A company that we encountered was having difficulty making a sale in Korea until they agreed to ship their product disassembled in three separate crates. Once received, the local representative assembled the parts and delivered the finished product to his customer. In overseas sales and marketing, you must be responsive to market opportunities. The marketer that is flexible, innovative, and creative will do well in international sales.

Exporting the completed product overseas and the formation of joint ventures involves an appreciation of time, understanding of cultural differences, and huge amounts of patience. In North America, we understand that time is money; business courses almost always include time management; and the growth of the fast food industry in the United States underscores our preoccupation with the value of time.

A true story where patience paid dividends occured in Mexico City a few years ago. My future joint-venture partner in Mexico finally agreed to our first meeting on a specified Tuesday morning at 10 o'clock. He said, "Stay in the hotel room, and I will call you when I arrive for the meeting." Well, as lunch time approached, he had not called. In fact, by late that afternoon, he still had not called. To shorten this true story, he finally called at the appointed time on Friday morning. The ensuing business and personal relationship generated millions of dollars in business, but the temptation on those first days in the hotel room waiting for him to call was to scrub the mission in anger. However, patience prevailed and the result was an incredible business relationship that has endured to this day.

To avoid getting ulcers in many countries of the world, you must understand that wrist watches often are simply worn for jewelry purposes because time can have very little meaning. In Hispanic countries, the Spanish word *mañana* literally translates into the English word *tomorrow* or *morning*, but in the everyday business language, it can mean simply, not today. Adapt to these and other overseas customs throughout the world as you are building personal relationships with your overseas trading partners and you will exceed your international business and social expectations.

EMPHASIS ON PRODUCT EXCELLENCE AND QUALITY

A discussion of the export sales of completed goods must emphasize that excellence sells. Quality control and quality assurance of the finished product and spare parts is essential for international trading success. Nothing is more costly or embarrassing than to be in an overseas location servicing your own product with spare parts that won't interchange. When this happens, the location is remote, replacement time is critical requiring costly airfreight, and the client's equipment is inoperative, requiring immediate service.

We had a customer located deep in the jungles of Brazil who needed parts and service for one of our products. We dispatched an engineer, complete with interchangeable parts, on a hurry-up basis to the remote, field location. Upon arrival, the engineer learned that the parts made in our own shop, which he hand-carried to the location, would not fit. We covered the expenses for the trip plus the cost and airfreight of a complete replacement unit. Quality control, important in all operations, is especially critical in international sales. The costs involved in solving needless problems is almost prohibitive, although essential in maintaining your corporate reputation of service after the sale. Someone once said, "Why does it seem like there is often a shortage of enough money to do something right the first time, but always unlimited amounts of money to correct problems?" The Japanese have learned that product excellence sells. The quality of Japanese products underscored by their international market penetration is well known.

Not long ago, former Secretary of Commerce William Verity was speaking about the disgrace of the foreign-trade deficit. He said, "If we don't produce quality, there's no way that we can get foreigners to buy United States products or get Americans to buy American products rather than foreign products." It is a known fact that quality is the priority in every market in the world. It is embarrassing that the United States taught the Japanese about quality.

THE EXPORT MANAGEMENT OR TRADING COMPANY

As an alternative to export entry as outlined earlier, you might prefer to take a more relaxed and less expensive initial approach to exporting your completed product. You might want to examine the merits of initiating international sales with independent exporters, often called Export Management Companies (EMCs) or Export Trading Companies (ETCs). These businesses account for approximately 5% to 8% of export sales from the United States.

These kinds of exporting companies usually have specific influence in certain markets and select their various product representations to suit that affinity. Often, they are able to combine shipments of different products to common destinations in single container loads to minimize freight costs. They offer economy of scale, important in global marketing for the smaller business beginning in overseas market development. Smaller manufacturers in the United States who are nonexporters are encouraged to seek out and employ an independent exporter.

The EMC, usually, represents several manufacturers, on an exclusive basis, with complementary product lines. They work on commission only, retainer fee plus commissions, or sometimes they actually take the title to the goods for resale. They function as a manufacturer's export department. In fact, they plan overall business strategy that can include finding and appointing international representatives and distributors on behalf of their clients. If you elect to use the services of an EMC, it should be a long-term arrangement, but with an understanding that you may elect at some time in the future to create and use your own export department. This will be especially true when you begin to visualize the need for strategic alliances. In any event, it might take a minimum of one year for your new relationship with the EMC to be mutually advantageous.

If the EMC takes the title to your goods, it becomes, for you, like another domestic sale. His overseas experience permits evaluation of his market, his overseas customer, and as a result, should minimize financial risks for you because he has assumed them by purchasing the product for resale. In contrast, you the manufacturer, might prefer to maintain control over pricing and clients. In this case, you would sell direct to his client, take the financial risk for the sale, and pay a pre-agreed commission to the EMC. This commission is usually in addition to his annual retainer fee. The EMC may function as your overseas distributor and may be required to inventory product for after-the-sale service. Depending on market forces and profit margins, the EMC may only be able to perform this service for the manufacturer where his network is already established.

The ETC, or export jobber, performs functions similar to the EMC, but usually operates without exclusive contracts and thus, has more freedom. ETCs usually purchase goods for resale and therefore take the title to the goods. The Export Trading Act permits these companies to apply for certificates of review that provide immunity from prosecution for activities that may otherwise be in violation of antitrust regulations from the United States Department of Commerce.

Both EMCs and ETCs offer certain advantages and disadvantages to the exporter. The major contributions are providing quick and easy entry into the export market; assisting manufacturer to focus on the export market; incurring less expenses by the supplier; affording an export learning opportunity for the manufacturer; and using international expertise in dealing with the many details involved in export sales. The major disadvantage is delegating the export opportunity and responsibility to a third party.

Mr. Stanley Epstein, president, National Federation of Export Associations, says advantages of using an export management or trading company include economies of scale (several manufacturers can spread marketing and logistics overhead across the operations of a single professional organization) and the skills necessary to complete a transaction are all under one roof—suppliers, buyers, banks, and other institutions that function as facilitators of foreign trade. The EMT–ETC frequently provides warehousing, receipt of goods from many sources, as well as packing and shipment. Trade channels are created for each product or market combination to distribute, transport, insure, finance, collect payment, and provide for aftermarket support.

Increasingly, the export trade intermediary becomes the risk taker, taking title to the goods and working with banks, credit risk insurance companies, and government agencies to provide the expertise required in carrying foreign receivables. As a result, export management and trading companies have become significant users of federal and state government export finance programs over the past two years.

In California, for example, the state's export finance office has worked actively with trade intermediaries. In Washington, the Export-Import Bank's working capital guarantee program has been heavily used by EMCs–ETCs. Under the United States Eximbank's direct access policy, which permits exporters to apply directly to its programs (rather than going through banks), trading companies have also become active users of its Intermediate Credit Program (in which exporters can borrow Exim funds, then relend them to foreign buyers).

The growing use of countertrade, which requires an exporter to buy back goods as a condition of sale, has stimulated greater activity by trading intermediaries. Many EMCs and ETCs offer the benefit of a worldwide network through which countertrade obligations can be fulfilled.

Overseas buyers have turned to United States trade intermediaries with growing frequency as well, since a single EMC–ETC can provide a network of multiple suppliers in a given industry sector. Often a United States trade intermediary can offer a sourcing function for an overseas company that needs assistance shopping in the American market.

American EMCs–ETCs tend to be small in size and entrepreneurial in nature, while their competitors abroad often are huge, worldwide organizations as in Japan, for example. The reasons for these differences are historical: European nations used trade intermediaries to deal with their colonies, and once these colonies were divested, the trading companies were found to be useful in maintaining financial links with former territories. In Japan and South Korea, huge trading companies have served a kind of quasi-government role in arranging raw material imports and spearheading market development abroad for a growing manufacturing base.

In Washington, government recognition of the unique value of trading intermediaries has helped create national awareness within the business community and among state governments and other official supporters of export development.

ASSEMBLY OF PARTS FOR LOCAL CONTENT

The assembly operation is usually the first significant activity of a newly formed joint venture. In this segment of the SAM strategy, all parts are manufactured in the United States and shipped unassembled to your distributor, representative, or joint venture partner. Special tools and required assembly jigs will need to be furnished in support of the operation. The parts are reassembled under your supervision in the host country with local labor. This phase permits training of host country personnel in the intricacies of making your product. Transfer of intellectual property such as trade secrets, patents, trademarks, and licenses is not required for this initial step in the new relationship. In the assembly operation, you are getting to know your new partner. Among other things, you will closely monitor anticipated market share increases as a result of this new function or activity.

Assembly activity meets most standards of local production for a specified time period if it is stipulated in the original agreement. You will need to carefully check the laws and regulations in each country regarding assembly. In most countries, assembly of parts is considered made in the host country, but usually not for an indefinite period of time. The purpose of assembly in the SAM strategy is to familiarize local labor with the assembly of your product while meeting requirements for local content. It is recommended that selected, skilled local personnel begin training in the United States manufacturing facility concurrently with the assembly operation. This decision is dependent on the amount of time required to master this first step of the joint venture.

In this activity of your joint venture operation, you are furnishing the same parts that you were selling in the finished product. Now, by adding local content, vis-a-vis local labor for assembly in the host country, you should see improvement in market share for product sales. You should ensure that you retain responsibility for management and quality control during assembly. This should be acceptable to your joint venture partner who in this phase will learn how to produce the commodity that is being sold in his country. Throughout this process, your new partner should begin to understand the value of your product, the importance of market reputation, the worth of quality control, and the necessity of after-the-sale service.

REASONS FOR THE ASSEMBLY OPERATION

This is the beginning of the formation of an overseas partnership that will perpetuate your presense in the marketplace. Local content will improve market share. This increased business will require that you expand production at home thereby creating more jobs in your United States company as well as in the newly formed joint venture.

In the new global economy, assembly will more and more become a requirement of international trade. Almost all developing countries insist on the employment of some natural resources, be it labor, materials, or services in the production of products that they consume. This trend will rise in the 1990s and beyond. In Europe 1992, there will be a directive insisting on product certification on European soil. This will involve some degree of assembly or manufacturing as a condition of market entry.

IMPORT RESTRICTIONS

It is likely that you will encounter prohibitive import tariffs or outright embargoes for classifications of assembled or disassembled product that you desire to import from your United States production facility. For example, we manufactured a generic product called a stabilizer for the American market. In many countries of the world, stabilizers were prohibited imports due to local manufacturing of similar products. While not exactly identical to our product, the terminology stabilizer was listed in the custom's agent book of prohibited imports. Webster's dictionary provides a definition for both stabilizers and centralizers. Strangely enough, the definition of each is about the same word-for-word. Therefore, the generic name was changed from stabilizer to centralizer and the product with the new name was cleared through customs without duties or questions.

Centralizer had the same maening to our clients as did the word stabilizer. International business frequently requires the exporter to be adaptive to circumstances.

When you are negotiating with overseas representatives to sell your product in their country, you should always keep the joint venture option for assembly and manufacture near at hand. Provisions for joint ventures as a natural extension of your overseas business development should be included in original distribution or representative agreements. Japanese automobile manufacturers entered the United States market using this identical strategy. During the past 20 years, they sold, then assembled, and now, manufacture cars in America. They, too, used SAM strategy.

MANUFACTURING OF PARTS

This phase begins the development of the true joint venture leading into significant increases in market share. Contributions of indigenous resources in addition to labor play a major role in this concluding activity of SAM strategy. Exchange of intellectual property is usually required during this activity. Technology transfer provisions and suitable agreements will be discussed at length later.

When manufacturing is in place, you should appeal to local authorities to consider placing like or similar imports on a list of dutable imports. In fact, customs may feel more strongly about protecting foreign investment in local enterprises and impose a ban on similar products. Afterall, you and your new partner, in forming the joint venture, have expended considerable time and monies to establish the production facility. You should be entitled to most favored treatment status from the local customs and excise people as a result of your investment in your local, joint venture production facility. You have much more at risk than a competitor, while afforded the same investment opportunity. You may prefer to continue to ship completed goods into your market if it can be continued without penalty.

CONSIDER LEVELS OF TECHNOLOGY TRANSFER

There are probably several levels of technology within your corporation. Let's say, you have experienced ten levels of product innovation during the past five years. Your productive research and development group anticipates additional innovations in the near term. You should assess your new host country market and introduce a level of technology commensurate with the capabilities of the joint venture. Many markets are not ready to absorb the latest and highest technological advances. Computerland, on Gorky Street in Moscow, is introducing early 1980s technology. The market is not ready for the highest level of portable computer sophistication, but it will be with time.

If you are selling at level ten in America, you may consider introducing technology to the joint venture at level three or level four. This level of sophistication may satisfy the current appetite of the market. If you were, for example, in the light bulb business, and the bulk of your rural market was without electricity, your initial level of introduction of technology for market access may be candles. As electricity is disbursed throughout the rural region, then the introduction of higher technology, in this case the light bulb, becomes feasible. You shouldn't reveal all of your know-how, even if a market can absorb the technology. In industrialized countries such as Europe 1992, where the latest and greatest high-tech is required, you can own the tools of production and thereby protect your proprietary interests.

When evaluating your manufacturing potential, you may have suitable products or technology on-the-shelf that can be easily and economically reactivated. This would add to your profit picture because product or project development costs would not have to be repeated. Yet, this technology or product may enter this new market and achieve the same enthusiastic results as it enjoyed in the United States, say, five years previously.

LDC TECHNOLOGY TRANSFER CHECKLIST

In most developing countries, technology transfers for partial to subsantial manufacturing must usually meet one or more of the following requirements in this checklist:

- It should be capable of developing and producing new products.
- It should be capable of improving quality and performance of products, reducing production costs, and lowering consumption of energy and raw materials.
- It should be favorable to maximum utilization of local resources such as labor and other services.
- It should be capable of expanding product exports to increase earnings of foreign exchange.

- It should be favorable to environmental protection.
- It should be favorable to production safety for worker protection.
- It should be favorable to development of managerial and other administrative skills.
- It should contribute to the advancement of scientific and technical levels of employees.

Compliance with one or several of the earlier requirements when providing technology transfers to developing nations should not be difficult for most small-to medium-size companies in the United States. Initially, consider providing intermediate technology in order that the transition from imports, assembly, and partial manufacturing is less costly, market acceptable, and occurs more smoothly. Start at level three and increase your technology transfer requirements to the joint venture as market demand dictates. Let the market drive the need and provide the income for introduction of new technology.

An interesting lesson was learned a few years ago involving premature transfer or disclosure of technology. The victim of this true story was one of the pioneers in the new transportable computer industry in the late 1970s. This manufacturer had a strong, growing sales base for his model 1, a pioneer transportable computer. His distributors were well stocked and sales were in an upward trend. One day, in the Los Angeles airport, reporters asked him about any upcoming new, and advanced technology under consideration at his company. Without thinking for a brief moment, and in the excitement of the moment, he announced the new, model 2, which incoporated many advanced features beyond the technology of the original model 1. Trucks began to roll into the plant in California with returns of the first model. Customers with major orders for the new second model expected to pay with merchandise credits from returns of the older model. Obviously, the small, but growing company was not able to endure the financial setback of accepting multiples of returned, now obsoleted units after their highest level of technological competence was publicly disclosed. You might say that timing was wrong for the interview in the airport.

KEEP SOME KEY COMPONENTS AT HOME

When considering the manufacture of parts overseas in a joint venture operation keep some key component parts close to home. Manufacture these critical items in your United States facility for shipment to the joint venture. This will permit you to exercise one additional element of control over the joint venture.

As an example, we manufactured a product that was bulky and mostly comprised of steel castings. The locking rings used to attach the product in its primary application were key elements of the design and operation of the product.

Rather than brokering and shipping cast steel from the United States, we deferred the production of the castings to the joint venture in the host country to satisfy the local content requirement. We continued to manufacture and supply the high-tech, high profit rings from the home office to the partnership. This operation permitted us to monitor production and disposition of product in the region where the joint venture was located. There were other elements of management and marketing controls written into the agreement, but keeping the manufacturing of the key component at the United States production facility was a huge comfort factor.

TRADE SHOWS AS A SALES TOOL

Trade shows that are coordinated through the United States Department of Commerce and other trade groups can be a useful tool in developing overseas sales and locating foreign representatives. They can be especially cost effective for meeting many people, customers and potential distributors in a central location at domestic or international shows. It is important to be staffed with suitable technical personnel in your sales booth to lend support to your marketing group at the shows. Also, ensure that the quality of your display booth and presentation of your product are at their best.

The United States Department of Commerce catalog and video/catalog exhibitions offer a low-cost, low-risk way to generate sales leads, whether you are looking for sales or representatives. Using the resources of United States embassies worldwide helps you to show your videos to potential agents, distributors, and other buyers in selected world markets. Their overseas officers provide the following services:

- Promotion of the event to a targeted business audience
- Displays of your catalog or video
- Staffing of people fluent in the local language to answer questions
- Trade leads and lists of visitors.

They keep your catalogs active after the show, using them in subsequent promotional events or featuring them in embassy commercial libraries. Custom tailored to meet the needs of small- to medium-size business, new-to-export or new-to-market firms, catalog, and video/catalog exhibitions have benefited thousands of United States firms since 1972. Every year commerce organizes several catalog and video/catalog exhibitions highlighting certain industries in selected markets. You participate by paying a small participation fee, sending catalogs or videos to the exhibition site, indicating your objective in each market, and responding promptly to each inquiry that you receive.

THE SCHEDULE B NUMBER

On January 1, 1989, the United States implemented the Harmonized Commodity Description and Coding System (HS) for classifying merchandise in international trade. Since that time, all shipper export declarations (forms 7525V, 7525V-Alt, 7513) have required that the revised 1988 Schedule B number be reported in item 17 on the form. A shippers export declaration is required to be submitted for virtually all export shipments from the United States. If you have difficulty in locating your new Harmonized System Schedule B number, call or write the United States Department of Commerce in your area. You can also call the Bureau of Census for information regarding the following categories: Industry Section Chief; Food, Animal, and Wood Section; Minerals and Metal Section; Textiles Section; Machinery and Vehicles Section; and Chemicals and Sundries Section.

GOVERNMENT ASSISTANCE PROGRAMS

The United States Department of Commerce, International Trade Administration, and the United States and Foreign Commercial Service provide excellent information for the new exporter. The commerce department generates data through its many agencies. If you want to know, for example, the population of children between the ages of one and five years old in Australia, the department can probably furnish that information from vast statistical compiling systems and data. If you want to know the per annum consumption of United States wine per country, this information is also available from the data bank.

A few of the many categories of services that the commerce department makes available to the new exporter include the following.

Comparison Shopping Service (CSS) offers a quick, accurate assessment of how your product will sell in a given market. For a reasonable fee, they will answer the following questions for you:

- Does your product have sales potential in the market?
- Who is supplying a comparable product locally?
- What is the usual sales channel for this getting into the market?
- What is the going price for a comparable product?
- Are purchasers of such products primarily influenced by price, or by other competitive factors, such as credit, quality, delivery, service, promotion, or brand?
- What is the best way to get sales exposure in the market?
- Are there any impediments to selling the product, such as quotas, duties, or local regulations?

- Who might be interested and qualified to represent or purchase your product in this market?
- Who might be an interested, qualified licensing or joint venture partner for your company?

Research specialists in the target country interview importers, distributors, retailers, wholesalers, end-users, and local producers of comparable products, if any, and inspect similar products on the market. The department usually completes your customized report within 45 days. This service is especially valuable to new, small exporters with few foreign contacts and limited overseas sales experience. This CSS service provides on-the-spot, current data that you need to make marketing decisions without the large travel, investigation, and other expenses associated with overseas research. While this service is helpful, the results of the survey must be tempered with other sources of similar information such as trade associations, manufacturers of similar products, peers, and competitors.

Export Contact List Service is comprised of a list of thousands of foreign compaies, stored on a database, who are interested in doing business with United States firms. These names have been accumulated by the department of commerce over a period of years at trade promotion activities carried out at United States embassies and other posts around the world. They screen each company and develop a business profile. The profile includes name, product or service, telex, facsimile, telephone, key contact, year established, number of employees, and relative size. Profiles are updated on the Commercial Information Management System (CIMS). The contacts that you need from their lists may include:

• Representatives	• Importers
• Manufacturers	• Retailers
• Wholesalers	• Distributors
• Licensing Partners	• Advertising Agencies
• Service Companies	• Banks
• Marketing Firms	• State Trading and Procurement Agencies

Many of the companies are buyers of commodities, raw materials, machinery, retail goods, specialty items, and other products and services. This ECLS service puts mailing lists, labels, or profiles at your fingertips. It saves time and costly in-country research if your product is suited for this type of new market approach. It is ideal for direct-mail campaigns to locate specific customers and to target business prospects by type of firm, import interest, country, and other variables. Overseas government agencies, trade associations, banks, and other organizations are also included in the Export Contact List Service database.

Foreign Market Research gets data that you may need quickly. Your exporting success could depend on how well you know your target market. But you probably don't have on-staff resources for expensive, time-consuming investigations. Turn to the export information experts of the Foreign Market Research and Trade Statistics services of the United States Department of Commerce to plot your best overseas sales strategies. They provide in-depth market data on selected products and industries in countries offering the best opportunities for United States goods. This convenient research service helps you select new markets, analyze new market conditions, formulate selling strategies, and enter promising foreign markets.

Matchmaker Trade Delegations match you with potential agents, distributors, and joint venture or licensing partners. The Department of Commerce does the background work—evaluating your product's potential, finding and screening contacts, and handling logistics. You, the potential new exporter, follow up with an intensive trip filled with face-to-face meetings with prospective clients and in-depth briefings on the economic and business climate of the countries visited. They offer:

· Prescreened prospects interested in your product or service

· In-country publicity

· Convenient sales avenues

· Business appointments scheduled for you through the United States embassy or consulate

· Thorough briefings on market requirements and business practices

· Interpreter

Matchmakers help the smaller business meet export sales objectives efficiently and economically. They generally target major markets in two countries and limit trips to a week or less so you can interview the maximum number of good candidates with a minimum time away from your office.

World Trade Data Reports (WTDR) screens your foreign customers and prospective clients. You are an exporter, not a gambler. You want to invest in sound transactions with reputable clients, but how can you check out customers half way around the world? That offer from Peru looks interesting, but you just don't know anything about Peru Imports, Ltd., in Lima, Peru. The WTDR program provides thorough, confidential background reports on potential trading partners—including buyers, distributors, agents, and retailers. WTDRs assess your potential customer's reputation and recommend whether to conduct trade with the firm and on what basis. United States businesses of all sizes use WTDRs to take much of the gamble out of exporting.

Commercial News USA , the high-profile export catalog of the Department of Commerce, can launch or expand your company's export sales—at a fraction of the cost of commercial advertising. With a single listing in *Commercial News USA*, you'll reach more business representatives and potential customers than you could in years of sales calls—without ever leaving home. Distributed worldwide, *Commercial News USA* reaches more than 100,000 screened business readers eager to know about new products. Especially beneficial to smaller firms, this convenient program can help you generate sales leads, identify profitable markets for your new products, and locate representatives, distributors, licensing partners, and buyers.

When two people are looking at the same potential marketing opportunity, one as an employee of a government and the other as a private enterprise exporter, evaluations could be different. You may not find your specific answer in these government programs, but much data and assistance is available to assist you in finding the answer.

COMMISSION STRUCTURE FOR OVERSEAS REPRESENTATIVES

The majority of smaller businesses enter export markets by the indirect sales method that calls for the appointment of commission sales agents, distributors, or representatives who will market your products before the in-country joint venture operations are initiated. After you select an agent, distributor, or representative, you need to formalize an agreement in writing to protect each party's interest. This contract, prepared by corporate counsel, will focus on mutual responsibilities for marketing services.

The overseas sales representative is usually compensated by commissions based on gross sales volume in his territory. There are many different ways to structure a commission arrangement with the overseas representative. If thoughtful pursuit of mutual objectives is employed in the development of the commission program, product sales in the region may exceed your expectations. Many companies, without much thought, simply say "If you get the order, we'll pay you a commission." This policy overlooks an understanding and appreciation of the true role of a sales representative. While this approach appears equitable from the company's point of view, a distributor may find this unworkable for several reasons.

Such a policy implies that commissions only accrue if the representative actually receives the purchase order. It would mean that the representative must be geographically on hand to receive each order. In actuality, he may have made the sale on your behalf, weeks or even months earlier. The buyer, when ready to procure the goods or services, may be required to place the order direct with his home office purchasing group. In many cases, clients are governed by corporate policy that requires acquisition of capital goods through a centralized purchasing organization usually situated in their home office. In such a situation, the sales representative would not be able to receive the order directly even though he generated the order and was physically in the buyer's office.

Such short-sighted commission policy implies that the company is reluctant to give credit for the overall sales effort in the region under contract by restricting commissions to orders actually received. From an experienced overseas manufacturer's point of view, this is the least desirable contract. Some territories such as Brazil, Indonesia, and India are tremendous in size. To insist that a representative be on hand to receive each purchase order in a decentralized region is somewhat unreasonable, if not physically impossible. In global selling, the point of sale can be difficult to determine. International sales should result from teamwork, between the manufacturer and one and/or more of his global representatives.

A more workable and fair approach gives credit where credit is due. The following commission structure works effectively for all concerned. To begin with, the written principal provides, as part of the manufacturer's representation agreement, detailed descriptions of the percentage of commission to be paid on the international sale of each item in their product line. Next, the activity for total commission paid is divided into three specific categories.

Territory

One third of the total commission is paid on final destination of shipment, if known. If unknown, this amount is accrued in a special account for future payments to representatives should an agent subsequently notify the company that the product has been received by a client in his territory. Export Trading Companies purchase on behalf of overseas clients. The shipping destination, as far as the company knows, is the ETC warehouse, say, in New Jersey. The ultimate destination for the product may be Nigeria, but this fact may be unknown to the company at the time of the transaction. Unless the representative knows about this specific purchase by his client in Nigeria, the allocation of territorial commission may remain unpaid indefinitely.

Product or Service Specification

A second one third of the total available commission is paid for product or service specification. This is the direct result of the representative visiting with the customer to sell him or her on purchasing your product. This is called *allocation of commission* for selling the product or service. Communication regarding these activities should be sent in report form to the principal on a timely basis. If the buyer places his order directly to his home office, a record is on file with manufacturer or with the principal. An effective way to ensure that you get the order is to have the client write the request for quotation with your exact engineering and product specifications, but without reference to your trademark or company name. This is a rewarding international marketing skill and usually involves a high-tech product, an operational technique, or an unusual service. Once the specifications are written around your company's product, patent, trademark, technique, or service, you then enjoy a proprietary position as a vendor.

Receipt of Order

The final one third of the available percentage is allocated for actually receiving the purchase order. If the specification for the company's product is complete, the principal should pay the the full commission on the basis of successful sales activity. In all cases where the representative clearly assisted in making the sale, he should be credited with this final one-third of the total commission. Actual receipt of the purchase order may be a physical impossibility. Afterall, the major victory is in securing the order specification with the manufacturer. For this system or method of commission payments to be effective, there must be continued communication between the representative and the principal.

GLOBAL ADVANTAGE OF THIS COMMISSION STRATEGY

This procedure, or a similar flexible program, has the added advantage in that it supports a global corporate strategy for commissioned representatives. Payment of commissions for services performed in differing geographical regions assures the company and representatives that credit is given where credit is due. Consider this scenario: Your representative in Australia is successful in having your customer specify your product. Your customer, however, will take ultimate and final delivery of your product in Thailand and expects after-the-sale service in that region.

In this scenario, you would pay two-thirds of the total commission to the representative in Australia for making the sale, and one-third to the representative in Thailand for territorial destination. This commission policy provides the agent in the final destination with income from the sale and delivery. Afterall, you will rely on him to provide after-the-sale service in Thailand. Territorial commissions, although frequently small, provide incentive and some reimbursement for sales and service expenses for the representative and cause him to work to earn total commission amounts by performing the three vital functions.

MONITORING PERFORMANCE

The distributor incurs substantial selling expenses for his principals. His physical presence in his country provides corporate representation without the corresponding fixed expenses. Territorial commissions go a long way toward covering daily overheads for foreign sales representatives. If your overseas marketer is clipping coupons, another name for depositing commission checks without any work activity on your behalf, you should quickly terminate the relationship. Reporting procedures, as required by the original written agreement, will provide clues as to the quantity and quality of work your representative is doing on your behalf.

The amount of commissions paid to a distributor is an indicator of the volume of business being consumated in his territory. A representative once said to a principal, "I have 15 accounts, and your company is on the bottom of my list in paying commissions." The principal replied, "Need I say another word about your performance?" Another performance clue is provided by a personal visit to the representative's home turf. Customer satisfaction in the geographical area may provide insight as to the extent of your representative's sales and service activities.

WRITTEN COMMISSION AGREEMENT

Reference is made throughout this text to the importance of mutual understanding of each party's objectives including the commission program. Clear written agreements (See Appendix A), properly understood by both parties, should preclude future misunderstandings and difficulties. The significance of this statement can best be explained by a true story that was extremely costly to a foreign representative. A customer, in the representative's territory, was earmarked by the principal as being ready to place a substantial order for capital goods in North Sumatra, Indonesia. The representative, who had maintained a long-standing relationship with the potential client throughout the Pacific Rim through other product sales, was asked to assist with the sale. The representative and company sales and engineering personnel began the pursuit of this large order.

The representative signed a formal contract with the company years prior to this event. After a considerable amount of time and money was expended by both the agent and the company in pursuit of this business, the order was placed directly with the principal's office in the United States. The commission on this sale was to have been substantial for the representative. Within a week of receiving the order, the agent was given 30 days notice of termination by the company in accordance with the provisions of the terms of the contract. The contractual and working relationship that had been in effect and profitable for both the representative and company for over four years was suddenly cancelled when the company was faced with the prospect of payment of such a large commission. This single commission earned was going to be many times greater than the annual salary of the international sales manager.

The representative protested for several reasons, not the least of which was for recovery of time and expenses in pursuit of this specific order. The principal simply referred to the paragraph in the agreement which essentially read, "commissions are due and payable on all orders 30 days after shipment into the representatives's territory." There was no specific reference made in the contract as to when commissions were accrued, such as at point of sale or time of sale. The principal saved a considerable amount of money, and the representative was contractually bound by that decision.

To make matters worse in this example, this same company moved a district salesman, new to international marketing, into the representative's territory a year before this cancellation. The employee received a copy of the commissions paid to the representative each month. Without understanding or caring about prior business risks and financial sacrifices employed by the representative in reaching a point of fair compensation in four years, the employee only saw big money going to the agent, and in his eyes, small money in his own paycheck. From the moment of his arrival, this new-to-international salesman began to undermine the long-standing relationship between the principal, his company, and the agent. In retrospect, the representative should have directly employed the required sales and service personnel who would have been under his direction and control. After the principal's service employee arrived in the territory, the situation was beyond the representative's direct control and resulted in termination of the long-standing agreement.

An upfront, clear understanding to the best of your ability in writing is absolutely necessary to prevent occurrence of the grief and sacrifice that resulted from the miscommunication and misunderstanding in the earlier example. The principal felt the commission was just too large and used legal and binding recourse to avoid the payment through the delivery clause that was purposely placed in the contract. That may have been acceptable, if it was clear at the outset that success would end the contract. Some American exporters set limits on agents. For example, they may say at $100,000 per annum commission level, we'll put in our own people. Smart export managers believe, if it ain't broke, don't fix it, since commissions are variable expenses based on successful market penetration and sales.

OVERCOMING THE RELUCTANCE TO PAY COMMISSIONS

Many United States smaller companies are reluctant to pay commissions. When an overseas agent begins to earn more than the chairman of the board, American companies tend to look for alternatives. This is a short-sighted approach unless the business plan, which should be known to both parties, called for termination of the agent when a joint venture operation is needed. Usually representatives are dismissed as a result of earning too much money for doing an excellent job.

Insurance companies have enjoyed corporate growth for years by compensating salesmen with commission income, but more importantly, by not tampering with the established commission schedule. Successful exporters increase the rate of commissions as volume of sales increase. Reluctant approaches to payment of commissions on behalf of many small- to medium-size companies have historically cost United States industry in overseas market share. Commissions are a variable expense that should be factored into the sales price of the product. They should be willingly paid because they result from successful sales performance. If the commissions paid or accrued side of the ledger is large, you can bet the order book is or has been full. The sales commission for a job well done is the beginning of building a foundation with your future joint venture partner.

You can always do the following calculation if a commission accrued amount makes you nervous. Simply divide the commission amount by the commission rate to determine your gross sales. If you paid a representative $25,000 last year at a 7% commission rate, your gross sales were over $357,000. It is important to continually think of the commission as a variable expense because nothing is owed until something is sold. The commissioned sales representative can make significant contributions to your bottom line. He is a cost-effective tool to improve market share in the export sales of completed goods.

TRANSITION FROM REPRESENTATION TO JOINT VENTURING

It should be clear in the beginning when the conversion from sales representation role to the joint venture will occur. If the transition is to be based on total annual commissions paid to the representative, an understanding of that amount should be spelled out in writing. The principal may say, if we are beginning to pay annual commissions of $150,000, maybe we should begin looking into the prospect of forming a joint venture. At this level of commissions, the total sales figures are indicating that an assembly operation or partial manufacturing of product may be needed to ensure retention and/or increase in present market share. The agreement may just state simply that the joint venture will occur in two years.

A manufacturer's representative agreement, if long-term in nature, should include a provision for joint ventures to complete the SAM strategy. Market development strategy should include terms of conversion as part of the original written agreement. The agent and principal should closely communicate regarding this point. Markets are dynamic and changing competitive forces can cause rethinking and drastic alteration of initial strategy. Host country laws can also change and directly affect your timing and approach to the market.

PRACTICAL CONSIDERATIONS FOR THE AGREEMENT

The Contents

When preparing the agreement, your corporate counsel should focus on the following points: the territory that is to be considered as the final destination of product; whether the agreement is exclusive or nonexclusive for that territory; the term of the agreement and type of notice and specific cause required for termination; the point in time that commission accrues, such as on receipt of order or shipment of order; the commission payment schedule per product; when payment is made, on receipt of payment from customer or 30 days after shipment; and the services that each party to the agreement will provide the other such as reports, and on what basis, timing, market feedback, and other information.

It should be clear at the beginning and made a part of the contract what investment the representative is required to make in regard to amount of inventory, sales personnel, service center personnel, or other requirements for support of the principal's market. If the contract is terminated, for whatever reason, provision for purchasing the representative's inventory and other assets used to support your marketing should be spelled out in detail.

Termination Clauses

The termination clause is a significant part of the contract between the principal and the representative. Usually, the document will read, "This contract is terminated by 30 days notice provided in writing by either party." This can serve the legal interest of the contract, but after years of experience as a manufacturer's representative and as a manufacturer, we insist that performance criteria for both parties be included in the contract. If there was to be a termination, it would be for a cause previously discussed and set out in writing in the agreement. This minimizes the possibility of personality conflicts, ego trips, personnel changes, or the worst case, someone's whims or wishes, causing cancellation of the contract. If reporting is a requirement, then the frequency, format, and anticipated content should be included in the contract. If service personnel were required, the number and their level of training and competence is stipulated. If the representative is required to have, say, two servicemen to maintain the contract, then it would be clear to both parties that failure to meet this requirement would be grounds for termination. If the representative is terminated by the company, then provision should be made for return of inventory to the principal.

This event should be provided for in the original contract.

On the principal's side, supply of updated and current visual aids and technical material, location and cost of training, frequency of visits to the representative's geographical area, and amount and description of specific head office support should all be provided for in the agreement. If the principal receives an inquiry from the agent's territory, it should be forwarded immediately to the overseas representative. Policy in this regard should be spelled out in the agreement.

Inventory as a Market Service

More often than not, you will require some local inventory in the host country if only to support after-the-sale service aspects of your representative's business. In some cases, substantial inventory may be required. Your handling of this may vary according to circumstances such as your credit policy, value of the goods, significance of the stock, political considerations, or simply, the ability of your representative to pay for the inventory.

You would be well advised to insist in all cases, where possible, that the foreign representative purchase the required inventory. This recommendation is made more in the interest of building market share than from the point of being paid, although payment is extremely important. If the representative has his own money in the inventory, a substantial amount of his time will be expended in selling these goods, resulting in reorders and market expansion.

He may suggest that you consign stock to him. This should be the absolute last resort and only considered if the inventory is made a condition of a substantial sale by an important client.

It has been our experience, that the consigned stock has a value to the representative equal to the amount that he paid for that inventory. This type of concern should always be covered in the terms of the original agreement. If your representative is in reality, a distributor, then inventory purchases should be a requirement for the agreement and territory assignment as a condition of contract. In some cases, contracts can be written to designate performance. If a given amount of volume of trade sales are generated per quarter, or even annually, the terms of the original agreement remain in effect. Trade can be mean sales to others in the territory or inventory purchases by the representative or distributor. What trade means to each party to the agreement must be specifically spelled out in the written contract.

If inventory is a requirement in your agreement with the distributor, provision must be made for its disposition if the contract is terminated. Different policies can apply depending upon who terminated the contract, but most companies would have a policy that would require taking back of the stock so as to maintain control over its final distribution. The terms and price of the buyback must also be provided for in the original signed agreement.

EXPORT PRICING TO SELL

There are many aspects to consider when pricing your product for export. Export management and trading companies, overseas representatives, intermediate suppliers, and others to be compensated in your export strategy must be provided for in your pricing. The number of distribution levels is dependent on your marketing strategy. How would you quote an end user, in an area where you have a sales representative, who makes this request from you directly and also from an export trading company that you recognize for a discount? To protect all of your third party suppliers, you should probably quote list or catalog price to the end user; quote list price less the standard trading company or jobber discount to your export company; while reserving the commissions, as per contract, for your territorial representative.

Your export price should be sensitive to time. Since you have longer time cycles in export sales, you should anticipate increased sales volumes and consider availability of overseas suppliers or components. You should anticipate complications in filling the order, especially in initial stages, and also consider payment terms if they involve special risks or costs, additional sales, general and administrative expense, representative's commissions, special discounts, and any product modification costs involved with the sale. You should be aware of the landed cost of your product in the buyer's location and keep well advised of your competitor's landed cost, too.

When quoting, you should be aware of the following costs and terms associated with the sale of finished product from your plant in the U.S.

Shipping Rates. Your freight forwarder will furnish this information, for inland freight from your plant to the shipping point, air or ocean freight, upon your request. You must supply him with exact weights and dimensions after the shipment is packed and ready to ship. This is a substantial element in determining your landed costs. This cost is reimbursable and should be included in your invoice to your customer.

Export Packing. This would be a percentage of the sales value, say 2% to 3% dependent on the product being shipped, or as quoted by a competent export packing and crating firm. This also is figured in landed costs and is reimbursed by your overseas client.

Shipping Terms. Ex works; Ex factory; ex warehouse; ex mill; ex silo; etc. It means, as is, where is, at the point of origin.

FOB (Free on Board). Free on board means on board the ship at which point the cargo passes across the ship's rails and the title is conveyed. The exporter pays all costs, though usually reimbursable, until goods are on board the ship. The terms are normally FOB vessel, or FOB any United States port. If the exporter quotes FOB airport, he is only responsible until he gets the goods into the hands of the appropriate carrier or agent of the carrier.

FOB—(Named Inland Carrier at Named Island of Departure). This means at some inland point, it is loaded on or into a carrier's specific vehicle (truck, railcar, etc.) to be transported by that and future carriers. If carrier is not named, mode of transport should be specified such as FOB Container, New Orleans, Louisiana. Every "valid" form of FOB leaves the goods on board or taken in charge of by some kind of carrier.

FAS (Free Alongside Ship). In this instance, the buyer rather than the seller must clear the goods for export and have them loaded on board. Title passes when the goods are delivered alongside the vessel and acknowledged, usually by means of a dock receipt. You only see this type of quote for a specific purpose which usually benefits the buyer.

Cost and Freight (C&F). This quote is followed by a specific overseas port of destination. It could be an airport or harbor. Seller accepts the responsibility for paying freight, loading, and other incidental charges, usually reimbursable, incurred to obtain the clean bill of lading. The buyer assumes the risks when the goods cross ship's rails, or are put into the hands of the named carrier at the airport or the carrier's agent.

Cost, Insurance, and Freight (CIF). This designation is also accompanied by a named port of destination. It means the seller incurs all charges for the buyer to include insurance, which are all technically charged back to the buyer. The most protection is in warehouse to warehouse coverage. Most shipments are insured to 110 percent of CIF value. Risk and title transfer just as in C&F and FOB sales. However, with CIF, the buyer has insurance when the title transfers and is protected against loss during transit.

It is important that your export quotation department use the services of a competent international freight forwarder. His expertise will be invaluable, not only with shipping schedules, but also in controlling costs involved with freight, freight consolidations, and insurance. Often, resourcefulness in calculating and reserving freight space and creative determinations of insurance costs can be instrumental in obtaining an order on price differential. While all associated costs added to the product sales price are for the account of the buyer, the freight forwarder will be invaluable in assisting you in determining landed costs for your client.

The pricing information as discussed in previous paragraphs relates to sales of manufactured product, which is fairly straight forward as to sales price, shipping, packing, sales commissions, and export discounts, where applicable. These parameters will become part of your export pricing policy. There is another aspect to pricing that may be worth covering in the event you get into negotiations whereby you are furnishing, for example, know-how, expertise, training, and equipment as part of a transaction as your contribution to the project. The value of your contribution must be agreed as being part of the cost of the package for the overseas buyer.

A specific example relating to this point occurred to my company in 1967 in Algeria. Our local representative advised us to quote a greater price than we expected to receive for the services and equipment. He advised, "Do this in order to be in position to offer a substantial export discount in the final rounds of negotiation and still be within the profit margins anticipated." He reminded us that Arabs by virture of their culture enjoy bargaining. This is noticed in the Souk or local market when they compete for your consumer business. In fact, it is insulting to an Arab merchant if you pay his initial asking price without horse trading for a discount on the final amount to be paid. This same culture can be found in major industrial negotiations for larger purchases, hence the pricing recommendation from our representative. The message was to be aware of the culture and be sensitive to its traditions, and always trust your in-country partner and follow his advice.

Anyway, the final quotation for the machinery and services was received from our home office, and we added a percentage mark-up to the sales price equivalent to the anticipated discount that would be given up in the final round of negotiations. All pricing was calculated with anticipated discounts and representative's commissions. The net to the home office would be the same and the trading exercise was in respect of the culture. A corporate officer in the United States, a long way from the delicate negotiations in Algiers, called and insisted that we go into negotiations with the final price that the company expected to receive to preserve and ensure corporate credibility. He didn't understand that our pricing procedure was creditworthy in the country where we were about to begin negotiations.

The meeting opened with our Algerian counterpart saying, "I just returned from a convention in Ontario, Canada, where I learned that you were going to overcharge a substantial percentage for your machinery, know-how, show-how and service contract; therefore, you must agree immediately to a discount in that amount or these discussions are here-by terminated." Obviously, with our revised pricing, there was no room for manuevering in the transaction and the trade was lost for the machinery and the consulting project.

TRAVEL TIPS AND USEFUL INFORMATION

Command of the English language will be a faithful traveling companion and prepare you for most business assignments. However, foreign usages of English have a way of sabotaging even the best sentence—even in England. We knew a Dunlop OMD salesman that traveled out of Grimsby, England, who used to say, "In the 'short span' of just over two hundred years, Americans managed to distort the most beautiful language in the world." As examples of the differences, Roger E. Axell in a book entitled, *Do's and Taboos Around the World*, (John Wiley & Sons, Inc., New York) cites an instance where the general manager of one of his firms' international division was complimenting a distinguished gentleman on the knickers he was wearing. Why did the gentleman turn crimson? In Britain, knee-length trousers are called *plus fours*, whereas knickers are ladies' underpants.

Axell continues by saying misunderstandings flow the other way, too. When an Englishman says a project will be finished "at the end of the day," he simply means that it will be done when it's done. A word as unambiguous as *backlog* can convey the wrong impression. To the British, a large *backlog* does not imply a list of orders waiting to be filled, but a hopelessly overstocked inventory due to inefficiency. On the other hand, when a Frenchman demands something, no offense should be taken. The French verb for ask is *demander*.

Axell says the word that gets Americans in Japan in the most trouble is *you*. To a Japanese, it is almost a violation of his territory, like jabbing a finger under his nose. At the very highest levels, Japanese businessmen do not expect to be addressed directly or even looked at directly. Those whom you deal with at other levels do not think in terms of self, but of company. "What do you think?" is not the point. What the "company thinks" is the point.

Axell concludes by adding, an American told his Japanese customer, "Our thinking is in parallel." The Japanese agreed, but after many months, nothing happened. Frustrated, the American asked, "Why didn't you act? We agreed our thinking was in parallel." The Japanese responded, "Yes, but I looked the word parallel up in the dictionary and it said 'two lines that never touch.'"

There are many do's and don'ts associated with international business travel. Obviously the list is endless because customs and traditions and cultural sensitivities are endless. During my initiation into the Middle East in 1960, learning how to drink Turkish coffee became an interesting experience. The first small cup was served. The waiter stood close and as the cup was emptied, he would fill it again. After many unwanted little cups of bitter coffee, a friend said, "Just wiggle the cup, and it won't be filled again."

Later that year, an amusing event that provided a culture clue happened during a visit by my father to Kuwait. He was the invited guest of a prominent Arab who at the time owned an automobile distributorship. After lunch, the cars were driven to the front of the palace for each of the guests. The host was driving a large Pontiac with all of the extras available at the time. His younger brother was driving a small Opel. My father asked the host why his little brother was not afforded the luxury of an identical, new Pontiac, to which the host replied, "What do you think we are, communists?"

The following checklist may prove to be useful reference for the new business traveler as well as the seasoned veteran:

TRAVELING CHECKLIST

1. **The eyes have it.** Keep a constant lookout for the glazed expression and the wandering or sleepy eye that tells you that you have lost your audience.

2. **"Is that perfectly clear?"** Don't guess, ask. Nods and smiles do not necessarily signify understanding.

3. **Stop and start.** Don't wait until the end of a speech or even a sentence before checking for comprehension. Never go on to B until A is thoroughly grasped.

4. **Spot quiz.** Don't take yes for an answer. Ask probing questions that prove how much your listener is really absorbing.

5. **After office hours.** If possible, meet with your opposite number for a quiet one-on-one double check of understanding on both sides.

6. **Shortcut shortcuts.** Avoid "i.e.," "ditto," "etc.," Say "we will" instead of "we'll" and "I believe your proposal is not acceptable" instead of "I don't believe your proposal is acceptable."

Axell adds these "quickies" as he calls them:

- Enunciate distinctly and clearly
- Overpunctuate with pauses and full stops
- Make one point at a time, one sentence at a time
- Paraphrase and ask others to do the same
- Avoid questions that can be answered yes or no
- If there is a misunderstanding, take the blame
- Use visual aids (photos, sketches, diagrams, graphs)
- Use both languages in visual presentations like flip charts, videotapes, and slide shows
- Put what you are going to say in writing "before" you say it
- Write and distribute a report on what was said as soon as possible after meetings
- Never use numbers without writing them out for all to see

- If possible, say numbers in both languages
- Send a follow-up telex, fax, or letter to confirm what was said by telephone
- Let your host set the pace of the negotiations
- Greet foreigners in their language, especially if it is an uncommon one like Arabic, Urdu, and Hindi
- In Japan, learn terms of greeting and departure phonetically so you will be understood
- Take a foreign language cassette with you to practice pronunciation as you go along
- Do not speak whole sentences in a language you have not thoroughly mastered
- One exception to the above: "Where is the toilet?"
- Never interrupt
- Don't ask rhetorical questions—give your listener an opportunity to reply
- Adjust the level of your English to your counterpart's
- Finally, whatever you may think, booze does not make communication easier or smoother.

BE READY FOR THE MEETINGS

It would be helpful to learn another language, learn to speak your own language better by writing it better, and learn more about the business climate and cultural differences before you attend business meetings in other parts of the world. For years in Eastern Europe, business meetings always included two or more of your counterparts. In meetings with overseas visitors, one person kept tabs on the other, and vice-versa. In short, they were spying on each other. The monumental political reforms in Eastern Europe in late 1989, hopefully, have eliminated that situation.

In Japan, corporations have experts in each area of expertise that could be covered during the meeting. These experts may include specialists in marketing, accounting, engineering, and law. Engineers attending technical meetings in Japan know their specialty perfectly. One engineer may be responsible for operational characteristics. Another may specialize in wear patterns of various materials. Each one is an expert in his area of responsibility, but may not know the workings of an overall, assembled system. However, when your project is completed, it will be a total quality package exactly as you envisioned in design and operation.

Several years ago, a business associate made a trip to Japan to visit a major shipyard to discuss plans for conversion of a railroad or flat-bottomed barge into a drilling ship. The manager had a complete set of engineering and conversion drawings prepared by his home office in California. The shipyard management met his flight from Singapore at 8 p.m. They asked if it would be possible to have a copy of the plans to review before the scheduled meeting at 7 a.m. the next morning. When he arrived in the meeting at the appointed time, there were over thirty engineers in the room. Each had a copy of a drawing for his specific contribution to the project. All of the personnel in the meeting had memorized drawing specifications in their field of expertise by the time the meeting began at 7 a.m. Each engineer stayed up all night learning the material that was to pertain to constructive discussions in his field of expertise in that meeting. The engineer responsible for a specific pump knew all there was to know about the pump. The same was true for the engineer in charge of generators. If a single specialist was asked how his expertise fit into the overall scheme of the project, he was not at a loss for words.

Usually, American businessmen travel on their own when making overseas trips. Modern hotels all over the world have excellent communication centers, secretarial services, translation capabilities, and other facilities to enable you to communicate with local businessmen and with your home office. Major accounting firms and legal groups have offices or correspondent offices in all major cities of the business world. If you need accounting or legal assistance, it is readily available. These facilities are there to assist you to be prepared for your next international business development meeting in practically any foreign country.

While living in Beirut in the mid 1960s, frequent trips to Cairo, Egypt were necessary. Comfortable hotel rooms were always difficult to find. The preference in those days was the Nile Hilton, which was always fully booked. In talking to the manager one day, he indicated one of his nagging problems was the quality of the commode handle return springs produced in Egypt. They didn't last very long as they stretched after only a few flushes. His problem provided a solution to my hotel accomodation needs while in Cairo. In exchange for keeping him supplied with return springs produced in Beirut, the manager would always have a room available.

5

Selecting a Representative or Partner

THE SELECTION OF YOUR SALES REPRESENTATIVE, DISTRIBUTOR, AND/OR OVERSEAS joint venture partner is one of your most important, if not the most important, decisions in international business development. It is a long-range contractual commitment with serious implications. Long-term commitments should never be made with short-term knowledge. It is imperative that you employ due diligence before making your choice because agreements are more easily made than terminated. Always ensure that the contract, when finalized, contains a clause that permits termination in compliance with the laws of the host country.

Consider all the reasons why you initially selected your representative. Your decision almost always involves consideration of his political as well as commerical influence within his own country. Evaluate what this influence could mean to your business strategy and position within his country if it were exercised negatively. This is one of many reasons why care must be exercised in the selection of your new partner, perhaps more care than you might employ in the selection of a corporate officer or board member in the home office.

EVALUATE YOUR SELECTION

The United States & Foreign Commercial Service of the United States Department of Commerce can be of assistance with this essential evaluation. They offer world trade data reports that provide a background check of potential trading partners for a fee. Your trading peers and competitors, vendors, Dun and Bradstreet, banks, creditors, and other suppliers can furnish useful information.

Often, your customer is willing to share information and assistance in the selection of your representative. Use caution here, however, as listening solely to your customer, whose intentions may be pure, can often produce unwanted results.

One of the most effective ways to do a background search is to visit with people who know or have done business with your prospective representative or joint venture partner. Personal experiences produce valuable clues to the likely performance of your future partner. They should be willing to share their experiences with you. Your new prospect will have a commercial reputation in the marketplace where he will represent your company. A few well placed questions with the right people should yield the answers that you are seeking.

SOURCES FOR FINDING A REPRESENTATIVE OR JOINT VENTURE PARTNER

Commercial Outlets

Your eventual joint venture partner, more often than not, will be your current distributor or agent with whom you have a track record of doing business. This is a desirable choice, if workable, because you would be building a future business on an established foundation. He or she is, in a sense, a known commodity to yourself, your company, and your clients. Most joint venture partners are selected from ongoing commercial relationships, but the degree of participation of your existing representative in the new joint venture will depend on his personal goals and financial resources.

It is possible that your current representative may not be interested in being a partner in an assembly or manufacturing operation. He may prefer to continue to work in sales as an employee or commissioned salesman for the joint venture. He is familiar with your product or service and should be qualified to recommend in-country candidates for partners who would be effective in joint venturing with you. This would have merit because the recommendation would come from an established relationship between parties with possible common commercial interests. Similar recommendations may come from friends, suppliers, customers, and yes, even competitors. Regardless of the source of the recommendation, you should use due diligence in checking out your potential business associate before you make a commitment to a new long-term contract. This is essential to minimize possible long-range conflicts and problems.

If you are in an overseas location interviewing and evaluating prospective representatives or joint venture partners, it is advisable to delay making your final decision until after you return to your home office. There is a tendency sometimes to act too quickly, and for this reason, a cooling-off period is defintely recommended. You don't want to make a decision based on emotion, but rather from considered judgment. A Swedish friend used to say, "Always think through international challenges with your brain, not through stomach reactions."

Also, after you return home, you'll have an opportunity to call other principals with whom your prospective partner may have business relationships. You can verify what kind of job he is doing for other principals. Are they pleased with his integrity? Are they satisfied with his performance? Has he lived up to their expectations? Did he deliver the increased market share? Did he comply with contract provisions of the joint venture agreement? Are they currently satisfied or looking for a new representative or partner? Answers to these questions provide relevant information needed to evaluate a new joint venture partner.

Government Agencies

The Foreign Trades Index or FTI can also be useful to locate agents and distributors for a minimal fee. The Agent Distributor Search (A/DS) locates these same representatives in targeted markets for a fee per country.

The Trade Opportunity Program (or TOPs) is another source for locating agents, distributors, and potential joint venture partners. This reference describes the country, the specific product in the present search, a brief description of the importer's business, and his name and address with a telephone and usually a facsimile number. If you cannot supply the specific product in question in the TOP inquiry sheet, you should, at minimum effort, contact this agent or distributor to initiate a relationship. If he or she is not interested in representing your company, they may know of a relative or friend in the import business that would want to represent your company. A phone call, as opposed to a letter, can expedite your business opportunity. It is certain to make a lasting impression on the party soliciting inquiries.

The TOPs program, which originates from American embassies in 186 countries in the world, is an excellent, free of charge, starting place for people new to exporting. Copies of inquiries from all over the globe can be obtained from the Department of Commerce, International Trade Division. With patience and perseverance you can build a network of international contacts with distributors, representatives, and potential joint venture partners without leaving your home base. You may need to work with the fax, telephone, and word processor to begin your network, but many people have earned a good living selling products and services through TOPs program leads.

Embassy or Consular Offices

This is a useful international medium for locating agents, distributors, or joint venture partners. You might need to travel to Washington, D.C., or possibly find a local consular office in an area near you, to effectively use these available services, but this is less expensive than traveling overseas to each country for data assimilation that may be locally available. You need to ask for an invitation to do business to obtain a visa for certain countries, like Saudi Arabia, for example. Sharing your business opportunity with a commercial officer in a foreign embassy or consulate office may provide the invitation, the visa, and valuable commercial information and introductions to help you realize expectations for your project in his country.

Each overseas embassy in Washington, D.C. has a commercial officer. He is charged with the responsibility of promoting exports from his country and attracting foreign investment into his country. He can provide you with information on trade, markets, needs, industrial directories, laws, lists of tariffs, import quotas and prohibitions, joint venture regulations, and other useful information regarding doing business in his country. A courteous and professional approach in these meetings will yield valuable insight for business procedures and recommendations for selecting your new business associate in his country.

A client called a couple of years ago asking for assistance in expanding international market share for his manufactured housing business. The intent was to form joint venturing or licensing arrangements in about a dozen pretargeted countries. The client intended to export parts of the buildings for assembly and finish in the host country. The client's instruction was to find joint venture partners in the targeted countries who would qualify for the terms and conditions of his licensing agreement. The licensee had to qualify without any special conditions. In short, gentlemen, here's the deal; take it or leave it. This, of course, was an outdated, old-fashioned approach to overseas business development, especially in developing countries.

The effective and workable approach is to identify the specific need or nitch, then adapt as necessary to satisfy that need in the mutual interest of all parties; but don't try to force product, terms, or conditions on anyone, anywhere. That archaic, ugly American business attitude simply will not work in the new, competitive globalized economy.

After explaining to the client that licensing a nonproprietary, nontrademarked, nonpatented product such as manufactured housing was going to be difficult, if not impossible, he emphatically said, "Go to each country and obtain facts to back up your assessments." As an alternative to that plan, it was suggested that a couple of weeks of research in the embassy row in Washington D.C. would identify potential joint venture partners and would be far less expensive than traveling to a dozen countries. The client agreed and the trip was made with interesting results.

Appointments with commercial attachés were easily arranged by phone after arrival in Washington. They are always anxious to discuss commercial opportunities that promote inward investment, hence, jobs in their respective countries. Therefore, it was possible to visit with twelve commercial officers of twelve countries without leaving an area of four square blocks from the hotel. In addition to obtaining lists of companies in civil engineering or construction work who could qualify as a joint venture partner, other pertinent information was learned at each embassy. Importation of plywood is prohibited in Egypt, unless for military or petroleum exploration purposes. Manufactured housing employs plywood. Also, Equador, in Central America, exports wood, albiet hardwood, but it was impossible to excite the commercial officer about importing wood of any type into Equador. Other information about public works projects and additional opportunity for schools, office buildings, clinics, and hospitals was uncovered. These visits were similar to visiting in the host country, but obviously not as informative.

There was sufficient information available to properly evaluate the project for each of the dozen targeted countries. The recommendation was to abandon pursuit of licensing nonproprietary technology that, when analyzed, contained too many materials indigenous to the targeted host countries. The research project in Washington, D.C. did obviate the need to spend one penny on an overseas trip to Egypt or to Equador. Although, in an effort to discredit the findings in Washington, the client sent three executives to Egypt at a later date only to verify the information and facts learned during the Washington D.C. trip.

Other Sources

Many sources of useful information to locate joint venture partners exist in various forms. Computer databases are available in some countries. These data compiling services attempt to match importers with exporters and vice versa in all areas of business. Trade publications and magazines can be effective in locating overseas partners, especially those journals that are compatible with your commercial interests.

International directories that list companies by product, company, location, and activity may also provide clues to potential representatives and joint venture partners. Use caution, however, when using massive data information sources, whether computerized or printed. As much effort as may be expended to keep these lists and databases current, business is dynamic and offices move, personnel transfer, and companies close. If you are trying to create a positive impression with an overseas company, it is embarrassing to ask to speak with someone who passed away two years ago. When a competitive overseas salesman offers to hand over his customer sales call and customer list to you, be careful, it may be out of date.

Don't forget the yellow pages of the telephone book when your are visiting a foreign country. Your future joint venture partner may have a full page advertisement in the phone directory. Your public library and the foreign trade office of the United States Department of Commerce also have yellow page phone books from some countries. Depending on your business interest, you can get leads for local representatives from your secretarial service in the hotel, the head waiter in a favorite restaurant, or a taxi driver. International business is similar to business in the United States, once the word is out in a network sympathetic to your request that you are looking for assistance in a given country, the grapevine grows. You will be inundated with opportunities to appoint a representative. Leads derived through these channels require due diligence.

WHAT YOU CAN EXPECT OF YOUR NEW PARTNER

Your selection of a joint venture partner in the host country will probably be the person with whom you have developed trust and trading experience. More often than not, your new partner will be your sales representative or distributor. You should expect continued performance and service from these associates after they become joint venture partners. It is difficult to discuss performance expectations from a distributor without impacting these same expectations from your joint venture partner.

Competing For Time

You selected your new joint venture partner or representative because you felt that he or she could make a positive contribution to increasing market share for your product or service in their country. More than likely, other overseas companies that he may represent selected this agent for the same reason. The fact that you have contracted with this new agent or representative places you in a position of competing for his time against his other business interests and accounts. Your objective, as the principal, is to see that he devotes most of his time to selling your product or service. To do this, you have to be a good international communicator and personally visit with him on a regular basis, in his territory. You must motivate him to be a team player much in the same manner as you motivate domestic sales representatives. He must feel that his contribution is important to the overall effort. Once that is understood, you should expect high performance from your representative on behalf of your company.

You should expect that your representative, and of course, the future joint venture partner to always work toward increasing your market share. One way that you can effectively compete for your representative's sales time is to structure a commission that offers more potential income than he receives from other principals. The cost of a sales call is fixed, regardless of whether the commission rate is 2% or 15%. If he travels, for example, from Singapore to Brunei, the cost for airfare, hotel, and the rental car are constant. If the total cost of the trip to Brunei is $600.00, he must look to sufficient sales volume to offset that cost. Given equal dollar sales volume, the 15 percent commissioned account is infinitely more rewarding to present to a potential client on this trip than the 2 percent account as selling expenses are constant.

Offsetting operating and marketing expenses with sufficient income is a compelling force for the representative to sell your product. This is not to suggest that income is the sole motivating factor, but it is a significant motivating force to keep your product line in front of your customers.

To further compete for his time, offer personal sales support by spending quality time with your representative and his customers. You benefit two ways by devoting your personal time to sales of your product or service within his territory with his clients, and increasing your personal exposure to his market, logistical problems, and service requirements. This activity also permits you to personally assess the job that he is doing for your company in his market. You can observe the customer's acceptance of your in-country representative or partner on a first-hand basis. When you return home, maintain constant communication with your representative from the home office through timely quotations, speedy deliveries, technical support, and after-the-sale service as required. Keep reminding him of his responsibility for increasing market share for your product or service while remaining alert to the need for joint venturing.

THE CROSS-BENEFIT PRINCIPLE

Your representatives's operating and selling expenses are offset by his income as in any business. Your new partner's income may emanate from many sources. You should expect him to be a prosperous representative, in the sense that his resources permit him to effectively represent your account. Of course, you recognize that the proceeds from one of his accounts may frequently fund activities on behalf of other principals, and vice versa. This cross-benefit principle is always at work with overseas representatives who must contract with more than one principal to ensure an income as circumstances and markets change. Most principals use representatives in the SAM strategy as a necessary first step. They anticipate that the initial arrangement will lead into long-range associations through joint ventures or other strategic alliances, but there are no guarantees for the agent or representative. For this reason, they must always work with multiple accounts or principals.

THE REPRESENTATIVE'S BELL COW

In the Pacific Rim, soon after starting a manufacturer's representative company, we were licensed to perform a pipe coating service on behalf of a principal. This account was considered a *bell cow,* that is, it permitted us to do work that could be completed, invoiced, and collected within thirty days. This short-term, immediate income could fund long-term marketing and sales activities that eventually would produce sizeable cash flow, but only months after the sales effort.

Commissioned sales representatives may make a sales call in May, and incur some expense, and a follow-up visit in July at additional expense, and maybe another follow-up sales call in September with additional expense before a purchase order is issued directly to the principal. After receipt of the order, the manufacturing process may require two months which means November shipping time may be 30 days into December; and if sold on extended terms, payment may not be received for 60 days or until sometime in February. Commissions are usually due and payable to the representative after the principal has been collected from the buyer. In this scenario, the agent, representative, or joint venture partner began sales activity in May, concluded the transaction in September, and collected earned commissions in February.

Due to this time delay from initiating sales until receipt of commission income, a representative must have a source of income to continue to make sales calls on your behalf. This is why the cross-benefit from principal to principal is critical. Once the sales/income cycle is in motion, after a couple years of work and effort, the representative enjoys a steady income. In start-up situations with your account, he'll be using income sources from other principals with which to promote your product or service.

In addition to the pipe coating service, by accident, we found another bell cow to see us through the start-up times. While visiting a potential principal who manufactured high-pressure, low volume chemical injection pumps, some glass was noticed in one corner of the plant. When asked what that came from, the engineer said, "Oh, we used to manufacture an ultraviolet light water-purifier a long time ago, but it didn't sell very well." When asked, "What was the distributor's price?" he replied, "They were sold to representatives for $75 each when we supplied them."

American companies moved into Indonesia and Malaysia in the early 1970s, and clean drinking water was foremost on the minds of expatriate personnel. If the units could be sold for $250 each in sufficient quantity where everyone was a winner, including the buyer, then this product would provide critical income to offset start-up and travel expenses for long-term achievements on behalf of all of the principals represented. The water purifiers were an instant success, and the immediate income from this bell cow kept the company fuctioning until major revenues were derived later from commissioned sales.

The lesson to be learned is simple: If you are to become a distributor or manufacturer's representative, you must have income for staying power until commission checks begin to materialize. Always try to establish your income before you establish your expenses. If you are a manufacturer, you want your agent to prosper while developing sales on your behalf. To do this, he or she must have a source of immediate income to offset personal and business expenses until the major sales develop. The importance of the bell cow cannot be over emphasized in start-up situations.

KEEPING THE REPRESENTATIVE FOCUSED

Your representative should devote sufficient time to your business for your mutual benefit. However, you should recognize that management of his time and activities will be increasingly more demanding of you and your company as your market share grows, and the joint venture operation begins. Your representative is an extension of you and your company and must be supervised and motivated in order to perform to your standards.

At a minimum, you have the right to expect that your new partner will represent your company or the joint venture to preserve and enhance your present market share, to protect your commercial reputation, and to sell your product in a lawful and professional manner. The representative is an extension of your company, your front-line marketer, and, in general, your on-the-spot man. You should expect that he will communicate product requirements, sales forecasts, service needs, competitor movements, changing government regulations, and an accurate and timely accounting of the marketplace under his supervision and responsibility.

One principal that we represented had a strict rule about communication. The contract read, "You shall communicate at least once a week with our home office, if only to say that you didn't do anything for us the past seven days." The communique need not be typed, but it was required on a regular basis. It made you think about your responsibility to the principal.

RESOURCEFULNESS IS AN ASSET

Resourcefulness is a significant asset to look for in an overseas representative or joint venture partner. It frequently is the major component for success in marketing in international locations. For example, in the 1970s, the seaport in Lagos, Nigeria, was blocked by numerous vessels, loaded with cement at demurrage, awaiting to be unloaded. A Nigerian National Company had an urgent requirement for tons of threaded pipe. Demurrage for any vessel calling in Lagos was approaching 120 days due to port congestion. The customer's requirement was pressing and it was obvious that delivery time, rather than price, would be the key to obtaining the order. Our representative, on his own initiative, traveled to the lesser known port city of Escravos, Nigeria, to determine the size and draft of vessels that were permitted to enter this port. Once these requirements were determined, a suitable, but smaller vessel was immediately located. The use of a smaller ship to unload in an alternate port permitted a delivery, FAS (free along side ship) within 14 days. Competitors were quoting delivery with an added demurrage cost and time delay of 120 days.

A few years ago in the Pacific Rim, the task of building and funding a machine shop and service business was accepted. An early return on the investment was anticipated by the parent company. In order to meet earnings expectations, two options seemed apparent to find sufficient work for the new center. The first option was to look at traditional sources of work that would provide an income sufficient to offset operating costs and provide an acceptable level of profitability. This option, however, would not meet the demand for an early payback of invested capital in the project.

The second option recognized that short-term success for the venture would come from nontraditional sources. The shop and services were new to this geographical area. Services that were being offered for the first time opened a new realm of salvage and repair options for customers that heretofore were not available. The task at hand became one of education. The customers had to be convinced that using the new in-region facility to effect repairs would be more cost effective than new, replacement purchases from overseas.

The task at hand was to find a suitable volume of work that could be performed to generate the sufficient dollars to affect the short-term payout on the investment. This would involve finding in-the-area, salvageable items that could be repaired for an amount much less than newly ordered replacement materials. The key was to identify a commodity that had been traditionally discarded all of these years because of a lack of repair facilities. After identifying that item, it would have to be sent to the new facility as soon as possible. About three months was required to round-up the machine work that had gone begging for years, but one day, seven barges loaded with work arrived at the dock. Recognition of a nontraditional opportunity resulted in a return on the investment on the facility in one-forth the time anticipated by the owners.

Resourcefulness includes the ability to recognize opportunity and adapt to markets as required. A partner that we had in Nigeria in the 1960s decided to import bicycles from Spain. The first shipment of the hand-painted bicycles arrived on time, but sales were less than encouraging. Early experiences in the Middle East revealed that frequently pilfered items, such as hand wrenches, were always chrome plated and sparkling in color. The same wrenches and other items that were finished in flat black were left untouched. A suggestion was made to order chrome-plated bicycles to improve sales. When the next shipment arrived finished in chrome, it was sold out within five days. The key was to identify what the market would purchase and supply the product that meets that particular demand.

COMMUNICATE EFFECTIVELY

Your representative or joint venture partner should communicate effectively. In the forefront of any international representative or joint venture agreement, there should be a section devoted solely to communication. You decided to employ a commissioned distributor in the first place because you were located thousands of miles from the market. Your most reliable source of knowledge about sales and competitive forces will be your representative or joint venture partner. You must, for your peace of mind, establish a commuication system that works for both of you. One principal that we represented requested a weekly report, and another principal wanted daily telexes. Whatever the system or requested means of communication, it should be included as part of the original written agreement. Always write down expectations of each party in the agreement to avoid potential and mutually expensive misunderstandings.

Overseas partnerships have been destroyed by rumor and misinformation that occurs when professional lines of established communication break down. Always acknowledge and compliment good reporting procedures by your representative. Always remember, the phone rings on both ends of the line. To receive good communication, you must also transmit good communication.

Your market is global in nature and is probably serviced by many sales representatives. Your company is responsible for producing and shipping product on a timely basis to several locations. For example, you may have quotations in progress that will impact production schedules should they all materialize in firm purchase orders on a given day. In order to plan for timely deliveries, you must be kept informed of potential market demand, likely product line requirements, and closing potential for quotations in the mill from each of your representatives.

AVOID PREPAYMENTS OF COMMISSION

You may, as a manufacturer, be requested by a potential representative to pay an up-front retainer fee in addition to commissions. It would be advisable to avoid that circumstance unless it is for a specific task that you request in addition to sales, such as an evaluation report of a plant site outside of his normal travel lanes, or for a report on his country that only you can use, for which he expends his time and money to obtain. You will find that representatives that ask for income before performance, in general, will be less than satisfactory for your purposes over the long haul. The manufacturer's golden rule for payment to representatives should be that commissions are to be paid when commissions are earned. This remuneration is made after sales are generated, not before.

OTHER IMPORTANT SERVICES

There are many other services that your representative or future joint venture partner can perform on your behalf. He can be useful in obtaining business visas for you and your corporate personnel. He should also keep you advised about all government tenders for products and services. If the government charges a fee for the documents, you should have a written understanding as to responsibility for paying for the paperwork.

Your representative or joint venture partner will from time to time, if he is active in the marketplace, uncover sales leads that may be useful for you in other geographical areas. For example, some clients may be multinational with offices and operations in many countries. Your representative in Turkey may learn of an upcoming bid in Argentina from a friend inside the Turkish division office in

Ankara, Turkey. If so, he should communicate that information back to you so that you can notify your Buenos Aries representative. International representative teamwork and mutual support should be actively endorsed. You should have an accounting system that compensates representatives for sales leads from all sources within your international marketing structure.

Your in-country representative should assist you in selecting and managing subagents, if required. When you start thinking about your in-country joint venture, he should provide help in researching the necessary data from his country that you will need for decision making. This would include recommendations for accredited legal, tax, and financial assistance within his country.

Your representative should collect invoices, delayed payments, insurance claims, and establish letters of credit, etc. If you require in-country permits or licenses, he should assist you in obtaining them. If you need guidance with customs or tax authorities, he should also be able to offer assistance. In addition to his commercial activity on your behalf, he should arrange accommodation, transportation, appointments, and total support during visits by you and your employees in his territory.

To summarize, you should be able to expect the same commercial responsibility from your authorized agent, representative, or joint venture partner as you would of a full-time employee of the company. Within these expectations, however, you may need to compete for his time with other activities, but this depends on your management and marketing capability. Use the tools as discussed in previous paragraphs to assist you in this endeavor.

WHAT YOUR NEW PARTNER WILL EXPECT OF YOU

You have just selected a representative or distributor to sell and service your present and future product line in a given territory or country. Once the contract is signed, mutual responsibilities begin. You and your new partner have agreed to enter a new market, develop sales and income, and look forward to assembly and manufacture in a formalized joint venture sometime in the future. Your new representative or joint venture partner will expect you to be able to perform and communicate, both of which, if executed professionally, will earn you his or her personal and corporate trust.

You are the owner of the intellectual property, the product, the sales approach, the track record, the service, and the trademark. You now have the responsibility to train your new partner in your business and in your product, but always listen to his ideas about market penetration and expansion in his designated territory. What has been working for you in Chile may not be applicable in Venezuela. You must adapt your business development approach to each country, and your representative's in-country knowledge is invaluable to you in making adjustments. Be attentive when he describes market needs. Again, you are in his territory. Let him make a contribution to writing the business plan. Review your in-country business plan together. Set goals together. Write down and define your anticipated progress, in time and in gross income, from sales, to assembly, to manufacturing. Establish a written game plan for progression that permits change should a new law, competitive force, or market shift dictate. You must be adaptable to cultural and ethnic considerations. The most important international business development attributes are resourcefulness, adaptability, and flexibility.

PREPARE AND EXPLAIN THE AGREEMENT

Prepare a concise, clear contractual agreement that explains in detail what you will provide for your representative. This may include home office services, sales support, literature, field engineering, and, yes, an explanation of how you plan to pay commissions. Ensure that the intent of your contract is communicated to the agent in terms he can understand. Do you intend that his commissions accrue from the time of sale or from the time of delivery? Do you have multiple considerations in calculating commissions such as point of sale, specification, or territory? These kind of questions should be discussed in great detail and made perfectly clear by you to your representative on the day of the signing of the agreement.

We represented a United States principal many years ago in the Pacific Rim. The product line was state-of-the-art and the company had developed an excellent after-the-sale service department over the years. They stationed a full-time salesman in our territory for mutual benefit. During a seven-year period, we jointly increased market share considerably and as a representative, we also developed a substantial worldwide service organization within our own company in support of this account.

In too many cases, mutual clients selected our service personnel over that of the principal. This should have pleased this manufacturer, but in time it became an irritant to the home office management group. Also, the owner of the company, in most cases, believed that the last person he spoke with on matters of interest to him was the expert. This could be true regardless of availability of factual information to the contrary.

To illustrate, a friend of his visited the plant one day after returning from a whirlwind around-the-world overseas trip that included the Pacific Rim. This visitor, for whatever reason, passed along inaccurate and negative information concerning our sales and service activities on behalf of this principal. He declared that some of our mutual customers that he had visited with during his trip were complaining about shortages of spare parts and competent field service in the Pacific Rim. None of his accusations was supported by the slightest evidence.

Our principal, for whatever reason, believed the rumor and misinformation, and cancelled our long-standing contract. Notice was abruptly received on the telex that we no longer represented the company as sales and service agents for that region. Our case was never heard by the principal. Therefore, we were helpless to change his mind. This was unfortunate due to the huge investment in parts, sales work, and, especially, the cost to replace our twenty-seven service personnel in the area. Clients were confused and dismayed at the action. That hasty decision, based on improper information, cost our principal, our representative company, and our mutual clients hundreds of thousands of dollars.

The point to be made here is as follows: Spell out in detail all elements of the agreement for mutual understanding, and especially, exactly what specific action or inaction can lead to grounds for termination of the agreement. This must be clear for both parties. Cancellation should not be permitted on the whim of someone, but it must be provided for, and hopefully, linked to specific performance. Your overseas representative or partner will expect guidelines to be written, explained, and honored.

TRAINING OF REPRESENTATIVE'S PERSONNEL

When agreements are signed and understood and the business and marketing plans are in effect, training of personnel should begin on two fronts, in the host country and in the home office. You must teach sales, engineering, manufacturing, quality control, and field service techniques to your new overseas group. Skills and tasks that your partner and associates are trained to perform early in the arrangement greatly reduce the future requirement for sending home office engineers and other vital personnel on a regular basis to the joint venture. You will retain the responsibility of periodic technical inspection trips to the host country site to ensure compliance with quality assurance standards once the assembly or manufacturing is in full operation.

When considering a joint venture in Eastern Europe or the Soviet Union, you should give serious consideration to training required personnel only in your home plant. Transition from controlled economies to Westernized free markets will be dramatic. To effect a workable transition, training should take place in an environment where a free market functions. This would not exist in Eastern Europe; just a few months into the free market experiment.

THE RELATIONSHIP NEEDS TIME

Rome was not built in a day, but it was completed. Keep your expectations high, but be considerate of the time required for the learning curve. The basic needs of people are virtually the same the world over. Be extremely sensitive to cultural differences you encounter in meeting these fundamental needs and in building long standing, enduring personal relationships. An allocation of sufficient time and patience, coupled with these principles of mutual contribution to a joint venture, will make it work for you and your partner. Meaningful business and personal relationships, in any culture, are created from mutual respect and trust, and this won't happen overnight. Again, commitment from the top of your organization is essential if you are to have time to accomplish this important task.

Over the years, many companies have sent personnel abroad with the expectation of overnight results. One company placed a competent and experienced salesman in Rome, Italy, to develop new export business in the Middle East. He was capable of accomplishing this task. After just one year, the company moved him back to the home office in Houston, Texas, and rewarded his efforts with a demotion. He was developing quality and trusting relationships in the market that would have shortly produced the anticipated result. The short-term, immediate profit focus of his company's management pulled him back from the marketplace prematurely.

THE GAMEZ PRINCIPLE

On the subject of building trust, it is important to review the GAMEZ principle, so called, because we learned it from a very successful Mexican businessman who proved that it is a workable concept to develop international relationships that lead to trade and joint ventures. He always said, "When in the United States, I work for you and your colleagues and follow your directives because, between us, you are the most familiar with business practices inside of your country. But when you are in Mexico, you and your colleagues will work for me and follow my directives since, between us, I am the most familiar with customs, traditions, language, and commercial practices within my country."

This is a significant statement of principle. It may not be exactly appropriate to your specific circumstance, but if you are just beginning to spread your wings into international business development, following the Gamez principle can only enhance your initial success. Nothing is more irritating to a foreign national than to greet an American businessman at the airport who, from whatever source, has become an expert on doing business in his country.

If you focus on your partner's personal needs and those of his country, you will succeed beyond your expectations. Always express your sincere belief in the worth and dignity of individuals regardless of their race, culture, and ethnic beliefs. In the new global and borderless economy, diverse cultures will increasingly become more interdependent on each other. The world must move towards solving the basic needs of all people as they drive for political and economic freedom; a process that most effectively begins when free international commercial trade exists among all peoples.

VISITS TO REPRESENTATIVE'S TERRITORY

Occasionally we would receive an itinerary, out of thin air, from an international marketing vice-president who worked for one of our principals notifying us of his impending visit to our territory in the Pacific Rim. His scheduled trip would read: Honolulu, 2 days; Tokyo, 3 days; Hong Kong, 3 days; Bangkok, 3 days; Singapore, 2 days; Bali, 3 days; and Sydney, 3 days.

In the first place, very little of his company's business was conducted in those large cities with the possible exception of Tokyo, Bangkok, and Singapore. This itinerary read more like a vacation than a work schedule. We'd always caution our overseas corporate visitors to write Denpaser, Indonesia, on their expense reports rather than Bali. It looked more professional to the nontraveled accountant who paid the expense account.

International executives, especially home-office types, would be met on arrival and whisked off to Central Sumatra in a helicopter to hunt tigers with a switch, as one principal duly commented. Not exactly, but most certainly the trip was necessary to call on customers in the jungles of Sumatra. Principals that will accompany you on field excursions to visit clients, regardless of difficulty, can be of great assistance to the joint operation. Some clients in remote areas would issue new purchase orders on the strength of a single visit from a home-based corporate executive who they perceived as going-the-second mile. This can be bonus business for you and your representative.

We desired and needed principals that would assist us with technical support and product sales backup with our mutual customers in Medan, North Sumatra; Duri, Sumatra; Djarkata, Indonesia; Brunei; Rangoon, Burma; Malaysia; and Balikpapen, Indonesia. When a principal arrived in Singapore, there was usually little time to reschedule his itinerary to meet the customer's requirements. Under such circumstances, the principal could have used his travel monies far more efficiently doing something else than traveling around the Pacific Rim. When the joint venture becomes operational, business demands and mutual involvement in the enterprise usually solve these kinds of concerns.

PLAN YOUR TRIP CAREFULLY

As you may know or will soon discover, international travel is extremely expensive. There are many excellent guide books written on this subject. Usually these books have a calendar of international holidays that could be a time saver when traveling in new territory. Here's one tip that will permit you to get more quality work time for the same daily travel cost. In Moslem countries, the Sabbath is on Friday, which means Thursday is their Saturday. If you are planning a trip to Europe and the Middle East, schedule the end of the week, Thursday and Friday, to be in a Christian country and schedule the weekend to be in a Moslem country. You can work on Saturday and Sunday in a Moslem country since that is the beginning of the Moslem work week. This planning permits you to work seven days a week during this business trip.

A list of holidays for each country is most helpful. If you are not informed, holidays can lead to unnecessary expense. One year, a principal wanted to call on the only potential customer in Rangoon, Burma. The plan was to meet him in Bangkok and depart from there to Rangoon. Arrangements were made and we arrived in Rangoon on schedule to find a five day national holiday in effect. Due to the remoteness of the location with respect to Malaysia and Indonesia, the only option was to wait in a hotel in Rangoon. You can be assured there are more exciting places in the world to pass five days of your working life than in a Rangoon hotel during a national holiday. On that trip, the representative did not do his homework adequately.

A checklist is helpful when you try to remember the elements to consider in a background assessment of your potential overseas sales representative and future joint venture partner.

- Name of the owner and managing director
- Date the company was established and reputation in the marketplace
- Banking and trade references
- Size and quality of the sales force with an emphasis on technical training potential
- Size of the company's annual sales turnover and total number of employees
- Product categories and type of market served
- Number of companies represented, names, and ones that are exclusive
- Type, number, and location of branch offices
- Type, number, and location of warehousing and service facilities
- Territory that is served on a regular basis and which personnel are directly responsible for results in which areas
- Primary category of customers that he serves

MEET YOUR NEW PARTNER ON HIS HOME TURF

Here's another tip that may come in handy during your representative search. If you have a prospect in a certain country, you should visit with him on his home turf rather than appoint him by mail. If this is the case as it should be, use care when planning your trip. Your potential partner may try to keep you on a rigid, all time-consuming schedule, which would preclude your visiting other prospects should he not prove acceptable to you. Remain flexible and keep your options open.

If this occurs in the United Arab Emirates, your diplomacy will be tested. In the former Trucial Oman States, now the Emirates, you must be sponsored for a visa and met at the airport by your sponsor. If the sponsor can be the customer or your end user, this is the optimum approach. However, if you are new to the area, the sponsor will probably be a prospective representative. If at some point, you feel he is not right as your representative, your diplomatic skills must come into play.

He sponsored your visit, and how do you get free to visit with others? It can be done with discretion, but above all, in that part of the world, you must do it in a way that preserves the dignity and honor of the party that invited you to his country. We always told the truth in a dignified manner. In Sharjah, for example, if you talked to someone else about your account, he was probably a cousin or brother of your original sponsor anyway. Information, while it appears to be closely held in most foreign countries, was almost always known to others with similar commercial dealings. If you have lunch with someone with a Japanese trading company in Rio de Janeiro, and you are of commercial interest either as an associate or competitor, the occurrence of the business meeting will be telexed, by the network, and known by all nine major Japanese trading companies in Tokyo the same day.

REPRESENTATIVES SHOULD AVOID FIXED INCOME CONTRACTS

In the early stages of starting a new manufacturing representative's business when cash flow is negative, you might be tempted to accept a fixed income from a principal. In doing so, you will have overlooked the fact that your expenses are variable. When you are responsible for all operating costs, you must have a variable income arrangement that permits full expense recovery allowing for profits.

This lesson was learned the hard way from a personal experience as a representative. We agreed to such an arrangement in the early days of forming our manufacturer's representative company in the interest of positive cash flow, we thought. A fixed monthly fee in lieu of commissions looked reasonable at the time and would be useful in paying some fixed overheads. A principal made an offer to fund our sales and service effort on his behalf on a monthly basis. He agreed to pay $600 monthly, and in return, we would run his errands, make his sales calls, and use our influence on his behalf all over the Pacific Rim.

It was quickly apparent that these activities on behalf of the principal involved substantial variable costs for airline tickets, hotels, communication, and ground transportation that far exceeded our fixed monthly income. And, when sales were consummated, there were no compensating commissions. When we counted our coins after a couple of months and terminated the arrangement, the principal said we were ungrateful recipients of his generosity.

Selecting your international business partner is a serious corporate move for you and your company. It is much easier to get into a contract than to get out of a contract. Whether you are contemplating a joint venture, license agreement, or a wholly owned subsidiary as your vehicle to doing business overseas, you will need to have host country employees and/or partners. If you want to do business in East Germany, you will need to employ an East German, and this applies in every country. Use one or all of the sources as outlined in this chapter for locating your new partner. Focus on the principles as discussed here, and above all, trust your judgment and common sense, and you'll be on your way toward making intelligent assessments and decisions about international partner selection.

6

Setting Up
a Joint Venture

LIMITED FINANCIAL RISKS

A JOINT VENTURE, BY ITS VERY STRUCTURE, LIMITS THE FINANCIAL RISK OF THE partners by spreading the total amount of capital required for the venture among the several partners. The participation in the joint venture by the local partner may further reduce risk by causing the venture, through his equity ownership, to be eligible for tax breaks, low interest loans, in-country government loan guarantees, and other incentives available in both developed and less developed countries. This residual benefit may reduce the amount of capital that you, the overseas partner, would be required to contribute to the joint venture.

In Scotland, for example, there are many government concessions including cash rebates for job creation, low interest loans for plant construction and/or expansion, and tax holidays for business development in the region. The government, through the Scottish Development Agency (SDA), provides multiple incentives if you create jobs and commerce in that country. Other countries in Europe 1992, such as Spain, Portugal, Italy, France, and Ireland offer similar incentives in an effort to attract inward capital and provide employment for their growing populations. Incentive programs will be discussed in detail later in this text.

THE BENEFITS ARE REAL

There are many economical as well as political advantages to international joint ventures. Risks of the venture are shared among the partners. Sharing provides a greater capital base for commercial activity that otherwise could be made available from a single individual. For this and other reasons, the overseas joint venture is an ideal tool for small- to medium-size companies to use in developing and expanding overseas business. Capital sharing reduces the amount required for the initial and on-going investment. The written joint venture agreement provides for a greater degree of management control by setting out management and operational aspects of the partnership well in advance of the commitment. Because of the structure of the enterprise, joint venture activities and specific duties can be closely defined in the written agreement among the partners.

In a joint venture, all of the partners share common purposes, interests, and responsibilities for positive results at the bottom line. Information and communication must flow freely among the partners. Each equity participant is usually an active member in the venture. Partners are working partners; they share risks, and contributions and, in general, make the partnership work to open otherwise closed foreign markets. The joint venture or joint enterprise may be the only viable vehicle in the future to do business in many foreign countries for the following reasons: investment laws may require that a local partner be involved in the development of resources within the country; due to cultural differences, local participation may be the only workable option; import duties and tariffs are discriminatory as to constitute an embargo; competitors may be assembling or manufacturing in-country in which case the market may be closed; and for numerous other considerations.

At the time of drawing up the written agreements, contributions of each partner are usually valued and qualified. You, as the partner from a developed country, may furnish intellectual property, technology, drawings, service technicians, and other assets. The local partner may contribute indigenous technology and know-how, materials, labor, logistics, etc. In any event, the value of each partner's contribution is usually in proportion to the success of the joint venture.

The primary advantage in setting up a joint venture overseas is to expand present market share. Sales enhancement will create a need for more employment both at home and in the host country of the joint venture. Vast new markets are opening everyday, especially in less-developed countries. Opportunities for industrial, agricultural, consumer, and service industry joint ventures are virtually unlimited. American small- to medium-size business has the expertise in each of these growth areas. America's awareness of the many advantages of joint ventures and the vital necessity of breaking out into the borderless, global economy to form these alliances must be increased during the 1990s.

TIME FOR DEVELOPMENT

By the time you have reached the stage of a written joint venture agreement in an overseas location, you and your corporation have committed extensive resources of time and money to accomplishing this objective. Joint ventures are expensive and require a commitment from the top of the organization. If your new joint venture partner is your sales representative, you may already enjoy some measure of cash flow from the association. After the joint venture is established as an extension of your own company, it will require a great deal of time management. You may have to visit the overseas location on a frequent basis. When the relationship changes from principal/agent to shared management control, a deadlock can occur at any time.

A joint venture is a long-term, serious commitment and requires time to sort out long and short term objectives and cultural differences. Joint ventures do not represent immediate profits or cash flow, but can be rewarding if you have entered a market for the long haul. Your reason for entering into a joint venture is to preserve and increase market share and improve the bottom line. The latest time estimate before you see a return on invested capital in joint ventures in the Soviet Union is five to ten years.

ANTICIPATE PROBLEMS

The number of participants in a joint venture is usually small because of the consensual nature of the management. Most international joint ventures are only feasible with a few partners. Even with common interests, conflicts can arise over profit-sharing expectations and individual commitment to the success of the enterprise. The initial written agreement is all important in that it should anticipate any pending disagreements or problems and provide for them in advance. This, of course, is almost impossible but many sample agreements from long-standing, successful joint ventures are available from legal experts for review. Seek competent counsel from international sources before entering a final contract. The joint venture agreement may seem difficult to negotiate and finish in the beginning of the relationship, but once finalized, it will be extremely difficult, if not impossible, to dissolve.

This book is not intended to be a substitute for competent international legal counsel that will be absolutely essential once the business development decision is made.

PRIVATE AND PUBLIC INTERESTS

There can be disadvantages in overseas joint venturing, especially when you try to join private and public interests. For example, when looking into joint ventures with government enterprises, you must be alert to social amenities and commitments that might not be apparent on the surface of the negotiations. In the late 1960s, we looked at buying a government-owned machine shop in Iran. Market research revealed that a demand existed for a shop facility. The state employed over 1200 workers in the shop. We estimated that with modernized and upgraded machinery and production techniques, the shop could produce four times the present output with fewer than 60 employees. The government of Iran said, "No problem, as long as you maintain all the medical insurance, retirement, and pension programs for life for those employees and their families that you don't need in the operation of the new business." That requirement made the project unworkable from a free market viewpoint and ended all further negotiations. The machine shop operation made sense for the government as a subsidized program to provide employment and social amenities to 1200 Iranians. Profit for the state-owned enterprise was not a consideration.

MAINTAINING EFFECTIVE CONTROL

International joint ventures are structured with certain characteristics. Each of the partners expect to share in the management of the company. International joint ventures are usually formed between corporations, state agencies, governments, or other types of legally incorporated entities. The partners have an equity position regardless if the venture is structured as a corporation or partnership.

Sharing between partners of the overall management and planning is fundamental to any joint venture. This joint activity includes working out the long-term business strategy, determining short-term tactical moves, and developing a plan for the evaluation of the performance of the joint venture. The size of the equity ownership by each partner usually determines management roles. In a two-way partner joint venture, a 25 percent ownership of equity is a practical minimum for effective sharing of management. Equity share can go as low as 10 percent in a three-way joint venture and can give the minority partner a voice in the management. In most joint ventures, the overseas partner can expect to participate, depending on the need for his contribution and negotiating skills, in as much as 49 percent of the equity issued by the host country joint venture.

Management sharing in international joint ventures may not be determined solely on equity holdings. The answer to how management will be shared can be as easy as answering a simple question, like, who needs who the most? The majority equity owner, who is usually the local partner, will need access to present and future technology, capital, management expertise, on-going logistical and service support, and an endless list of other requirements that only the minority, or overseas partner, can furnish, especially at start-up. The written joint venture agreement must outline specifically management control that often will be determined by contribution.

REASONS TO CONTROL THE VENTURE

You, as the small- to medium-size business, want to control the joint venture, especially in the early life of the enterprise. You will have written agreements which will be only as good as the intent of the parties. You need some time and business experience with your new partners before you relinquish control of your contributions, which at the outset, may be significant to you and the joint venture. Without substantial contributions from the overseas partner, joint ventures in developing countries would be difficult, if not impossible for the host country entity. Contributions such as your name, your trademark, and your business reputation require security and protection.

In addition, there are many other reasons for controlling the joint venture from your view point as a foreign investor. You are the partner that has the highest experience level with managing the manufacture and sales of your product or service, irregardless of equity holdings. In fact, your host country partner should welcome this, especially in the early stages of the venture. You will be expecting a return on your investment. Until you have developed a track record with your new partner, you will want to control the enterprise to ensure that your share of profits are repatriated on a timely basis.

Also, you are probably a global operation. If not, the fact that you are taking this first step in joint venturing indicates the development of a long-term strategy. This joint venture becomes one of many elements in your global marketing and international business development strategy. If you have an operation in Malaysia, for example, that produces certain items in your product line, you might not want that joint venture to sell into, say Thailand or Indonesia who are in conflict with your overall global marketing strategy. In order to prevent this from happening, you need to control the joint venture overseas marketing.

If you have a situation whereby the risks, investment, and costs of operation are insignificant, you should be able to gain control through equity ownership, but what would you own? In most countries, especially the developing ones, the laws are written to ensure that the host country partner owns the majority of the joint venture. In some countries, this rule of law is changing. In Mexico in the past two years, there has been a relaxation of ownership requirements in order to attract inward capital investment. Equity participation is taking a back seat in some countries to job creation. In Europe, you may own any or all of your business enterprise. In developing countries, you must carefully check the laws. Attitudes can be hostile toward foreign majority-owned companies. The American attitude that you notice from time to time towards Japanese cars produced in the United States is an example of this hostility. This absence of the understanding that capital follows opportunity breeds suspicion about foreign investment in America.

Minority ownership does not necessarily mean giving up control, even if there are only two partners. The written agreement may provide management control for the minority holder in view of contributions of technology, capital, and know-how. Some local laws may be written in such a way as to protect the rights of minority shareholders. Your attorney should be able to furnish information regarding rights of the minority partner in each of your targeted countries. For example, a 26 percent equity position can challenge the majority in Germany; in France, more than one-third gives the minority certain rights; and in Korea, 25 percent gives the owner rights to prevent changes in the articles of association or incorporation. You can write the by-laws of joint venture to require unanimous consent on vital issues to the joint venture. The 12-member nations of EC 1992 vote on two categories of issues in Brussels; those issues that require majority consent, and those matters that require unanimous consent.

METHODS OF CONTROL

If you own a minority position, you should have a capable resident manager placed in the local corporation in a high position to look after your investment. He should have sufficient respect of the local partner as to exert positive influence on him. If ownership by locals is divided among several shareholders, large voting blocks have effectively been dissolved. You should assist in the selection of these passive investors. Ideally, you should have a written management contract, if lawful and enforceable in the country where you have the joint venture. This gives you effective control of the corporation, regardless of your share holdings.

In all circumstances in joint venturing overseas, you must control the marketing function of the enterprise. If you control the disposition of the production of the joint venture, you effectively control the corporation. This is accomplished by a contract between the overseas partner or the United States small- to medium-size business and the joint venture. You must control exports of product or services outside of the host country of the joint venture. In fact, you should establish a marketing or sales company to contract for all of the export production of the joint venture. Production and marketing can also be controlled through technical assistance and trademark agreements.

When establishing the joint venture, you can stipulate in the written articles of incorporation various classes of voting and nonvoting stock. The by-laws can set out when certain stock is issued and which stockholders may vote. An independent audit is another way to control the joint venture. The use of an internationally known accounting firm that has an office in the overseas host-country is excellent, but if necessary, compromise, and use a competent local firm. In order to promote goodwill, you may only want to control certain aspects of the joint venture that are important to your shareholders in America such as the annual budget for expenditures, pricing as it effects your global activity, expansion as it relates to requirements for additional investment, dividend payments that affect your income from the operation, debt that may or may not be guaranteed by you, and other phases of company development.

There are other practical management procedures to establish and maintain control of overseas investments. Quaker Oats, for example, evaluated a specific market in Central America a few years ago. Market potential was not large enough to support a corporate investment in a company plant but significant enough to enter by more creative means. They decided to form a wholly owned subsidiary as a marketing company in Nicaragua. The marketing company then contracted with a local company to manufacture the Quaker Oats product line on an exclusive basis, which meant they could only sell to the Quaker Oats marketing group situated in the country. Investment was minimized, but more importantly, marketing of the Quaker Oats product was under the direct control of the wholly owned subsidiary, even though all of the product was manufactured by a locally owned company.

THE LETTER OF COMFORT

We had a costly experience in the Pacific Rim years ago that involved a lack of understanding of the letter of comfort as an absolute control mechanism, a document frequently used in Pacific Rim countries. A letter of comfort, used primarily in the Far East, is simply an assurance by one of the partners in a joint venture that they are comfortable with their investment and the management of the company. This letter is usually directed to a bank when an extension of a loan or an expansion of a credit line are under consideration by its lending officers. It is not a guarantee, but it is intended to give comfort to the lender that the joint venture partner submitting the letter is pleased with his investment and plans to remain faithful to the joint venture.

Most banks in the Orient that deal with trading companies everyday will extend additional credit beyond the normal debt to equity ratios when they receive a letter and the business plan that specifies the application of funds. A schedule of repayment is made. In our case, asking the minority partner to write such a letter spelled the beginning of the end for our manufacturing representative company. Although we owned 60% of the stock in the company, the letter of comfort that enabled us to borrow beyond our credit limit effectively transferred complete control of the corporation to the 40% shareholder.

On the basis of the letter, we overborrowed to fund expansion into Oman in the Middle East. Shortly after the loan was granted, the minority partner, a corporation, announced that they were assuming all management control of administration and finance of our company, effective immediately. Obviously, we protested, but quicky realized that we had given away our company on the strength, not of a financial guarantee, but of a letter of comfort. There was no fiscal responsibility on the part of the writer of the letter. The minority partner simply said, "If you do not accept our new arrangement whereby we control the company, we'll withdraw our letter at the bank and your loan will be called." And, we, the majority owners had the most to lose in relative terms of investment, reputation, and commitments, and thus had no choice but to comply with their demands.

Losing management control of the joint venture was devastating, given the vitality, growth, and accomplishments of the company prior to selling shares to the minority partner. The difficult reality was having to sacrifice a once-in-a-lifetime opportunity for business development coupled with the loss of relationships in Oman due to circumstances beyond our control. The superior attitude of our minority partners and our ineptitude in not recognizing the controlling power of a letter of comfort signaled the end of the Pacific Rim joint venture.

GETTING YOUR RETURN ON YOUR INVESTMENT

Once you have decided to form a joint venture in a given country, you will begin making an investment marked by many things such as your time and that of your associates, capital, intellectual property, equipment, technical services, and other tangible services. You should expect a return on this invested capital which can be achieved in many ways. There will be many factors that weigh on your achievement of the return on invested capital. In Russia, for example, an overseas partner can only take out the original investment in the form of hard currency profits generated by exports from the joint venture. This law is under the control of the central bank that regulates foreign exchange dealings. Also, local tax laws will affect the time in which it takes to achieve the return on the investment.

A recent example of a joint venture that was recently finalized in the Soviet Union underscores the value of resourcefulness in negotiating for return on investment. The joint venture was structured 40% for the United States partner, and 60% for the Soviet partners. The new entity was capitalized at $9 million, and the United States partner agreed to a technology transfer of know-how to manufacture tools for the critical Soviet industry for $3.6 million in credit towards his 40% investment. This credit fully vested the American partner without any requirement to advance cash to the venture.

The Soviet joint venture, with this new exportable technology applied for a hard currency commercial loan equal to three times the capitalization, or $27 million from the Soviet government. The Soviet-American joint venture also obtained approval from the government to use these hard currency funds to purchase 100 finished and operational units from the American partner over a three-year term.

The loan proceeds provided convertible financing for the joint venture to purchase needed equipment from the American partner. In exchange for $3.6 million in appraised technology, the United States company received orders in excess of $25 million, which provided a net income well over the $3.6 million and a retained working interest of 40% in the joint venture, in addition to ongoing license and trademark fees for the life of the venture. The Soviet government loan will be repaid from Soviet export sales to Algeria, Iraq, Libya, and Iran where Soviet-made technology is acceptable. This marketing will be under the control of the American partner who will integrate this activity with his or her overall international sales strategy. Nationalized industries within these target market countries remit hard currency to the Soviets for their purchases. This will permit the United States-Soviet joint venture to retire the loan obligation within the specified term of borrowing.

You can also begin recovery early in the operation by collecting up-front fees for licenses granted to the joint venture to begin operations. This fee will probably be due and payable on a quarterly basis throughout the life of the joint venture and should be carefully spelled out in the written agreement. You will be required to furnish on-going home office technical support. You should be reimbursed for these services. Include a substantial profit margin when determining pricing for these services. Again, include this schedule in specific terms in the written agreement. An independent trademark agreement will also provide additional cash flow towards the investment return.

A prudent course to follow when considering a joint venture in the Soviet Union or Eastern Europe is to inflate your budgeting figures to compensate for unforeseen circumstances. If you think you will conclude your agreement within four months, add an additional twelve to eighteen months for good measure. If you think your negotiating expenses for travel, hotel, meals, and other expeditures will be $150,000 in one six-month period, double or triple your estimates. In developing countries, business transactions require a much longer time than you originally anticipate. With this fact in mind, plan for the worst and if you conclude agreements in record time, then you will create savings in the bank.

You own equity in the joint venture. You anticipate that this investment will be profitable. As the joint venture becomes profitable, net worth should increase causing appreciation of the value of your equity. This is another form of return on investment. You probably employed the SAM strategy in the formal joint venture. Initially you will be supplying all of the required supplies and parts for the assembly operation. The sale of these supplies and finished parts to the venture with a gross income percentage built into the pricing will also provide investment return. Since you control all marketing rights of the enterprise, you will have opportunities to sell products and services supplied by the joint venture. Profit margin on these export sales from the joint venture will apply toward your investment.

A written agreement, clear in every aspect, has been emphasized throughout this book. Where specific work is to be performed by the overseas partner in addition to the supply of capital, parts and supplies, and know-how, pricing and payment terms for this contribution must be carefully defined in writing. Each task must be identified explicitly as to what it is and what it will cost the joint venture. A third party to verify the quality of the invoices is advised to prevent future misunderstandings.

CHECKLIST FOR GETTING PAID

In circumstances where you, the overseas partner, supply technology, goods, and services:

- Specify when payments are due and provide for interest or penalties for late payment.

- Have as much of the payment as possible made up-front in a lump sum. Establish a payment schedule that will keep the cash flow positive throughout the project and index otherwise future payments to inflation.

- Describe all permissible withholdings such as taxes, social security, retentions, and provide that no other withholdings can be made without prior approval. Performance bonds or stand-by letters of credit are preferable to retention at the end of the contract.

- Carefully spell out the payment mechanism and whenever possible, require irrevocable, confirmed letters of credit to be established at the beginning of the venture.

- In the event that approval of invoices is required prior to payment, stipulate that approval is deemed given unless specifically denied in writing within a specific period after submission.

- Demand payment in hard currency to avoid the effects of foreign exchange fluctuations.

- Anticipate future changes in regulations dealing with repatriation of profits, royalties, and other forms of return on investment from the venture. Hard currency deposits in offshore accounts or letters of credit payable in hard currencies are useful precautions.

- Purchase insurance coverage against extreme restrictions on convertibility of local currency.

- Avoid the risk of unfair local administration by including local taxes as reimbursable costs to the joint venture.

Most of the recommendations in this text may be achieved, but from a practical viewpoint, you may have to settle for less than the optimum. You can expect resistance when negotiating your agreement as in any business transaction in the United States. What is presented here is the ideal circumstance to strive for while minimizing business risks as much as possible.

We operated a profitable, joint venture in Oman in the early 1970s. This was long before stock certificates were authorized or issued in that country. The basis for the agreement was a hand shake and the Sultan's word was impeccable. This is mentioned, not to suggest such an undertaking in the 1990s in any country, but only to illustrate that if you perceive a market sufficiently important to your overall business strategy, you, as the commercial officer of the company, should be as flexible as you can in negotiating agreements. Contract form is not universal. People and circumstances do alter formats. Stay within the law by all means, but remember why you are negotiating to form a joint venture.

A situation occurred a few weeks ago with a client that wanted to introduce a potential joint venture partner to her contacts in Estonia, a Baltic Republic within the Soviet Union. The new prospective joint venture partner was asked to sign and notarize a noncircumvention, nondisclosure agreement complete with a pay order before that partner could be introduced throughout Estonia by our client. The document transmitted was too complex for this company, which was new to international trade. They did finally send a letter that contained some loose, but meaningful noncircumvention language. We were flexible in accepting this document knowing that Estonia is a small country in which our client has significant commercial and political clout to protect her disclosures.

Use the same business sense that you employ in your domestic operations to guide you in your international decisions, but with the further realization that you must rely on teamwork more so than perhaps you have in the past. Your new team for overseas business development may include your banker, attorney, freight forwarder, tax accountant, packing and crating company, the United States Department of Commerce and/or one of its agencies, private consultants, and/or an export management company. Negotiate joint venture agreements from the same win-win posture that you employ in your domestic business activities.

7

Structuring the
Joint Venture

THE HOST COUNTRY PARTNER SHOULD HAVE SIGNIFICANT INPUT FOR THE STRATEGIC business plan that should be jointly agreed and accepted. Once the plan is agreed upon, it is necessary to decide how the plan is to be implemented in a shared management structure. If you are planning a venture with a government agency, be aware that strategic objectives of joint venturing with a local government may be significantly different from those of the private sector. In the Iran machine shop example, the government was placing the emphasis on providing jobs, training, and social benefits without regard to profitability and competitiveness of the venture. The communist and socialist economies in Eastern Europe are being confronted with this problem in their transition from state-controlled economy to a free-market system. It will require unyielding determination by the people to ensure conversion of the system. East Germany, in May 1990, is confronting unemployment for the first time in its brief 41-year history.

When you form the joint venture you have effectively taken a new business partner. Each of the parties to the joint venture will have a vested interest through contributions of various forms and an anticipated return on investment. Management should be shared among the partners in a manner that permits effective, profitable operation of the enterprise, yet permits participation by everyone, which underscores again the importance of the selection of your overseas partner. The strong continued emphasis on the value of communication and good partner selection are the two most important ingredients for successful overseas joint ventures.

THE FORM OF THE AGREEMENT

Joint venture agreements take on many forms. There is no specific joint management structure that will ensure safe passage in dealing with the requirements of all parties under any situation. When considering the structure, you will need creative organizational talent. Each partner will be taking a different risk, in type, and in value. The length of time that the parties intend to operate the venture will impact its structure. Some partners, especially the overseas partner, will have other business interest elsewhere. The degree of integration between the in-country and off-shore interests of the partners must be considered. The business function of the joint venture must be addressed in its initial structure. The overseas partner may have two distinct product lines, one commodity manufactured for application in the mining industry and another for specific industrial applications. The joint venture may be structured to service only the mining industry due to the new partner's affinity in that nitch of the in-country market. A separate joint venture may be considered with a different in-country partner to serve the industrial market. The organizational structure of the mining venture would be functional to sell one product line to a single market. Frequently, divisional structure is preferred for economy of scale. If the host-country partner divided his marketing and servicing activities to meet both objectives, mining and industrial, the joint venture could be fashioned for both markets and could sell distinctly different products under the control of a single organization.

The structure of the joint venture must take on a form that is suitable to meet the objectives of the enterprise and those of each of the partners. Good business planning, effective open communication, consideration of cultural sensitivities, and mutual understanding of the reasons for the partnernership in the first place are essential elements of a successful joint venture. If you have correctly evaluated market potential, selected the right partner, and done your homework with respect to needs of the host country, the joint venture will expand market share for your goods and services and meet your anticipated return on your investment.

DECIDING ON THE MANAGEMENT

You may select one of several orgaizational methods to structure the organization. In the Pacific Rim joint venture, we used the board of directors as the highest level for making decisions. Any disputes by the various partners were resolved at this level. The majority shareholder was named chairman of the board. In developing countries, there may be a compelling reason to appoint an influential local person in business or government as chairman. The board, comprised of the partners, manage the company. The members are usually not employees of the enterprise but represent the integration of their investment with the objectives of the joint venture. The board is the final resolution of conflict and should be kept small in order to function effectively. When considering functional meetings, it is useful to remember the popular definition of a two-hump camel. It is a thoroughbred race horse designed in a committee meeting.

In the United States, we call the operating officer of the company the chief executive officer, or CEO. In international operations, he is usually known as the managing director, and like his United States counterpart, is responsible for implementing board decisions and running daily operations of the company. He is a profit-center manager who must remain keenly aware at all times of the partner's interest. International designations for his supporting management team are known almost universally as the financial director, the technical or engineering officer, the personnel officer, the marketing officer, and the purchasing officer.

In many cases, the board will also appoint a managing partner. He is usually responsible for interfacing between the partners and the internal management of the company. The managing partner's operational role and power is dependent upon the length of time the joint venture will be in effect, the scope of the venture, and the will of the board or partners. The power of the managing partner can vary from absolute to limited which would be that of overseeing the internal management process. Usually, the managing partner ensures that the planning, organizing, staffing, directing, and controlling functions of management are in place and properly operating to meet the partner's objectives.

A system of management control is used by partners to ensure that the provisions of the joint venture agreement are being honored. They may also want assurances that all is going according to plan. Control systems provide for performance measurement and evaluation of the attitudes and effectiveness of internal management.

There are many useful techniques used for implementing management control systems. The most obvious is to require financial reports on a timely basis as close to real time as possible. We always submitted a monthly operating statement and balance sheet. Our chief financial officer liked to focus on the all important three Bs as he called them; bookings, billings, and backlog. This type of operational information is useful and revealing about the state of the joint venture for any reporting month. It is obvious that visits from home office personnel is a useful control function. When our partners would visit the joint venture, a board meeting was convened so that they would be privy to any and all of the information that they needed to take back to their management overseas.

With the advent of high-capacity modern portable computers, it is reasonable to have an operating statement in the form of a spread sheet on a daily basis. With such computing capability at one's finger tips, endless what-if scenarios can be generated to evaluate the effect on annual earnings of the smallest anticipated expenditure or changes in market share. An executive once said, "In corporate meetings twenty years ago, the budget went to the department whose leader had the loudest voice and most staying power in meetings. Today, with a lap type computer, suggestions in the board room can become operating statements within a matter of minutes for immediate management evaluation."

In addition to the monthly financial statement, an annual audit is conducted and the results distributed as confirmation of monthly operating statements and balance sheets. If a minority partner with a substantial investment in the joint venture used a certain auditing firm for his annual statements such as Arthur Young or Arthur Anderson, we would try to use the same firm in the local area. This provides continuity for the partner. If there was a compelling reason to use local auditors, such as cost differentials, this fact would also be presented to the partners.

Planning for the venture was done jointly. A significant management control system is to review actual performanace against capital budgets, strategic objectives, and short-term accomplishments. A thorough review of the joint venture in early stages of development is recommended to uncover any troubling aspects that may be developing in sales strategy, management, accounting, services, distribution, production, or profitability.

FORMING THE JOINT VENTURE

Due to the diversified nature of a joint venture, each organization will be unique to its purpose. You need to consider several aspects when deciding on the management that will be required for the joint venture. Meeting short-term goals usually requires an agressive approach to managing a business. The feasibility of this depends on the relative strengths of the partners, the duration of the project, and the integration of the joint venture's activities with each partner's interest, risks, and contibutions. The selection of the partner who will have the dominant role in management could be determined by a majority shareholding, a substantial contribution and subsequent risk of capital, technology, marketing ability, and know-how, or lastly, simply by host country government edict.

Joint ventures with longer life expectancies usually require less intense management styles. A long-term objective means that the joint venture must build on the internal strength of its management. This will require time and patience on behalf of the managing partner. As the internal management grows in strength, it will grow in independence. This is in contrast to the early years when the venture depended entirely on the overseas partner for staff, technology, training, know-how, service after-the-sale, and other vital support functions.

Any variation, each with their own differences, may be considered in forming the joint venture. Whichever you chose as your workable model, cover all aspects of the formation of the joint venture in a written agreement prepared with competent international counsel. You must somehow couple purpose, management, and marketing with the equity relationship of the partners.

You have probably been selling products and services in the host country from your United States facility. Market or outside forces have now caused you to initiate negotiations to form a joint venture. With your prospective partner, you need to identify the opportunity and the mutual benefit to forming the venture. You begin by focusing on the strategic business plan that you will develop together to determine what is involved in realizing the objectives of the plan. You need to reach an agreement on the products and/or services to be provided by the joint venture. More than likely, this may be a commodity or service that you are currently importing and could easily adapt to assembly in the host country. After deciding on the product or service, you should reach an agreement as to the market to be exploited and the organizational structure that will be required.

Soon, you will reach a round of negotiations, with attorneys, tax, and accounting experts, that will focus on the more detailed aspects of the formation of the venture such as financing the enterprise, compensation of management, ownership of factories, offices, real estate, and other considerations. A list of checkpoints for a joint venture is an essential tool for the small- to medium-size business at this stage of the negotiations. Use this to ensure that all elements of forming a joint venture will be thoroughly explored and discussed by the professionals that you have employed to prepare the agreements.

CHECKPOINTS FOR A JOINT VENTURE AGREEMENT

- Decision as to the type of local entity to carry out the business
- Time limits within which the local entity is to be formed and in operation
- Conditions precedent such as government approvals and guarantees, United States revenue rulings, insurance, and others
- Responsibility for obtaining government authorizations including exchange control authorizations and customs permits, and for bearing the expense
- Financing of the local entity
- Contributions of the partners including cash, technology, and management expertise
- Decision making at the shareholders' level: simply majority interest or qualified majority; veto powers with regard to major amendments to the Charter, or Articles of Association of the enterprise; major changes to the business plan
- Decision making at the management level: powers of the managers; limitations on the powers of management; veto power in selected situations
- Pricing and manufacturing policies and responsibilities
- Compensation of management

- Ownership of factories, offices, and real estate
- Countries to be included in the manufacturing and sales territories
- How to solve discrepancies and differences of opinion between the joint venture partners
- Policy as to distribution of profits
- Royalties to be paid for the utilization of intellectual property rights by the joint venture
- Assuming that intellectual property rights are involved, who shall be the owner of such rights which are developed by the joint venture? Under what conditions will the partners be allowed to use such intellectual property rights
- Transferability of interests in the local entity
- Grounds on which the partners may be entitled to withdraw from the joint venture
- Reasons which may entitle partners to force a partner out of the venture
- Which country's law shall govern the joint venture agreement

As the proposed agreements take on more form, drafts will be needed. Usually, the partner contributing the greater amount of management expertise, technology, or capital provides the first documents. By this time, they are detailed as to the day-to-day operations of the venture and contributions of each party. The use of detailed checklists are useful to ensure all of the important issues are addressed.

After the essential information has been obtained, analyzed, and correlated, the actual drafting of the agreements can begin. The agreements usually consist of the joint venture agreement itself, which covers the establishment and operation of the enterprise, and the related license agreements that govern the use, by the joint venture, of the technology, and other intellectual property of the partners.

Management information is included in this text as a guideline to the formation of your joint venture. In each and every circumstance, new and unsuspected issues may arise. Your task, entering the world of international joint ventures as a small- to medium-size business for the first time, is to maximize your opportunities for greater market share while applying common business sense principles to minimize risks. You have probably observed that most, if not all, of the outlined management principles exist in one form or another in your present domestic United States operations. Therefore, if international business activity is that similar to your domestic operations, why haven't you looked at overseas joint ventures before as an expansive marketing, job creating, profitable business development option?

8

Antitrust Factors

THE PURPOSE OF THIS SECTION OF THE TEXT IS TO EXPLAIN WHAT YOU, THE SMALL-to medium-size business, should be aware of with regard to antitrust as it impacts joint ventures. It is not the intent of this book to get involved with law but rather to explore relevant information that will be useful to the small- to medium-size business. It is doubtful if any legislation such as the Sherman or Clayton Acts will have any impact on your company, but it is important that you know that such legislation exists. Always rely on the services of corporate counsel when such complex legal issues arise.

The Sherman Act was written to prohibit restraint of trade and formation of monopolies. The substantive provisions of the Sherman Act that concern joint ventures are as follows:

> Section 1. Every contract, combination in the form of trust or otherwise, or conspiracy, in restraint of trade or commerce among the several states, or with foreign nations, is hereby declared to be illegal . . .

> Section 2. Every person who shall monopolize, or attempt to monopolize, or combine or conspire with any other person or persons to monopolize, any part of the trade or commerce among the several states, or with foreign nations shall be deemed guilty of a felony . . . .

The Clayton Act prohibits specific trade abuses such as price discrimination, conditioned sales made subject to the exclusion of seller's competition, acquisition of assets and equity of any party to a commercial transaction that would lessen competition or create a monopoly, and the use of interlocking directorates among large corporations. The substantive provision of the Clayton Act, which deals with acquisition of stock or assets, and affects joint ventures reads, in part, as follows:

> Section 7: [N]o person engaged in commerce or in any activity affecting commerce shall acquire, directly or indirectly, the whole or any part of the stock or other capital share and no person subject to the jurisdiction of the Federal Trade Commission shall acquire the whole or any part of the assets of another person engaged also in commerce or in any activity affecting commerce, where in any line of commerce or in any activity affecting commerce in any section of the country, the effect of such acquisition may be substantially to lessen competition, or tend to create a monopoly.

In the Antitrust Guide for International Operations (1977), the justice department discusses typical joint venture situations and states there are three essential inquiries in determining the legality of the joint venture:

1. Whether competition in a given market is unreasonably restrained by the creation of the joint venture
2. Whether the joint venture has any unreasonable collateral restraints
3. Whether the joint venture is a bottleneck monopoly which must be accessible to all interested parties on a reasonable and non-discriminatory basis

The justice department essentially concludes that it will not challenge the creation of joint ventures if:

1. They do not eliminate any significant competition between the partners themselves
2. The costs and risks associated with the project are high enough to prevent the partners from undertaking the task individually
3. The venture is not unduly broad in scope and duration
4. There are no unreasonable collateral restraints of trade
5. The venture does not eliminate potential competition in a concentrated market

As a general rule, joint venture partners are not required to give the members of the industry outside the joint venture access to essential assets of the joint venture that would disclose the joint venture's technological or economic advantage. The Department of Justice currently expresses the belief that by requiring such access the incentive for firms to achieve specific, legitimate goals would be destroyed. The department feels that it is better to have enterprises outside the venture compete with the venture, either individually or by creating other joint ventures.

ANTITRUST GUIDELINES TO USE
WHEN STRUCTURING THE INTERNATIONAL JOINT VENTURE

While it is difficult to be very accurate about how much market power is too much or how much efficiency benefit is necessary to outweigh loss of competition due to ancillary restraints, the following guidelines may help in the effort to create a joint venture that fulfills the needs of the partners and, at the same time, does not contravene relevant United States antitrust laws:

Identify the Appropriate Business Objectives of the Partners

It is natural to seek as much contractual protection as possible when dealing with a competitor, potential or actual. However, a careful analysis of the venture will focus on the essential business objectives of the partners. Nonessential objectives that create problems should be eliminated at this point. The partners should then be told which of the main objectives are permissible and which create antitrust risks. If possible, offer legally acceptable alternatives to troublesome proposals rather than rejecting an essential objective out-of-hand.

Limit the Scope of the Joint Venture to Principal Objectives

Having determined the principal objectives of the joint venture and having eliminated those that are not legally permissible, prepare a statement of the scope of the joint venture. The objective should be a narrow statement of the venture's purposes rather than a listing of prohibitions that draws attention to negative aspects of the venture.

Require both parties' concurrence in any change in the venture's governing documents (including purpose clauses). A good example of the usefulness of a written statement of scope is the GM-Toyota joint venture. The memorandum of understanding expressly stated that the venture would be limited in scope to this vehicle and this agreement is not intended to establish a cooperative relationship between the parties in any other business. The actual agreement adhered to the narrow scope and this was one of the primary determining factors that lead to ultimate approval of the venture by the commission.

Tailor the Size, Power, and Duration
to That Necessary to its Purpose

While a joint venture can be struck down for being too large, lasting too long, and having too much market power it must be remembered that a venture that is too small and limited in scope can also be struck down as being unneccessary, or one that deprives necessary access to participants in a market where access to the venture is essential for effective competition. The size, power, and duration must be appropriate to both the scope of the venture and the relevant market.

Avoid Collateral Restraints Not Necessary to the Venture

Ancillary restraints need not be formulated in the least anticompetitive or most procompetitive manner possible. However, they are most likely to survive if they are necessary for the venture to work. The joint venture partners should make an assessment of the degree of antitrust risk they are willing to take. In view of potential *per se* treatment given to collateral restraints, it is wise to use them only if they are essential to the success of the venture (especially those which limit, restrict, or prevent competition) and even then, only if they are drafted as narrowly and precisely as necessary.

Avoid Unintended Spillover Effects

The more protections against accidental spillover collusion contained in the agreement, the more likely the joint venture agreement will survive the complex balancing of efficiencies and anticompetitive effects that take place in rule of reason analysis. This will be true whether scrutiny is at the time of joint venture formation or in the future.

Apply Antitrust Criteria That Are Relevant to the Market

Realistically appraise the size and market power of the firms in the relevant industry. Study the behavior of these firms to determine the behavioral norms. Find out whether the industry is concentrated, and whether entry into the market is easy or difficult. Remember that the venture is being formed and its behavior will be judged in the context of the industry in which it operates at the time an inquiry is made.

THE EXPORT TRADING COMPANY ACT

The Export Trading Company Act of 1982 states that export trade certificates of review can be issued by the secretary of commerce with the concurrence of the attorney general. The antitrust standards for issuance of a certificate of review incorporate three criteria that are presently in the Webb Act—1, 2, and 4 below, and add one new standard, 3. Certificates will be issued for associations that:

1. Result in neither a substantial lessening of competition or restraint of trade within the United States nor a substantial restraint of the export trade of any competitor of the applicant;
2. Do not unreasonably enhance, stabilize, or depress prices within the United States of the goods, wares, merchandise, or services of the class exported by the applicant;

3. Do not constitute unfair methods of competition against competitors engaged in the export of goods, wares, merchandise, or services of the class exported by the applicant;

4. Do not include any act that may reasonably be expected to result in the sale for consumption or resale within United States of the goods, wares, merchandise, or services exported by the applicant. (Section 303a)

Since export joint ventures by definition involve foreign trade or commerce neither the Sherman Act nor section 5(a) of the Federal Trade Commission Act will apply to an export joint venture unless the challenged conduct has a direct, substantial, and unreasonably foreseeable anticompetitive effect on a protected interest, in either domestic United States commerce, United States import commerce, or export commerce of a person engaged in such commerce in the United States.

The Department of Commerce has issued guidelines that discuss the eligibility requirements, certification standards, and analytical approach that departments of commerce and justice will use to determine whether to issue a certificate (50 Fed. Reg. 1786 Jan. 11, 1985). The department of commerce has also published regulations describing the application procedures (50 Fed. Reg. 1804 Jan. 11, 1985). To obtain free copies of the guidelines, regulations, or application forms, or to get preapplication counseling, contact the director, Office of Export Trading Company Affairs, International Trade Administration, Room 5618, United States Department of Commerce, Washington, D.C. 20230.

The Export Trading Company Act of 1982 (the ETCA or the Act) is intended to increase United States exports of goods and services primarily by removing two impediments: restrictions on bank investments and certain export financing, and the uncertainty regarding the application of United States antitrust laws. To remove the impediments, the ETCA makes several changes to applicable banking and antitrust laws. These changes are reflected in four titles, which, for the most part are independent of each other.

Title I establishes in the department of commerce an office to promote the formation of export trade associations and export trading companies. By providing a full range of export services, an export trading company can function as a one-stop export intermediary for United States producers of goods and services. Title II permits eligible banking entities to acquire, subject to certain limitations, up to a 100 percent of the stock of an export trading company. It also reduces certain restrictions on export financing.

Title III provides for a certification process that enables businesses engaged in export trade to determine in advance whether their proposed export conduct will have specific protection from liability under federal and state antitrust laws. Title IV clarifies how the Sherman and Federal Trade Commission Acts apply to export commerce.

Many, and perhaps most, export activities are currently permissible under United States antitrust laws. But members of the American business community have long expressed uncertainty about the application of United States antitrust laws to their export conduct. The purpose of the act is to encourage United States exports, particularly small- to medium-sized firms, by minimizing any antitrust uncertainty about proposed export conduct. The act reduces the uncertainty by establishing a procedure that permits persons engaged in export trade to receive a certificate that sets their limits of antitrust liability before they engage in such conduct.

9

Financing and Insurance

GENERAL DISCUSSION OF EXPORT FINANCING

FINANCING IS AN ALL-IMPORTANT INGREDIENT FOR COMPETING IN INTERNATIONAL trade and is frequently the deciding factor in concluding a sale. European and some Pacific Rim governments have long recognized the need and value of supporting the private sector through creative financing. Lenient credit terms and low interest rates assist their industries to compete in the global marketplace. While there are institutions in place in the United States to provide competitive sources of trade finance, the structure is cumbersome. United States businesses competing in world markets have frequently discovered that applications for available government resources can be difficult and time consuming. Paperwork is excessive, and compliance with stringent rules and regulations can be difficult. In many instances, qualifying for international trade finance loans can be as difficult as qualifying for domestic balance sheet borrowing.

International traders consider the product and financing as a single package. If you can solve the most difficult problem in advance, transaction financing, and offer that as a package with the product going into the marketing presentation, you have provided a significant service for the foreign client. This type of trade advantage is available to overseas competitors from the many trade merchant banks situated in overseas financial capitals of the world.

The small- to medium-size business often depends on traditional domestic sources of finance to support growth into the international market. This is rarely an option as few domestic banks, with the exception of multinational institutions, have the staff or facilities to handle an international transaction. The difficulty for the small business to attain financing is the reality that big banks can't finance them because they are too big, and small banks can't finance them because they are too small.

THE NEED FOR TRANSACTION FINANCING

United States exporters have an urgent need for more creative sources of export and joint venture financing. Fortunately, more nonbanking sources of export trade assistance are growing across the country. These newly formed institutions vary in size and the scope of financial services that they offer, but all share a common commitment to financing exports for the small- to medium-size business.

A prevalent problem for many new exporters is selling beyond their means of finance. A small trader or broker may have a confirmed international purchase order from Lima, Peru, accompanied by an irrevocable, confirmed letter of credit opened in his favor for the entire export sale. Assume that the sale is for $25,000 worth of automobile spare parts with a cost of $19,500. The exporter has made the sale, but is now faced with payment to the auto parts supplier to obtain delivery. He approaches his local bank who may reply, "What is a letter of credit, and/or where is Peru? You don't have that much net worth." He then asks his banker to provide a letter of credit or guarantee for the auto parts supplier. His banker again replies, "This bank will not provide back-to-back letters of credit, especially one backed from some foreign source." If the letter of credit from Peru contained an assignable clause, the exporter or broker could transfer or assign the letter of credit to the supplier. This assignment or transfer would disclose his auto parts supplier to his client in Peru, a tactic, if repeated often with other clients, would soon put him out of business.

The small exporter needs a dependable source of off-the-balance-sheet financing that will bridge funds and conclude the transaction. He holds an asset in the form of a self-liquidating financial instrument that will pay the full value of the transaction upon presentation of shipping or other stipulated documents. The problem is paying the supplier to effect shipment. Frequently the time lapse from payment of the supplier, shipment to the freight forwarder, and delivery to an airport or seaport, and presentation of shipping documents to receive payment may only involve a few days.

Consider this additional scenario: you have just received your first large international purchase order complete with supporting financial documents. This order for your product places serious strains on your internal financial capability to purchase raw materials, pay for labor, and cover other costs related to the ultimate delivery to the port of shipment. Trade financing would assist you in this instance with the preshipment working capital you require to complete and ship the order. A trade finance bank would use your buyer's purchasing and financial documents as security for your borrowing. They will employ due diligence to validate your buyer's documents. Also, the trade finance bank could become an invaluable ally when you look to countertrade as a vehicle to finance joint ventures.

THE FUNCTION OF A TRADE FINANCE BANK

Traditional banks, lending, and/or guaranteeing institutions are not geared to provide preshipment working capital that the small- to medium-size overseas trader almost always finds in short supply. Our worthy global competitors, however, have access to numerous and flexible methods of finance from overseas lending institutions that include international trade merchant banks that thrive on funding overseas commercial activities for foreign competitors. In major financial centers throughout the United States, you can find specialists that call themselves trade merchant banks in the European and Pacific Rim tradition. These institutions, with access to and support from other major banks, have the expertise to provide competitive financing through various options. Instead of viewing their roles as simply lenders, they have essential roles in export transactions and combine marketing and administration with financing. In becoming quasi-partners in each transaction, they are in an ideal situation to look at transactions in terms of commercial viability. They don't finance the company; they finance the trade, the sale, or the transaction.

The most difficult task the small- to medium-size business faces in the global economy is trade financing. Most small- to medium-size businesses, after entering export markets, soon find themselves overtrading. The value of the order book becomes much greater than their capitalization. At this point, they are disqualified from consideration by the domestic banking system because they did not meet the quick asset tests of liquidity, even though they have the ability to obtain purchase orders. These aggressive and successful marketers require sources of trade financing, such as transaction funding, because they don't qualify for balance sheet lending. There is a pressing need in the United States for more trade merchant banks to finance export sales and joint venture needs of United States small- to medium-size companies.

GOVERNMENT LOAN GUARANTEE PROGRAMS

There are government institutions and programs that can provide some answers to export finance, namely the Eximbank. New and changing globalized market conditions have caused more programs to be readily available for the small- to medium-size business. Collateral requirements, quantity of paperwork, and time required to complete a program leading to funding may be excessive depending the window you're going through and the quality of your application. Eximbank has a lower working cap of $10,000 and may take three to four weeks for approval, but some applicants have been approved inside of 10 days. You are still required to satisfy your local bank, through balance sheets, that they should coguarantee the balance of the loan with Exim. Usually, however, by the time you get through all the process, your overseas client may have placed his business elsewhere. To be truly market effective internationally, your financial package should be clipped to your offer to sell.

There are special program requirements for state and federal loan guarantee programs depending on which way you borrow. A cash flow projection depicting monthly activity and cash balances is a vital tool to determine cash needs and to monitor borrower progress after disbursement. This cash flow projection must be submitted with the application to cover anticipated activity during the term of the export revolving line of credit program. Monthly progress reports are to be submitted by the borrower to the lender. Discrepancies between the projected cash flow and the progress report will provide an early warning of problems to the lender so that appropriate preventative servicing actions can be taken.

ALTERNATIVE SOURCES OF FINANCING

Several alternative sources of export financing are revealed in a special report written by John Chewning, entitled, "Filling in the Gaps," in the January/February 1990 issue of *Export Today*. There are a number of organizations that provide specialized financial services for exporters including international leasing, maquiladora financing, foreign exchange services, financial facilitation, and advisory services. Also, a number of venture capitalists are using their access to capital to assist exporters.

Trade finance banks provide the full range of international services you would expect from a bank, but can usually out perform most banks. Global trade is their expertise, and they can process export financing transactions more efficiently and profitably than traditional banks. This, coupled with their expertise in export financing, permits them to take on a greater variety of deals and accomodate smaller clients than banks could profitably. Even the larger trade finance banks don't have the large overhead and administrative costs prevalent in most banks, which enables them to justify profitable smaller financial transactions.

Several foreign, quasi-governmental agencies can offer United States exporters competitive financing for sales to buyers in their countries. The terms offered are often more attractive to purchasers than those offered by the United States Export-Import Bank or commercial banks in the United States. Due to inward pressure to balance their trade surpluses with the United States, three countries in particular—Japan, Taiwan, and South Korea—boast of their own export-import banks that are quite active in financing imports from the United States.

There are several other trends that promise greater export financing flexibility in the near future. First is the growing potential of trade paper brokerage. Forfaiters and factorers have been using this method for several years. After buying receivables from traders, many companies in turn sell this paper in secondary markets. There is talk on Wall Street of developing investment tools from trade paper. If export financing becomes an attractive investment option, who knows how many companies will want to join the bandwagon. Another trend is the proliferation of private credit insurance companies; a form of quasi-financing.

The use of private credit insurance to hedge risk, and thus lesson financing needs, is understood by few small- to medium-size United States businessess. While it is not suitable for several markets or particular transactions, it can prove a less costly alternative to straight export financing.

CONSIDER AND PROVIDE FOR THE COST

The one major complaint often associated with these alternative methods of finance is the cost factor. They are frequently more expensive than traditional bank services. The exporter, when facing the choice of losing a trade or sharing some of the profits, has a clear choice especially when the trade shows great profit potential or leads to additional market penetration. As more and more firms adapt or emerge to meet the growing need of export financing, increased competition will reduce the costs of these needed financial services. Always determine the out-of-pocket cost of alternative financing in advance of using the service. This cost should be included in your selling price for the goods or services sold in international markets. If you don't factor this substantial cost into your selling price, you may find alternative financing too expensive for your operation.

A TRADE MERCHANT BANK SURVEY

The following survey by John Chewning in "Filling in the Gaps," *Export Today*, provides comprehensive examples of new and emerging services in the international finance field, and who some of the participants are, and what sort of services they offer. The list is incomplete and the companies are not endorsed by this text. The purpose is to present a cross section of companies and services to create an awareness of what is available to the small- to medium-size United States exporter.

Most small- to medium-size business in the United States will experience overtrading in international market development. They become cash-poor, but purchase order-rich. The problem becomes one of funding difficulties created by marketing success. Often, balance sheets of growing, expanding companies will not meet bank criteria or government regulations for lending purposes.

Bristol International, Ltd., a trade merchant bank in Dallas, Texas, formed by exinternational bankers, offers trade or transaction financing or financial engineering services for the small- to medium-size business that usually have problems with normal bank financing for legitimate international transactions. These dynamic, growing exporters are frequently termed 'net users of cash' and their balance sheet usually reflects ratios that fall short of commercial bank lending parameters. They are usually denied additional working capital.

Trade finance banks say they look for positive answers to basic questions as presented in a litmus test. Essentially, the bank uses these criteria as a measure of the worth of the transaction. Unlike factoring where the invoice is sold after shipment, the trading bank is buying the risk of manufacture or production of a service. He almost becomes a joint venture partner with the supplier as they share a common interest, such as producing the order or service and collecting for the transaction.

A LITMUS TEST

1. Are the principals involved in the transaction honest, reputable and experienced in their business?

2. Is their offshore buyer or seller legitimate and is their purchase order or letter of credit verifiable through reliable sources?

3. Is the prospective client prepared to relinquish control of the transaction in terms of structure, paperwork, logistics, freight, and other aspects?

4. With reference to an export transaction, are the goods actually presold? With regard to imports, can the offshore supplier actually deliver to the buyer's specifications?

Trade finance banks such as Bristol say they feel good answers to the preceding questions are more critical than the client's balance sheet. They look at the balance sheets, but typically they usually reflect overleveraging, under capitalization, and a shortage of working capital. If after due diligence Bristol approves the transaction, they will usually finance preshipment working capital up to some substantial value of the inventory exported or goods imported.

The Trading Alliance Corporation, New York, was incorporated by former trade finance bankers at Manufacturers Hanover who felt they could serve the trade community more efficiently by going out on their own—where they wouldn't be hampered by the rigid cost accounting formula that many banks use to determine creditworthiness. TAC looks at the performance potential of an international transaction rather than the balance sheets. TAC management becomes involved in the transaction to determine each client's particular needs and, depending on their analysis, can provide a number of specialized services including:

- guaranteeing letters of credit
- extending credit terms to buyers
- making advances against receivables
- alleviating working capital problems by buying raw materials or components against firm orders for finished products
- arranging back-to-back and specialized letters of credit
- assuming the role of the buyer of record in the transaction to satisfy the credit concerns of the suppliers
- taking title to the goods
- assuming or mitigating customer non-payment risks
- managing foreign exchange risks

In addition, TAC can become involved in other aspects of export transactions such as contract negotiations, transportation and distribution, sourcing, insurance, countertrade, and product and market research and development to complement its export financial services.

Another trade merchant bank, World Trade Finance, Inc., Los Angeles, was formed only last year, but is already active in helping firms export overseas. It, too, looks beyond the balance sheet to determine the viability of an export transaction. Prior to forming WTF, Mr. Hodge, marketing director, worked for the California Export Finance Office, where he became familiar with the various federal and state sources of export financing. WTF specializes in using state and federal loan guarantees for its clients. Funding can be obtained from WTF for working capital to source raw materials and components, or to meet foreign buyer credit terms.

WTF's fees are comparable with those of commercial banks, but will take on transactions that would not be acceptable to most commercial banks. By isolating the export transaction, WTF can lend money without interfering with the client's current lines of credit. WTF also becomes more involved in export transactions than traditional export finance providers and will take an active role in negotiating terms of sale, foreign risk protection, and collections.

The Initial Funding Corporation, New York, caters to small- to mid-sized companies whose existing credit lines are fully used and/or won't support export sales, or whose assets are fully leveraged. It looks at the possible profitability of a transaction. After scrutinizing the particulars of a sale, IFC can provide:

- letters of credit
- direct loans
- credit insurance
- factoring
- specialized forms of financing

IMF specializes in financing textile and fashion, automotive, chemicals, plastics, and capital goods exports, but will consider transactions in any industry sector.

Trade merchant banking works for imports too. For example, a toy importing company known to a merchant bank had a capital base of $2 million. They also had $8 million in purchase orders from reputable buyers such as Toys-R-Us and Walmart. The overseas seller required that the buyer post letters of credit. The importer's bank said that the letters of credit would be posted when he deposited $8 million cash in the bank as collateral. Obviously, the toy importer with a $2 million capital base was not in the position to deposit $8 million in cash. They contacted the transaction bank who suggested that they ask their clients for domestic letters of credit. This imported toy was a hot-selling item, therefore the clients agreed to open domestic letters of credit for the importer. Armed with these letters of credit, the trade bank was able to obtain an $8 million line of credit to support the required overseas letter of credit.

ACCOUNTS RECEIVABLE OPTION

Cambridge Trading Services Corp., Boston, Mass., specifically caters to small-to mid-size market companies. They offer cash up-front upon shipment. Components of Cambridge's financing include:

- 90 day open account terms
- 80% cash upon shipment without a balance sheet loan
- 95% credit insurance without deductible
- no minimum annual volume
- Cambridge takes title to the goods
- elimination of documentation responsibilities

THE FORFAIT OPTION

Another financial tool to consider, especially when trading with developing countries in Eastern Europe, is forfait, a simple system of trade finance. The importer agrees to pay the exporter with promissory notes or bills of exchange guaranteed by an acceptable bank. The exporter then exchanges the notes with a forfaiter for cash before shipment. The forfaiter has no further recourse to the exporter and collects from the importer or his guarantor when the notes become due and are payable.

Originating in Hungary and traded in London and Switzerland primarily, forfaiting is a viable option that serves the interest of both the buyer and seller because the buyer can negotiate extended payment terms in the secondary money markets and the seller gets his cash immediately. You, the seller works with the buyer to obtain a clear, concise, irrevocable and unencumbered promise to pay for the goods purchased. Provision for warranties and/or potential disputes that could arise from the sale of the goods or services are covered in separate documentation. The seller of the goods discounts the paper and sells it in the secondary money market in a forfaiting market in London or Switzerland. The seller, at this stage, is removed from the transaction (nonrecourse) and the holder of the paper and buyer of the goods settle on the repayment terms. This can work in the interest of the buyer, who may need an extended period in which to pay for the goods or service.

In effect, forfait permits the buyer to purchase goods on his own terms, or at least on more acceptable terms than would be available from the manufacturer. United States banks will not, in general, participate in forfaiting. If the buyer's paper is unacceptable on its face in the money market, an EVAL stamp is required. EVAL stamps ensure that there is a banker's acceptance or banker's guarantee that the amount of money due to the holder will be paid by that bank.

Interest costs to the importer are usually tied to the London Interbank Rate (LIBOR), plus a premium if there is a currency or political risk involved for the period of the notes. Also, there will probably be commitment fees, depending on the length of time of commitment between the export of the goods and exchange of the notes for cash. Forfaiters are generally European banks, insurance companies, and finance companies with their activity centered in London or Switzerland, although increasingly, forfaiting is being offered by American companies. These forfaiters have availability and appetites for paper which vary depending on their sources of funds in various countries. Most forfaiters specialize and buy notes from several countries where they have special knowledge or relationships with local financial institutions.

British-American Forfaiting Company, Inc., in St. Louis, Missouri, although several banks and general trade finance companies offer forfaiting, has the distinction of being the only forfaiting broker in the United States and only one of two in the world. According to David McGhee, BAFC's president, forfaiting programs vary enormously between providers and over time. BAFC attempts to use the forfaiting program most advantageous to a particular client or transaction by arranging nonrecourse trade financing through established European underwriters. Bank guarantees from the importing country are normally required. BAFC's services are available for exports to more than 100 countries.

Among the benefits of BAFC's variety of programs are:

- Nonrecourse payment to the exporter at shipment
- No political, currency, or commercial risk
- No bad debts or collection problems
- Frees working capital
- Cash received at shipment or by selling existing receivables
- Buyer credit does not tie up exporter's credit lines
- Deferred payment may help create additional market share
- Agents and distributors may build up large inventories while deferring payment
- Sales into high risk countries are facilitated
- Financing commitments available up to two years in advance
- Credit periods up to 12 years
- Grace periods up to two years
- Multiple currencies available
- Miminum transaction—$50,000
- Competitive costs usually passed to the buyer/exporter

Morgan Grenfell Trade Finance, Ltd., New York, is a subsidiary of Morgan Grenfell & Co., Limited, the London-based trade and merchant banking organization. MGTF was formed to provide exporters with the services of a forfaiting house, a common financing entity in European markets. MGTF has financed exports to over 100 countries and has the capacity to finance both large and small transactions.

FOREIGN EXCHANGE MANAGEMENT

International Monetary Exchange in Elizabeth, New Jersey, specializes in providing foreign exchange services to a variety of charitable organizations. While many banks and brokerage houses are heavily involved in currency trading, relatively few help the exporter to manage foreign exchange to maximize profits in overseas export sales. IMEX secures for its clients interbank exchange rates for world currencies. These rates are designed to give clients flexibility and the opportunity to better control their costs, obtain competitive financing, and increase profit margins. The company's goal is to provide clients with a complete foreign exchange department, independent and without the ongoing expenses of an in-house operation.

A relationship begins with a discussion of a client's requirements and the capabilities of IMEX o fill those needs. On the basis of currencies they expect to be trading, clients are introduced to new banking relationships. Lines of credit for foreign exchange transactions are established in the client's name. Through IMEX, clients are able to deal as easily with the world's more exotic currencies as with free-floating daily convertibles. In addition to trading these currencies with dollars, interbank rates are also negotiated with the major cross rate exchanges. Included in the functions performed by IMEX are:

- Spot, forwards, and futures exchange transactions
- Debt/equity services
- Exchange related advisory services

Compensation is determined in advance by a fee schedule prepared for each client. IMEX never has access to the client's funds. All controls and disciplines are in place for the protection of the client.

FACTORING

Factoring was introduced about 25 years ago in Europe and the Far East as an asset-based lending technique to improve liquidity, provide credit protection, and fund working capital for companies in the textile, apparel, and furniture industries. Its primary benefit is in allowing buyers to purchase on open-account terms, which does not tie up existing credit lines for either the exporter or the importer. By providing a means of turning receivables into cash, factoring eliminates the cost of collections and the risk of bad debts.

Used extensively in the textile industry in the United States to finance domestic transactions, factoring is emerging as a way to finance international trade, and in a wide variety of industry sectors. International factoring is carried out through a group or network of factoring companies. Factors Chain International, based in Amsterdam, is the largest network of factorers, with 90 member companies in 35 countries. Another major factoring network is the International Factors Group, headquartered in Brussels, Belgium. Some major factorers have set up their own networks.

Factoring works in this manner: An exporter approaches a United States factoring company (usually a subsidiary of a foreign bank, although a few American banks are getting involved), which is either a member of one of the international groups or has an established network of its own. Fellow members or allied companies in the foreign country will establish a credit line for the importer and guarantee the risk for the United States factorer. They will also be responsible for collections from the importer. Based on the guarantee, the United States factorer can in turn guarantee the exporter, thereby eliminating his credit risk. The United States factorer or an authorized bank can now provide the financing. The foreign factorer collects the debts and forwards them to the exporter, via the United States factorer.

Heller Financial, Inc., New York, has formed alliances and joint ventures with commercial and merchant banks in most foreign countries, and is the leading factoring company in many markets. Usually, companies with a high volume of repeat business and a $1 million or more in annual sales are the best candidates for Heller's factoring services.

The exporter provides Heller with an aging of accounts receivable, at which point Heller credit analysts will establish credit lines for the exporter's customers. As the exporter ships to his customers, he invoices them in the usual way, but with instructions to direct payments directly to Heller. When the exporter requires funds, he can draw against the account set up in his name. The operation is designed to provide credit approvals faster than conventional methods. While primarily a tool for the furniture and textile industries, Heller can provide factoring for a wide range of commodities and manufacturers. In addition to factoring, Heller can offer other specialized export financing services, such as:

- Credit risk protection
- Local financing in the import country
- Off-balance sheet financing
- Array of cash management and investment banking services

INTERNATIONAL LEASING

Plymouth Commercial Funding, Inc., New York City, accomodates leasing transactions both domestically and internationally, and specializes in high-technology and capital goods. It considers international financing on a case-by-case basis, and facilitates transactions between United States companies and foreign buyers by offering the importer the benefits of depreciation, fixed monthly costs, capital conservation, and preserved credit lines. Plymouth also acts as a broker of used computer technology and provides trading company services for high-tech products.

MAQUILADORA FINANCING

Inter-American Holding Co., San Diego, California, seeks capital appreciation through equity and equity-related investments in labor-intensive manufacturing operations whose production can be relocated into a Mexican maquiladora. Its services are targeted to companies with sales of $10 to $50 million in the following industry sectors: furniture, auto parts, metal products, low-tech electronics, sporting goods, boats, and machinery. Companies should have a labor rate (fully burdened) of $8.00 an hour or more, a labor cost component equal to 18% or more of the cost of goods, and have at least 100 direct labor positions that can be relocated to Mexico. Manufacturing should be assembly line versus job shop in nature.

IHC provides manufacturing start-up and administration know-how; political insight and skills; and acquisition identification, evaluation, financing, and production relocation. Through the establishment of a maquiladora, companies can reexport products to the United States at competitive prices, or export to third-world countries. IHC intends to liquidate each investment in 18–36 months through dollar sales to Mexican buyers.

GENERAL/MISCELLANEOUS SERVICES

Asset Management, International Financing and Settlement, Ltd., New York, has a wide network of financial resources in Europe and the Pacific Rim. They also have offices in Tokyo, London, Hong Kong, Milan, and Vienna. The company's main skill is constructing packages for international traders with diverse financial needs, stemming from complex growth and transactional variations. For companies that are engaging in more extensive international transactions, AMIFS can put together a financing package including the following:

- International trade financing, including forfaiting
- Nonmonetary trade financing, such as countertrade and clearing
- Debt-to-asset conversion of LDC government, trade, or private sector debt
- Off-balance sheet asset management financing
- Marketing facilitation through the use of trade alliances
- Investment merchant banking for growth and development
- Technology transfer and project financing

Intercontinental Credit Corporation, New York, is the financing division of Pan American Trade Development Corp. (PATDC), a trading company. Because of its relationship with a trading company, it can take title to merchandise should this be required. Export financing services include:

- Confirming: offering short and medium-term credits to foreign buyers
- Forfaiting
- Debt-equity swaps, capital transfers, sale of nonresident accounts, arbitrage, retirement of debt via exports
- Countertrade, barter, and offset

PATDC is active in trading, brokering, warehousing, and processing commodities such as steel, forest products, and rubber, and various manufactured products. It has associated with companies in Brazil, Venezuela, Mexico, Columbia, and Belgium, and has representatives on all continents with the exception of Africa.

A.I. Trade Finance, Inc., New York, is a wholly owned subsidiary of American International Group, Inc., one of the largest American-based international insurance companies. It specializes in:

- Forfaiting
- Buyer credits
- Facilitating government export finance programs
- Trade finance services

Trade Financial Services, Corp., New York, considers itself a cross between a bank and a trading company, and is willing to take on the complexities and risks of export financing in touch-and-go transactions. TFSC has designed its programs to suit companies with four types of export financing needs: additional lines of credit for export growth; financing based on opportunity rather than balance sheets; faster turnaround on letters of credit and documentary services; and a reduction in bureaucracy that can make financing international sales time consuming and costly.

TFSC gears itself towards smaller companies needing more straight financing, firms needing assistance in structuring export financing packages, and companies looking for a third party between customers and suppliers. Among the services available are:

- Export collections
- Trade banker's acceptances
- Full range of letter of credit, plus letter of credit bill discounting
- Supplier financing and compensation trade
- Credit, contract, and international shipping documentary services
- Buyer financing
- Asset-based financing
- Off-balance sheet financing
- One-off transaction financing
- Project financing

The Houston Group, Houston, Texas, is an investment banking and project consulting firm that has developed a close relationship with major Japanese industrial organizations including substantial banks. Through these resources, the Group is able to offer financial services for major project activities on a recourse and nonrecourse basis. In addition, the Group can assist in the development of financing packages that may include barter and/or trade transactions. The company's primary areas of interest are in Far Eastern markets, especially Japan, Indonesia, China, and South Korea.

Particular fields of interest for project and trade financing are in the process industries, such as petrochemical, cogeneration, refinery, pulp, and paper. Services include financial information and packages that secure financing, establish the economic feasibility of projects, and organize subsequent findings into packages to use by lending institutions. The Group is also interested in finding technology, processes, and/or equipment that can be exported to Japan for domestic use, and it is currently developing licensing agreements between United States companies, as well as sales and service agreements for American products.

International Capital and Resource Development, Inc., Oklahoma City, Oklahoma, offers a full range of international management, consulting, and banking services. The global banking services include:

- Offshore lending and the establishment of foreign currency bank accounts to settle all kinds of documentary transactions
- Use of underlying documents as well as trust receipts, trust agreements, and security agreements
- Worldwide transfer of funds
- United States government and private guarantee loan programs
- Foreign government support programs
- Establishing a global bank network
- Irrevocable letters of credit
- Foreign exchange transactions

F. Marti & Company, Inc., New York, specializes in export financing for sales into Latin America. It categorizes itself as a confirming house. In some instances, it will take title to the goods, and in others it facilitates short-term financing. The firm gears itself to the small company, usually financing transactions of $10,000–$50,000—sales too small for conventional banks that are wary of Latin America in any case.

Minnesota Trade Trust, Minneapolis, purchases insured export contracts, as well as other insurable commercial and government accounts, from both new and established growth companies. MTT finances exporters when they can secure their assets by focusing on the credit-worthiness of its client's customers, letters of credit, insurance, and other security factors. Financing is designed to extend flexible cash flow, payment terms, and timely financing at competitive rates. Clients are supported with management assistance and the resource facilities of a business development center, which are under contract from an MTT affiliate.

Trade assets of the Trust are backed by bank guarantees or insured by American Credit Indemnity Company. This permits the Trust to include its investors in a diversified portfolio of highly secured trade contracts.

Diversified International Group, New York, through its group of 10 offshore companies, provides several international merchant and investment banking services. As owners, purchasers, traders, and sellers of crude oil products, coal, agricultural commodities, and precious metals, DIC maintains overseas facilities that afford access to European and Middle East markets. Through these markets, it can offer exporters prime bank letters of credit and bank performance bonds. The company will also purchase and invest in accounts receivables, foreign government obligations, and existing letters of credit.

FINANCING CONSULTATION

ADF International Finance, Los Angeles, California, is an international organization of merchant bankers and consultants with additional offices in London and Sydney. Billing itself as international treasurers for hire, ADF assists small and mid-size business with multinational financial needs. By exploiting its expertise and resources, ADF helps its clients obtain international financing tools such as:

- Working capital lines of credit for export
- Short and medium-term non-recourse buyer credits for credit-tight developing countries
- Accounts receivable financing for international subsidiaries, distributors, or end users
- Forfaits
- Multicurrency vendor leasing programs
- International loan sales

Additional consulting services provide expertise in control of foreign exchange exposure and international cash management, frozen funds, and currency repatriation from developing countries and countertrade.

Owens International Credit, Inc., Clearwatyer, Florida, offers exporters a number of services to boost overseas sales, including international credit reports, FSC utilization or formation, and through its sister entity, Owens International Insurance, Inc., a wide range of credit insurance. Owens assists exporters in meeting their financial needs by facilitating the use of:

- Receivables financing
- Buyer's financing
- Eximbank programs
- International loan packaging
- Factoring
- Specialized financial instruments

FOREIGN BANK SUBSIDIARIES

Midland International Trade Services, New York, is a subsidiary of Midland Bank Aval, Ltd. MITS offers U.S. exporters a number of financing options. MITS has access to a worldwide network of specialist teams with strong product experience, and particular strength in Latin America. MITS prides itself on a flexible approach designed to manage complex trade transactions. It can take title to the goods and track goods in channels of trade. It can also offer 100% nonrecourse trade financing. Other MITS services include:

- Advisory and transactional structuring
- Nonrecourse export financing
- Trade-related project financing
- Facilitation of Eximbank and FCIA programs
- Foreign government subsidized export financing, especially for Brazil, Mexico, Venezuela, and Argentina
- Forfaiting
- Trade-related interest rate and foreign exchange services
- Asset-conversion services in developing nations
- U.S. bankers acceptance financing
- Trade loans/advances/refinancing
- Letters of credit
- Documentary/clean collections

Creditanstalt–AWT Trade Finance Company, San Francisco, California, is a joint venture between two Austrian companies (a bank and a trading company). Creditanstalt–AWT (CAWT) offers a variety of export financing services in the European trade and merchant banking tradition. Their services include:

- Short and medium-term forfaiting transactions
- Countertrade options including advance purchase, buyback, offset, and clearing/switch
- Facilitation of Eximbank/FCIA programs
- Revolving buyer credits
- Pre-export financing
- Private insurance coverage
- Secured lending

The company specializes in creating client-specific packages comprising several facilities. CAWT also provides advisory services, market research, foreign sales representation, and joint venture structuring between United States, Soviet, and East European companies.

INNOVATIVE BANK PROGRAMS

Security Pacific–The Sequor Group, New York, recently developed a program aimed for a growing need in the export community, especially among small and mid-sized companies: the demand for open account terms of sale on short-term export transactions. Called the Accelerated Cash Management Exports, the bank will provide 100% credit and collection facilities for export transactions. If an exporter needs to finance a short-term transaction, ACME can advance funds prior to maturity. The exporter pays interest only on the required advances, at a rate based on the cost of funds.

Bank of Boston, New York, has established a unique program to assist a greater range of small- to mid-sized exporters. The Bank is allowing a number of smaller banks to use its Trade Key software to facilitate their letter of credit operations; it is also giving them access to its international staff and vast overseas network of financial institutions. By combining the international resources of a larger bank with smaller banks' abilities to work with smaller customers, this program makes it both feasible and profitable to work with exporters that might otherwise have been unable to obtain traditional bank export financing.

The program is flexible and can even be provided in another bank's name for its own customers. Solutions designed to increase international trade transactions are tailored to the goals of each bank by reducing costs, increasing productivity, and enhancing profitability without major capital expenditures. The Bank can also design other export financing tools and factoring for smaller banks.

THE OVERSEAS PRIVATE INVESTMENT CORPORATION

The Overseas Private Investment Corporation (OPIC) began operations in 1971. Organized as a corporation and structured to be responsive to private business, the agency's mandate is to mobilize and facilitate the participation of United States private capital and skills in the economic and social development of less developed, friendly countries and areas.

Currently OPIC programs are available for new business enterprises or expansions in approximately 100 developing countries or areas around the world. Assistance is not available for projects that adversely affect United States employment, are financially unsound, or do not promise significant benefits to the social and economic development of the host country or area.

As a self-sustaining agency, OPIC has received no public funds beyond its original start-up appropriations. However, it has recorded a positive net income for every year of operation, with reserves currently standing in excess of $1 billion.

While private investors have the capability to assess the commercial aspects of doing business overseas, they may be hesitant to undertake long-term investments abroad, given the political uncertainties of many developing nations.

To alleviate these uncertainties, OPIC insures United States investments against four major types of political risks.

Inconvertibility

This protects the investor against the inability to convert into United States dollars the local currency received as profits, earnings, or return of capital on investment, and futher against discrimininatory exchange rates, but not for devaluation of host country currency.

Expropriation

This coverage protects the investor against confiscation or nationalization of an investment without fair compensation.

War, Revolution, Insurrection, and Civil Strife

This coverage protects an investor against losses due to war (declared or not), revolution, or insurrection. In addition, coverage is available against losses due to civil strife such as politically motivated violent acts including terrorism and sabotage.

Business Income Coverage

OPIC is now offering Business Income Coverage (BIC) for political risks. The coverage protects a company from interruptions and resulting loss of income (suspension of operations) caused by political violence and expropriation.

American investors planning to share significantly in the equity and management of an overseas venture can often use OPIC's finance programs for medium to long-term financing. To obtain financing, the venture must be commercially and financially sound, within demonstrated competence of the proposed management, and sponsored by the investor having a proven record of success in the same or closely related business. OPIC furnishes financing through either direct loans or loan guarantees.

To foster private investment in the developing world, OPIC offers two major investment encouragement programs.

INVESTMENT ENCOURAGEMENT PROGRAMS

Feasibility Studies

An investor's decision to do business in a developing country frequently hinges on the ability to investigate and analyze the potential of a specific enterprise. To meet this need, OPIC can provide funding assistance for feasibility studies. Under this program, OPIC will reimburse an investor for up to 50 percent of the study's costs (60 percent for a small business-sponsored study). In all cases, maximum OPIC participation is $100,000.

Special Project Grants and Loans

OPIC also offers grants and loans in support of host country nationals involved in OPIC-supported projects. Funding is generally provided to businesses on a concessional loan basis in amounts not exceeding $50,000. The actual amounts and terms of funding depend entirely on the nature of the undertaking.

For investors seeking business opportunities in developing countries, OPIC offers a computer data system that can match an investor's interest with specific overseas opportunities. This service, known as the *Opportunity Bank*, allows United States firms to submit a description of their business, type of investment sought, and the developing country or countries of interest. Upon request, the information can be matched against similar information submitted by foreign business seeking American investors.

A domestic firm or foreign entity can register itself with the Opportunity Bank at no charge; a modest fee is charged for "match" requests. The Opportunity Bank is designed to foster the exchange of investment information. No determination is made by OPIC as to the accuracy or reliability of information submitted.

THE EXPORT-IMPORT BANK OF THE UNITED STATES

The Export-Import Bank of the United States (Eximbank) was created in 1934 and established as an independent United States government agency in 1945. The purpose of the bank is to aid in financing and to facilitate exports. Exim receives no appropriations from the United States Congress. Since inception, Exim has supported more than $120 billion in export sales, and has paid more than $1 billion in dividends to the United States Treasury.

Exim is directed by statute to offer financing for United States exporters that is competitive with the financing provided by foreign export credit agencies to assist sales by their nations' exporters, to determine that the transactions supported provide a reasonable assurance of repayment, to supplement, but not compete with, private sources of export financing, and to take into account the effect of its activities on small business, the domestic economy, and United States employment.

Foreign Credit Insurance Association (FCIA), a group of United States property, casualty, and marine insurance companies, cooperates with Eximbank to cover repayment risks on short and medium-term export credit transactions. More than 350 commercial banks work with Eximbank to provide funding and participate in the commercial risks of medium-term transactions. Exporters, buyers, and bankers are invited to call, write, or visit Eximbank for more detailed information. Participating commercial banks, FCIA, and export insurance brokers can also assist applicants.

In 1989 alone, Eximbank assisted in over $6.6 billion dollars of international sales of which small business accounted for over 27 percent of the total. Small business from 1984 to 1989 had been averaging up to 22 percent of Eximbank's business. Historically, Eximbank had been the mecca of financial assistance for the Fortune 500 companies. In recent years, as the international marketplace began to change, it became apparent that Eximbank's programs needed to better reflect this changing trade environment. Thus, the bank has undertaken a major overhaul of its programs designed to provide greater risk protection to lenders and to be accessible to the widest variety of potential sources of export finance.

SMALL BUSINESS ADVISORY SERVICE

To encourage small business to sell overseas, Eximbank has a special office to provide information on the availability and use of export credit insurance, guarantees, direct and intermediary loans extended to finance the sale of United States goods and services abroad.

Briefing Programs

Eximbank offers briefing programs that are available to the small business community. The program includes group briefings and individual discussions held both within the bank and around the country. For scheduling information, call (202) 566-4490.

FINANCIAL SUPPORT PROGRAMS

Eximbank's financial programs are generally available to any United States exporting firm, regardless of size. The following programs, however, are particularly helpful to small- to medium-size business exporters and may be applicable to your needs.

Export Credit Insurance

An exporter may reduce its risks by purchasing export credit insurance from Eximbank's agent, The Foreign Credit Insurance Corporation (FCIA). Policies available include insurance for financing or operating leases, medium-term insurance, the new-to-export policy, insurance for the service industry, the umbrella policy, the trade association policy, and the multibuyer and single-buyer policies.

FCIA Coverage

- Protects the exporter against the failure of foreign buyers to pay their credit obligations for commercial or political reasons
- Encourages exporters to offer foreign buyers competitive forms of payment
- Supports an exporter's prudent penetration of higher risk foreign markets
- Gives exporters and their banks greater financial flexibility in handling overseas accounts receivable

FCIA Offices

40 Rector Street, 11th Floor
New York, NY 10006
(212) 227-7020

The office serves New England, New York, New Jersey, Pennsylvania, Delaware, District of Columbia, Maryland, and Virginia.

20 North Clark Street, Suite 910
Chicago, IL 60602
(312) 641-1915

The office serves Ohio, Indiana, Michigan, Illinois, Wisconsin, Minnesota, North Dakota, South Dakota, Iowa, Missouri, Nebraska, Kansas, Kentucky, and West Virginia.

Texas Commerce Tower
600 Travis, Suite 2860
Houston, TX 77002
(713) 227-0987

The office serves Louisiana, Oklahoma, Arkansas, New Mexico, North Carolina, South Carolina, Texas, Mississippi, and Tennessee.

Wells Fargo Center, Suite 2580
333 South Grand Avenue
Los Angeles, CA 90071
(213) 687-3890

The office serves Alaska, Washington, Oregon, Hawaii, California, Nevada, Arizona, Montana, Wyoming, Colorado, and Utah.

World Trade Center
80 Southwest 8th Street
Miami, FL 33130
(305) 372–8540

This office serves Florida, Alabama, Georgia, Puerto Rico, and the U.S. Virgin Islands.

New-To-Export Insurance Policy

Eximbank offers through FCIA a short-term (up to 180 days) insurance policy geared to meet the particular credit requirements of smaller, less experienced exporters. Under the policy, Exim assumes 95 percent of the commercial and 100 percent of the political risk involved in extending credit to the exporter's overseas customers. This policy frees the smaller exporter from first loss commercial risk deductible provisions that are usually found in regular insurance policies. This special coverage is available to companies that are just beginning to export or have an annual export credit sales volume of less than $750,000 for the past two years.

Umbrella Policy

In late 1984, Eximbank introduced the umbrella policy to insure the receivables of companies with only limited export experience in international trade. These policies are available to commercial lenders, state agencies, finance companies, insurance brokers, and similar agencies to ensure their client's export receivables. Exporters are eligible if they have averaged annual export credit sales of less than $2,000,000 for the past two years and have not used FCIA in the past two years.

Working Capital Guarantee

The Working Capital Loan Guarantee Program assists small business in obtaining crucial working capital to fund their export activities. The program guarantees 90 percent of the principal and a limited amount of interest on working capital loans extended by commercial lenders to eligible United States exporters. The loan may be used for pre-export activities such as the purchase of inventory, raw materials, manufacture of product, or marketing. Eximbank requires the working capital loan to be secured with inventory of exportable goods, accounts receivable, or by other appropriate collateral. Eximbank will guarantee loans for up to 90 percent of the value of eligible collateral.

Eximbank/SBA Working Capital Co-Guarantee program

To more effectively reach small business with its working capital guarantee authority, Eximbank concluded an agreement in August 1984 with the SBA to extend co-guarantees under SBA's Export Revolving Line of Credit (ERLC) Program. By participating on an equal basis with the SBA, Eximbank effectively increases the SBA's guarantee authority from $500,000 to $1,000,000. Thus, if an exporter qualifies as a small business and needs to borrow less than $1 million in working capital funds, both Eximbank and SBA resources are available. Under this arrangement, SBA will continue to consider amounts below $200,000 solely for its ERLC program. Eximbank will continue to provide guarantees covering working capital loans or credit lines to companies that are not small business.

Direct or Intermediary Business

Eximbank provides two types of loans, direct loans to foreign buyers of United States exports and intermediary loans to fund responsible buyers of United States capital and quasi-capital goods and related services. Both the loan and guarantee programs cover up to 85 percent of United States export value, with repayment terms of one year or more. Direct loans of any size and long-term loans to intermediaries (more than $10 million or over 7 years repayment) are offered at the lowest interest rate permitted under the OECD arrangement for the market and term.

Medium-term intermediary loans (less the $10 million and 7 years) are structured as stand-by loan commitments. The intermediary may borrow against the remaining undisbursed loan at anytime during the term of the underlying debt obligation. There is a prepayment fee if it is triggered by prepayment of the foreign borrower.

Guarantees

Eximbank's guarantee provides repayment protection for private sector loans to creditworthy buyers of United States capital equipment and related services. The guarantee is available alone or may be combined with an intermediary loan. Most guarantees provide comprehensive coverage of both political and commercial risks, but political risks coverage is also available. It covers 100 percent of the principal amount of the financed portion. However, the exporter or the guaranteed lender, must provide Eximbank with a counter-guarantee of 2 percent of the commercial risk on all medium-term loans of $10 million or less.

In the event of default, the guaranteed lender must file a claim no less than 30 and no more than 150 days after default. The claim will be paid within five business days after receipt.

Repayment Terms

Eximbank-supported financing follows the repayment term guidelines customary in international trade. For capital goods sales, the guidelines are:

Contract Value	Maximum Term
$50,000 or less	2 years
$50,001–$100,000	3 years

Contract Value	Maximum Term
$100,001–$200,000	4 years
$200,001–and over	5–10 years, depending on the nature of the project and the OECD classification of the buyer's country.

Loans for projects and large product acquisitions, such as aircraft, are eligible for longer terms while lower unit value items such as automobiles and appliances receive shorter terms.

Program Selection Chart

Exports   **Appropriate Program**

Short-Term (Up to 180 days)

Exports	Appropriate Program
Consumables	Export credit insurance
Small manufactured items	Working capital guarantee
Spare parts	
Raw material	

Medium-Term (181 days to 5 years)

Exports	Appropriate Program
Mining and refining equipment	Export credit insurance
Construction equipment	Commercial bank guarantees
Agricultural equipment	Small business credit program
General aviation aircraft	Medium-term credit
Planning/feasibility studies	Working capital guarantee

Long-Term (5 years and longer)

Exports	Appropriate Program
Power plants	Direct loans
LNG and gas producing plants	Financial guarantees
Other major projects	
Commercial jet aircraft and locomotives	
Other heavy capital goods	

THE INTERNATIONAL FINANCE CORPORATION

The International Finance Corporation (IFC) was established in 1956. It is an affiliate of the International Bank for Reconstruction and Development (the World Bank), and derives its status and power from an international agreement (Article of Agreement) among its member countries. Membership in IFC is open to all governments that are members of the World Bank. The Corporation has 125 member countries.

Principal Activities

- Direct investments in individual productive private enterprises
- Project identification and promotion
- Helping to establish, finance, and improve privately owned development finance companies and other institutions that assist development of the private sector
- Encouraging the growth of capital markets in the developing countries
- Creating in the capital exporting countries interest in portfolio investments in enterprises located in the developing countries
- Giving advice and counsel to less developed member countries on measures that will create a climate conducive to the growth of private investment

IFC will invest in any type of enterprise in the developing countries that meets its investment criteria. Its past investments have been primarily in manufacturing. Other areas of investment include (but are not limited to) mining, tourism, utilities, and agriculture projects.

Government participation in an enterprise that is otherwise eligible for IFC financing will not necessarily preclude an IFC investment in that enterprise. IFC is prepared to support mixed enterprises, such as joint ventures between private enterprise and government. Each case will be examined in the light of such factors as the extent of government ownership and control, the nature of the enterprise, efficiency of management, and the possibility of increasing private ownership in the future.

Every venture in which IFC invests must hold out the prospect of earning a profit and must benefit the economy of the country in which it is made. IFC will not finance any venture which, in its opinion, cannot provide sufficient private capital on reasonable terms. IFC will invest in a venture only if there is provision for immediate or eventual local participation. If necessary, IFC will, in appropriate cases, join in an underwriting or other arrangement that will make shares available to local investors either immediately or in the future. IFC attaches great importance to the extent of the sponsor's participation in the share capital of an enterprise. IFC will never be a majority shareholder.

PRIVATE EXPORT FUNDING CORPORATION

The Private Export Funding Corporation (PEFCO) finances United States exports. The Company, which is owned by fifty-four commercial banks, seven industrial companies, and one investment banking firm, makes medium-term and long-term fixed interest rate export loans when such terms are not available from conventional private sector lenders. All of PEFCO's export loans carry the unconditional guarantee of the Export-Import Bank of the United States (Eximbank), regarding timely payment of principal and interest. Eximbanks's guarantee represents the full faith and credit of the United States.

PEFCO's involvement is usually limited to loans that have final maturities at least five years from the date of commitment; PEFCO will not make an offer for less than $1 million. Individual loans have ranged from approximately $1 million to $225 million with an average being about $21 million. Most of these loans were made to foreign purchasers of United States goods and services. In the case of lease transactions, loans have been made to commercial or special purpose lessors.

Frequently, PEFCO joins a lending group that includes one or more commercial banks as co-lenders, and Eximbank, as co-lender and guarantor. PEFCO's participation in export financings has ranged from a modest portion of a total loan to the entire financed amount. Generally, the company's loans are repaid from maturities due after those of the commercial banks and before those of Eximbank. In the event that Eximbank is not a co-lender, PEFCO's loan is usually repaid from the later maturities.

COUNTERTRADE AS A METHOD TO FINANCE JOINT VENTURES

Countertrade is a generic term that means exchanging one item of value for another item of value, something for something, or simply, quid pro quo. This 'something' can be almost anything such as soy beans, vodka, ships, oil, radios, perfume, wood carvings, and yes, even hard-currency cash.

This practice of barter or commodity exchange has been around since the beginning of mankind. It has recently grown in prominence as a method of financing trade and joint ventures between commercial enterprises and less developed countries.

MANY FORMS OF DISGUISE

Counterpurchase. The most common type of countertrade where a seller agrees to purchase a set amount of goods from the country that purchases from them.

Offset. This is a variation of the same theme whereby the seller guarantees to use goods and services from the buyer's country in the product he is selling (local content).

Buy-back. In these transactions, sellers of capital equipment agree to be repaid from product produced by that machinery.

Barter. A simple swap of one good for another. It is simple, but rarely employed in international trade.

Switch trading. A complicated form of barter that involves a chain of buyers and sellers in different markets.

Free markets are now in vogue in Eastern Europe, but it will take some horse trading, common in preperestroika days, to get these countries into the global economy. Countertrade accounts for about 25 percent of east-west trade and it is expected to flourish in days ahead. Countertrade is often costly and inefficient, but as more and more enterprises in the east try to engage in foreign trade, they will have little choice as long as they are short of hard or convertible currency but to use countertrade on a more frequent basis.

Key Test Questions

When considering countertrade, the first task is to identify a commodity or product produced in the developing country in sufficient quantities that make it attractive for export. Caution should be exercised here by asking yourself two significant key questions:

If the product is excellent for countertrade, why isn't the host country already exporting it to generate hard currency?

If you accept the product in countertrade, will you be able to find a market that will permit you to convert the product into hard currency?

Examples

Some may say countertrade is hideously complex and risky business, and it can be, but a simplified example may possibly work for you in this manner. Let's say that you desire to sell a United States-made product to a company in a developing country with stringent central bank foreign exchange controls. In short, the prospective purchaser will be unable to pay for your product with hard currency upon presentation of the required documents. However, there may be a way to make the sale, but it will mean additional work and creativity on your part to turn the problem into an opportunity with countertrade.

Perhaps, heretofore, you have been selling your product to buyers in a developing country with access to overseas foreign exchange. But, now, to make a specific sale you need to switch roles, and in a sense become a salesman for the developing country or a supplier inside the country. Your task is to generate a commodity, United States dollars, by selling a product produced in a developing country to customers in developed countries. With the hard currency generated from this activity, you can pay your company for products and/or for underwriting the start-up and operating costs of a joint venture. You can earn income from each activity: the product sale, the countertrade, and the joint venture.

Armed with a product or commodity, you now look for a market in a developed country. The size of the transaction is governed by the dollar requirements of the sale of your product in the developing country. It may not, however, be an even dollar for dollar trade. You will need to generate the funds required to cover your sale from fall-out such as gross profit or commission from the countertrade. The structure of the transaction is dependent on who is involved, what is needed, and how it is to be financed.

If the developing-country commodity or product is for sale for X amount in United States dollars, you will sell it in a developed country with convertible monetary standards for X plus some value, say Y, also in hard currency. If Y, or your recovery, is sufficient to cover the sales price of the product that you are trying to market into the less developed country, then you have completed your mission by ultimately creating the commodity, United States dollars, in an amount sufficient to pay for your company's product.

A more complex example of countertrade may occur in this manner. Suppose you target host country A for a joint venture, but your future partners don't have the hard currency to support the intended partnership or joint venture. However, your new partners have various other assets that you feel are essential to the joint venture in host country A. And, the prospects for the business are tremendous if you can help solve their currency problem. Here's where you really earn your wings in international marketing. You learn that in host country A there are several producers of goods that meet international quality standards. You and your prospective partners identify those items that you feel are exportable from country A. Now you must determine which countries could be importers of these same goods. Once identified, they are called target countries B and C.

Therefore, host country A, where you want your joint venture, with your assistance, becomes an exporter to target countries B and C through countertrade to produce the hard currency to finance your joint venture in host country A. An ability and technique of being able to locate saleable products and define multinational markets can provide you with a competitive edge in global trade. It permits you to overcome the reoccuring stumbling block to forming joint ventures in developing countries.

Developing Countries

All developing countries have natural and commercial resources that with creative marketing can find a home in the international marketplace. The countertrade may involve several commodity exchanges in several countries before the end result is convertible cash. However, once the requirement for hard currency is satisfied, the joint venture may proceed as any normal business partnership.

Recognition of one or more trading opportunities as an extension of your principle business activity can result in countertrade. These new opportunities alone can be a rewarding and exciting international business. If market recognition is effective, the joint trading enterprise can be profitable well in advance of the actual start-up of the working joint venture. In short, cash profits from the upcoming joint venture could be a bonus to an already profitable relationship that was developed solely to fund the original project.

This text is not intended to oversimplify an often complex activity, but if you understand the historical basis of trade and barter, you already know the fundamentals of countertrade. Complexities can arise from execution of required financial instruments frequently encountered during the process. International trade merchant banks can be helpful in facilitating a transaction by providing various trade financed options along the path to your desired result, but you as the marketer, must instigate the commerce. The bank will support the trade if there is collateral in place for each step of the way. Countertrade usually facilitates this test since a commodity or finished product is fundamental to each transaction.

The global economies of the 1990s will dictate that creative international marketing must embrace an ever-increasing understanding of countertrade and the opportunities that it affords in a global market. Markets and joint venture prospects that otherwise would be denied for lack of hard currency can now be developed with confidence through countertrade. If you possess the skills to recognize and implement multinational trading in support of product sales and joint venture creation, your value as an international business development executive increases as global marketing becomes more complex and competitive.

Eastern Europe and/or the Soviet Union

PepsiCo, Inc., a multinational corporation, is a much larger operation than the small- to medium-size business to whom this text is directed, but their operation in the Soviet Union is an excellent example of how creative marketing can lead to excellent international business opportunities through countertrade.

Several years ago, they looked at entering the Russian market. The problem they encountered was in repatriating profits in hard currency from sales inside of the Soviet Union. Hard currency was unavailable. PepsiCo had to find an exportable product that had international appeal. They settled on Stolichnaya Vodka, a commodity that could be resold in the West for hard currency. This was a classic countertrade until, in 1989, it became evident that the demand for Pepsi syrup in the Soviet Union was becoming much greater than the demand for Stolichnaya vodka in the United States.

In April of 1990, the Soviet Union and three western partners, including America's PepsiCo, signed an agreement that involves exchanging $1.5 billion worth of ships built under contract in Soviet shipyards by a Soviet-Norwegian joint venture for PepsiCo syrup to offset the imbalance in vodka/syrup. In an earlier deal struck in January of 1990, Russia agreed to swap $30–40 million worth of vodka for coffee from Brazil.

The PepsiCo, Inc. countertrade ageement in the Soviet Union called for a $1 for $1 product exchange. This means that for every United States dollar of imports, they agreed to export a United States dollar of Soviet product. PepsiCo also negotiated a similar arrangement in China for $1 for $1 exchange in countertrade. When they went to India, the result was somewhat different, but nevertheless creative. India's market represented a far larger middle class, hence a larger potential market for their soda than either Russia or China. The agreement with the Indian government, finalized in September of 1988, called for a $1 to $5 exchange or for every United States dollar of imports into India, PepsiCo agreed to take five United States dollars of Indian exports. This agreement was concluded in the interest of generating hard, foreign exchange on behalf of India. Additionally, PepsiCo agreed to assist India with the development of certain agricultural projects within the country.

Another known multinational American corporation provides an example of how to develop opportunity in a less developed country through countertrade. McDonald's has entered the Soviet Union for the long haul. In early 1990, they opened 20 outlets in various cities in the Soviet Union. They will operate with local currency. Rather than import requirements for their foods as one might expect, they have embarked on a program to develop segments of agriculture in support of their needs. For example, they have imported a potato from the Netherlands that is doing well in Russian soil. They will supplement this with their own onions, beef, and other needs. When George Cohen, CEO of McDonald's in Canada, was recently asked how they would repatriate profits, he answered, "There are lots of apples and tomatoes in the Soviet Union, maybe someday we'll process apple pies or tomato paste for export, for now, we plan to recycle rubles for internal growth in the Soviet Union."

Mr. Cohen also commented that McDonald's ran an advertisement in Russian newspapers for 500 potential employees for twenty new McDonald locations. The ad ran for three days. The post office called and said, "When are you going to send a truck to pick-up your mail?" McDonald's received over 12,000 applications for 500 jobs. This is indicative of the size of the labor force in the East Bloc that is ripe for employment in the private sector. If you are considering the Soviet Union, the time to get in is now while costs are at rock bottom. In two to four years, entry costs will be much higher.

Events of the summer of 1989 with regard to the President's visit to Poland and Hungary, and subsequent events in the fall of 1989 leading to the dismantling of the Berlin wall and an opening of Brandenburg Gate in Berlin signals an end to the cold war. Political and economic reforms that are underway in several countries in Eastern Europe and in the Soviet Union seem to be unstoppable. This will open new economic opportunities for entrepreneurs creative and flexible in their approach to today's world markets. Mr. Lech Walesa, a leader of Poland, was recently on television in America saying, "Without joint ventures by American companies in Poland to effect economic reform, our political reform will fail." He is inviting United States small- to medium-size business to his country and newly envisioned free markets, but Poland's problem is, as is often the case in developing countries, their deficiency in hard currency.

This is where creativity comes into play on behalf of the seasoned international business executive or entrepreneur. Before writing off this opportunity, you should determine what Polish people produce that would be exportable to other nations. In this way, as described in earlier paragraphs, you would be able to generate the hard currency that you require for the joint venture in Poland. Admittedly, this requires effort and some financial commitment on your part, but if Americans are going to increase world market share going into the year 2000, we must begin now, at the beginning of the 1990s decade, to create opportunities for United States small- to medium-size business expansion into the global economy.

Multitudes of possibilities for countertrade exist in Eastern Europe. Yugoslavia, for example, produces beautiful consumer goods such as furniture. They have ample raw materials and an excellent labor force. They need American marketing skills, know-how, and ingenuity to convert their resources into products that can be used for local consumption and exportable commerce. The door is open for joint ventures and current products exist to permit finance with countertrade. What is true in Yugoslavia, is true in all of the Eastern European countries and the Soviet Union. Some countries are a little farther along than others in their desire for political reform, but be alert to new opportunities as they arise.

Romania is the most agressive and enthusiastic Eastern European countertrader. They have signed a $1 billion deal with Candu, a Canadian atomic energy company, to construct a nuclear reactor in Romania for railway wagons and coal. In Russia, countertrade has been used to fund about 10 percent of its most recent 800 joint ventures.

The Soviet Union, in similar circumstances as Eastern Europe, needs internal economic reform to match their new political reform. The Russians are desperate for overseas joint ventures, or joint enterprises, as they are called, to support the reforms promised under Perestroika. Countertrade, in many instances, may be your most effective option to recover hard currency from an investment in a joint enterprise in the Soviet Union. Otherwise, if you invest hard currency as part of your contribution to a joint enterprise in the Soviet Union, your only other alternative to recoup this investment is from earnings realized from exports goods and services that are paid for by overseas buyers in convertible currency. Your return on investment is restricted to profit taking in hard currency earned only from exports of goods or services produced by the joint enterprise. Countertrade may be a more attractive element in doing business with the Soviet Union.

Czechoslovakia has a pearl on the horizon for countertrade. In 1850, Tatra Coachworks began making carriages. In the 1930s, they began manufacturing automobiles for the public. The Tatra automobile, before World War II was gaining international acclaim for design and performance. Today, each vehicle is produced by hand by the least expensive robots in the world. Tatra has the expertise, buts lacks the manufacturing know-how and technology to mass produce automobiles and trucks. When they achieve production capability, their products will surely have convertible currency value in the west.

Entrepreneurs are overheard everyday, "I've got a line on this unique product or needed service that will sell in Eastern Europe and the Soviet Union." Counterparts in the east are encouraging product and service entry with many creative schemes. Finding something to sell in the east is simple. Finding a source of convertible currency is the real challenge.

A more productive approach than looking for things to sell may be in finding exportable commodities in Eastern Europe and the Soviet Union that meet world standards. While this will not be easy by anyone's measure, countertrade will open the doors to unlimited earnings for sales to Eastern Europe and the Soviet Union.

Risks

Countertrade can be costly. In addition to paying commissions to middlemen, companies that export to the Council for Mutual Economic Assistance (CMEA), in Eastern Europe, should include an extra margin or subsidy in quoted pricing. Whatever time and expense that you calculate to conclude a countertrade transaction, double or triple that estimate. After all, you may have to substantially discount East European product to move it in western markets. This is especially true of manufactured products due to present day quality standards that are far below acceptable world standards. Add to this burden, the hidden cost of finding a buyer and insurance to cover the risk on nondelivery, and countertrade becomes an expensive way to do business. However, it may be the only way to transact business in some cases.

In their 1989 book, *Exporting from Start to Finance*, Dulat and Wells offer the following comments on countertrade. The opportunities for countertrade are virtually limitless, which is probably what makes it so difficult and time consuming. Your first point of negotiation should always be to minimize the percentage of the sale that is to be compensated in some form of countertrade. Your leverage point will go from excellent, for goods the countertrading country really needs, to close to zero, or 100 percent countertrade, for nonessential consumer goods.

Even though you are dealing with a private party, that party is often being controlled by its government because it is only through the government that import licenses and foreign exchange can be obtained. They continue by saying, count on much higher costs than in conventional transactions, even if you plan to handle the import goods yourself. If you are planning to have a countertrade house or an ETC handle the resale, the cost could be as much as 20 percent. Even then, it would be difficult to get third party help for a deal of less than $1 million. Check the penalty clauses and determine what happens if the penalties should apply, and what the downside risk is. Even though the penalties seem vague, you can assume that any uncompensated infringement of your agreement will mean the end of trading days with that country.

Dulat and Wells conclude by commenting, while countertrade can be a potent marketing tool and sales achiever, and in some situations, a profitable and wise thing to do for the bold trader, in most cases it is better to avoid countertrade if possible. In other words, do not go out looking for countertrade, let it find you. Apart from the obvious risks, it will have a tendency to slow up the pace of doing business because of the slow negotiations and the relatively large number of proposed transactions that do not materialize. It will be interesting to note what becomes of the office of barter in the Department of Commerce, as created under the Omnibus Trade Bill. The office is supposed to monitor barter activities internationally, as well as enterprises seeking barter. The same trade bill also establishes an interagency group of countertrade and offsets.

While the comments of Dulat and Wells have merit and should be considered before undertaking countertrade, the downside risks may be outweighed by the opportunity of establishing a productive joint venture in a developing country. With exciting developments and apparent new and unlimited opportunities opening up rapidly in Eastern Europe, the small- to medium-size business may need to rethink the position that countertrade is too difficult. It may represent the only option for market entry in some cases. And in fact, once the procedure of countertrade is established in a given circumstance in a given country, and product lists and outside markets are defined, the activity will be almost self-perpetuating as a provider of hard currency in support of the continuing joint venture activity.

A humorous incident occurred a few years ago involving countertrade and a communication problem. A young man, without much understanding of international commerce, worked at an order desk in Houston, Texas, for a major steel manufacturing company in the United States. One day the phone rang, and a customer in Mexico wanted to order a substantial quantity of steel pipe. The customer said that he wanted a barter deal. The young man thought he said a border deal since the point of delivery was to be Laredo, Texas, a town on the border with Mexico.

It was never entirely clear why the pipe was shipped from the mill without all the documents being in order, but it was shipped. The young man received a frantic call later that week from his freight forwarding agent in Laredo, saying, "What are we going to do with all of this cotton?" The young man replied, "I don't know anything about cotton, this pipe was sold FOB, Texas border. The agent retorted, "You misunderstood, this purchase is a barter transaction." The steel company accepted delivery of the cotton, sold it immediately, and a seemingly costly misunderstanding resulted in a gross income beyond initial expectations.

Countertrade requires unique skills in recognizing opportunities, old-fashioned horse trading, and marketing. It may sound simple as conveyed in this text, but it can be complex because it requires that you, the marketer, have an understanding of world markets and the diverse opportunities in the global economy. Often, export management companies can be useful in assisting the small-to medium-size company with barter opportunities due to their diversified customer base and multiple looks at various trading opportunities. Countertrade is not conducive to specialized thinking, it requires flexiblility in the understanding of the concept and the rewards. Hopefully, American small- to- medium-size business will recognize the immense value and importance of countertrade as a financing and marketing tool for trade expansion well into this decade and the 21st century.

LETTERS OF CREDIT

There are several ways that an overseas buyer may fund his purchases from you. Except for cash with the order, a preferred method of payment for exporters is a confirmed, irrevocable letter of credit confirmed by a prime United States bank. This letter is opened by an overseas bank at the request of the foreign purchaser in favor of you, the exporter, and represents a guarantee of payment subject to conditions set out or stipulated in the letter. The conditions outlined in the buyer's letter of credit should be a mirror image of the terms and conditions of sale as you presented in quotation form on your proforma invoice.

For export or joint venture financing, the letter of credit is possibly the most well-known international financing instrument, the most complex, and the least understood by the exporters entering international markets for the first time. Letters of credit can be used to fund joint ventures. Dulat and Wells, in *Exporting from Start to Finance*, offer clear definitions of terms and conditions pertaining to the use and understanding of international letters of credit. Their explanations are presented in the interest of clarity and interpretation.

The letter of credit requires an opening bank, a paying bank, a buyer, and a seller. The opening bank issues the letter of credit on behalf of the buyer who is obligated to reimburse the credit extended by this bank. The paying bank (*nominated bank*) is the bank on which drafts (also known as *bills of exchange*) are to be drawn under the credit. The seller is the party to whom the credit is issued.

He is also known as the beneficiary, the exporter, and the shipper. In order to understand the terms of the letter of credit, certain definitions need to be clarified.

Revocable vs. Irrevocable

Always insist on an irrevocable letter of credit placed on a prime United States bank. Irrevocable means that once the L/C is opened, it cannot be altered or changed in any manner without the expressed consent of those directly involved, especially the exporter. Revocable letters of credit have little, if any commercial value and are seldom used in international commerce. However, unless the letter of credit specifically states it is irrevocable, it is deemed to be revocable.

Confirming vs. Advised

Confirmation by a prime United States bank is preferable because you would have a promise from an American bank to pay, based on its own evaluation of the documents in place by both the buyer and the overseas issuing bank, although it does cost you or your customer additional fees. The confirming bank will then negotiate the letter of credit, usually in three days or sooner, if it is from a strong bank in a stable, commercial country such as Germany, France, Japan, or the United Kingdom.

If the letter of credit is advised, the advising bank in the United States clearly states it is acting as an advising bank and that the credit conveys no engagement on our part. They will verify that the documents are in order and send the documents to the issuing bank for final examination and compliance. The issuing bank may designate the advising bank to be the paying bank. If the advising bank chooses to accept the responsibilities of the paying bank, it also becomes the negotiating bank. The letter of credit continues to convey no engagement and payment, if made, is usually made with recourse.

Straight Credit vs. Negotiated Credit

A straight letter of credit can only be paid at the counter of the paying bank, which in the case of straight letters of credit will usually be the issuing bank or its American branch or prime correspondent.

A negotiated letter of credit can be presented at any bank, even though a different advising bank may be involved. Depending on a negotiating bank's relationship with the confirming or issuing bank, including the possibility that the issuing bank keeps a transfer account with the negotiating bank, having negotiated on your behalf, the negotiating bank may pay you. The payment will usually be made with recourse, and possibly only after you sign a letter of guarantee or your own bank furnishes a letter of indemnity for you. These documents are based on your credit and are a promise to pay the bank if the issuing or confirming bank does not pay the negotiating bank for any reason.

Sight vs. Usance

When it is due is an important component in a letter of credit. Letters of credit are usually due on-sight, meaning that the exporter is paid as soon as the paying bank has determined that all documents are in order according to the letter of credit and that funds are available. If the buyer has asked for extended terms, the letter of credit will be a usance credit and will state that the draft be drawn at a certain number of days after sight, meaning that the exporter will be paid in that many days after negotiation or acceptance of documents.

Bills of Lading and Other Transport Documents

A transport document of some kind is a key item in the negotiation of most operating letters of credit and when arranging for the shipment, you must exercise great care to receive a document that is acceptable under the credit. Until you have some actual experience in dealing with acceptable transport documents, use your documentary department of your international bank, trade merchant bank, or your freight forwarder. This is especially important if you contemplate negotiating the credit with anything other than the on-board bill of lading from a regularly scheduled ocean vessel, or in the case of air freight, an airway bill issued by a regularly scheduled airline, or its agent.

Transport documents that are clearly unacceptable under any letter of credit are bills of lading issued by a charter party (a party chartering a vessel in its own name and then contracting for cargo); bills of lading for vessels propelled by sail only; bills of lading that state the cargo is being loaded on deck, unless a statement is written to accept this loading; or bills of lading issued by a freight forwarder, unless an ICC approved FIATA combined transport bill of lading form is used (however, this would not be valid if a marine or ocean bill of lading is a letter of credit requirement).

In all cases, the transport document must be clean, meaning there can be no exceptions or qualifying statements as to possible defective conditions of the shipment. The preceding were all negative statements. On the positive side, look for these key statements or conditions on the document to assure that they comply with the terms of the letter of credit:

- An original signature on the bill of lading by an agent for the carrier or as master or responsible employee of the named carrier, preferably on the carrier's own form
- The bill of lading indicating that the goods are: a) dispatched, taken charge or loaded on board, or when a marine bill of lading is required. b) loaded on board or shipped on named vessel

- A full set of originals (usually three) has been issued if more than one original was issued or required
- The transport documents meet all other stipulations in the letter of credit

Shipping and Expiration Dates

A letter of credit with requirements that you cannot comply with is worse than no letter of credit at all. The exporter may request an extension, but the buyer is under no obligation to provide the extension. In all cases, consider the intent of the buyer who opens the letter of credit. If friendly, he is likely to be understanding should you require an extension; if hostile, he is unlikely to grant extensions that could cause problems in shipping and collecting.

The exporter must be sure to have sufficient time before the expiration date to get all the required documents to the bank. This includes making allowance for the time for the steamship company to issue the bills of lading, adequate for all paperwork and deliveries, and especially time to get the invoices, packing lists, and other documents notarized and/or certified. This may include various government agencies and offices of foreign representatives in distant American cities. Often, it takes the steamship company up to 10 days to issue bills of lading after loading. There is no way to correct a discrepancy of late shipping or late presentation of documents.

Clean and On Board

These terms are so common to letter of credit and shipping terminology that explanations are frequently overlooked. *Clean* refers to bills of lading and other documents accepted by the receiver, agent, or shipper without notations or any exception as to the condition of the goods. *On board* occurs when the merchandise crosses ship's rails and the tackle is released. For air shipments, a clean receipt is obtained when the merchandise is placed in the hands of the named carrier or its agent at the airport.

Partial Shipments Allowed

Virtually all letters of credit will specifically state that partial shipments are or are not allowed. Partial shipments are allowed if not stipulated to the contrary. It is a good idea for the beneficiary or exporter to request that the letter of cedit allow for partial shipment although both parties may agree that only one or two or some other stated number of shipments will be made and so specified in the letter of credit. This permits the exporter to collect against that portion of the order shipped, even if for any reason, it is less than the total amount of the letter of credit. If partial shipments are not permitted, the letter of credit is only valid when the shipment is complete.

About or Approximately

If "about," "approximately," "circa," or some similar word is stated in the letter of credit when referring to quantity or value, there is an allowable variance of 10 percent of that specified quantity or value, but the total draw down cannot exceed the value of the letter of credit. In case of specified installment shipments under a partial shipment clause, if any one such shipment is missed, the entire L/C becomes invalid, not just for that shipment, but for all shipments unless otherwise stated. Many types of variances may be stated in this very adaptable instrument.

Transshipment

This is used to describe a situation in which the goods are off loaded from one carrier and placed on another carrier, vessel, or conveyance. If the transport document indicates from origin to destination, it will be accepted in the normal course of events. However, it should be clear in writing if transshipment is permitted or not permitted, and if permitted, under which circumstances.

Amendments

All primary parties to an irrevocable letter of credit, including opening and confirming banks, must agree to any amendment. The buyer is under no obligation to initiate an amendment, and the seller need not accept any amendment put forward by the buyer.

You should become aware of the intentions of your buyer when negotiating the sale, i.e., is he a wanting, willful buyer or just purchasing from you because you are the only supplier that can immediately deliver his needs? Sometimes it is evident that a certain amount of hostility exists at the point of sale and negotiations for an extension of time at some future date would be impossible. In contrast, you may have the feeling that your buyer would be willing to assist you through time extensions if delivery became a problem. In any case, you should make these determinations early in the sales negotiation.

Transferable Letter of Credit

The right to transfer a letter of credit to a second beneficiary can be very useful, even though requesting it from your buyer indicates some financial weakness on your part. It permits you to transfer the proceeds of the letter of credit, in total or in part, to your suppliers. The transferee must then also take full responsibility for the letter of credit performance conditions, just as if it were the initial beneficiary.

If you are acting as a broker or manufacturer's representative, a major disadvantage in transferring or assigning letters of credit is in revealing your source to your buyer. Next time, your buyer may try to go direct to your suppliers. If you must resort to this procedure, ensure that you have a notarized, executed hard copy of a combination nondisclosure, noncircumvention agreement with both the buyer and the seller. This is for your future protection.

Assignment

Unlike the other phrases explained in this text, assignment is not a standard phrase within a letter of credit, but it is included here because of the confusion between transfer and assign. Unlike transfers, a letter of credit may be assigned regardless of the conditions in the letter. The beneficiary gives the bank first rights to the letter of credit and the bank promises the assignee will receive the stated share of the proceeds before the bank pays the balance to the beneficiary. Assignment is a right of a beneficiary that can be useful as long as the assignee is willing to accept an assignment of proceeds as a form of payment. To do this, a supplier must have confidence in the letter of credit and the ability of the beneficiary to perform under its conditions.

Revolving Letter of Credit

A revolving letter of credit may be accomplished in many ways. It can be opened for a certain dollar amount for a given period of time and automatically replenished each time a draw down is made. Such a letter can be accumulative or nonaccumulative for given time periods or quantities, and it can be limited in amount by time periods or in total. This letter can also be amended by the buyer to replenish at specific intervals.

Our Pacific Rim operation negotiated an effective revolving letter of credit years ago with a government agency in India. The agency was able to appropriate $.5 million dollars in a relvolving line that was replenished to its original amount at each draw down. The purpose of the instrument was to fund imports of critical emergency items that must be imported in a moments notice. These requirements, being urgent and having top government priority, could not be deferred for the length of time needed to establish a single letter of credit for normal purchases of imported material. The revolving letter of credit, with a red clause, functioned well, and as a result, availability of emergency supplies kept the Indian project going without lost time for over two years.

Special Clauses

There are three commonly discussed special clauses of which the red clause is the most often mentioned. It effectively provides for passing to the seller the credit standing of the buyer. It permits clear advances (no bills of lading need be presented) to finance the exporter's performance of the contract before shipping. A red clause is accompanied by a statement that appropriate documents will be forthcoming. Obviously, this clause is rarely seen except in special situations, as in the Indian example and close relationships between buyer and seller.

A variation of the red clause is called the green clause, and is very similar. It also permits a draw down of clear drafts, but requires the subject goods to be stored in the name of the paying bank until documents are received.

A telegraphic transfer clause is the second most often mentioned special clause. It requires the issuing bank to pay an invoice amount to the order of the negotiating bank, upon receipt of a tested telex, indicating that the required documents have been received in good order and are being forwarded. The purpose is to speed up the payment, especially if you are not geographically located in a financial or export center.

The third clause, the evergreen clause, provides a periodic expiration date with an automatic extension, unless advance notice is provided, and it usually states an ultimate, fixed date. It can be used in standby or revolving letters of credit where a long validity is anticipated, and also when the issuing bank and/or account party may wish to periodically assess their risk exposure.

Special Documents

1. Copies of telexes, facsimiles, or other communications

2. Consular or embassy certifications

3. Import or export licenses

4. Acceptance certificates or statements

5. Inspection certificates, usually by a third party

6. Certificates of origin

7. Proforma invoice

Letter of credit preparation and evaluation is a subject of study in and of itself. Letters of credit should be written and evaluated by bank experts and the terms of payment should be checked by your freight forwarder in advance of preparing your proforma invoice.

In the general discussion of this chapter, we mentioned a problem encountered in Okinawa in the 1970s that precluded acceptance by the buyer or a perishable product that was subsequently dumped overboard. There was a minor discrepancy in the letter of credit. Such discrepancies may include errors in arithmetic or spelling; misspellings, or failure to copy misspellings in the letter of credit; obvious corrections—the bank wants clear originals; drafts drawn on the wrong party or not properly declared or signed; and party to notify is not properly stated or omitted. To avoid most of the mistakes that lead to discrepancies and collection problems, you need to study the terms of the letter properly, allow sufficient time to fulfill the terms, and pay attention to every detail.

Letter of Credit Checklist

Check these items on this checklist against those that you request from your buyer when he prepares a letter of credit against your proforma invoice. Review the checklist again when the letter is received. Additional details and assistance is available from brochures at all major regional banks, money center banks, and trade merchant banks. Items to consider when you request a letter of credit:

- Name, address, and telephone number of beneficiary
- Total value and total quantities
- Irrevocable
- Strong and reputable issuing bank
- Is it confirmed?
- A local and convenient paying bank
- At-sight or usance
- Payable in U.S. currency
- Latest shipping and expiration date
- Latest date for receipt of letter of credit
- Partial shipments allowed
- House bills of lading or NVOCC bills of lading allowed
- Terms of sale, such as FOB vessel (named port), C&F, CIF
- Shipping point(s)
- Documents required
- Is it transferable?

Above all, consider the relative fees and charges among your possible choices of paying and confirming banks. It is equally important, if not mandatory, that you check on the strength and reputation of the issuing and confirming bank. For example, many letters of credit have been received from developing countries from banks in those areas that don't exist.

You are selling the goods or making an investment in a joint venture. You have answered an inquiry by submitting a quotation and/or proforma invoice. The proforma invoice is a pre-issued invoice to permit the overseas buyer to establish the letter of credit. All of the items on the letter of credit checklist should have been detailed on your proforma. The buyer, in writing the letter of credit, should be following your terms and conditions of sale exactly as stipulated in writing in the proforma invoice.

Checklist on Receipt of Letter of Credit

- Is it revocable?

- Is the paying bank of good reputation and is the currency transferable in the event that bank is overseas?
- Does it need to be confirmed in the United States?
- Is the seller's name and address spelled correctly and are there other misspellings that might create discrepancies?
- Are the dollar amounts and quantities per your quotation?
- Is it payable at-sight, or if a usance credit, is it agreed?
- Are the shipping terms correct, FOB, CIF, others?
- Are the documents required as agreed?
- Can you provide insurance as required?
- Are letter of credit fees and costs as agreed?
- Is there sufficient tolerance as to quantity, and is the word "about" or an equivalent word necessary?
- Is the merchandise correctly described?
- Are partial shipments allowed?
- Is transshipment allowed if necessary?
- Is there sufficient time to meet the latest shipping and negotiation time-table?
- Can you ship from the stated port of embarkation?
- Is the shipping destination as agreed and possible?

(NOTE: This is an important consideration, and can sometimes cause expensive problems. As an example, a few years ago we were quoting a bulk commodity C&F Lattika or Tartous, the ports of Syria. Without checking the draft or capacity of these ports, we were quoting in lots of 25,000 metric tons. The buyer, fortunately, pointed out that 18,000 metric tons was the maximum load that a ship could transport and clear the channel into the port. Had we shipped the original amount, it would have been quite costly.)

- Is the registration of the flag vessel permitted to call in the port of destination? Are they prohibited?
- Is the shipping destination as agreed and possible?
- Will the style and type of transport document you will receive be acceptable, such as a house bill of lading versus on-board ocean bills?
- If a named vessel or carrier is stipulated can you comply both as to availability and voyage timing?
- Do you have the time to obtain the consular legalization and other documents required?
- Are there inspection or mandatory PSI problems?

- Can you provide a packing list by carton?
- Can you meet marking and labeling requirements?
- If you need to ship on deck, is it permitted?

Many exporters and exporting companies feel that all transactions should be done only with letters of credit. There are many situations, however, in which letters of credit may not be to your advantage or fit the nature of your product and your shipping patterns. For example, a small apparel supplier who makes many, small partial shipments of low value may not want to employ a letter of credit due to the costs. The letter of negotiation costs of each shipment will represent a large expense and many of the conditions may be restrictive and cumbersome. This can, in turn, cause many requests for amendments, which can be costly for both buyer and seller, and strain the working relationship. You should consider shipments of $5,000 to $10,000 as a minimum under letter of credit terms when negotiating expenses. In some cases and with some banks, these amounts are too small for economy of scale.

Dulat and Wells point out that a survey in the October 1987 issue of *Exporter Magazine* revealed some astounding facts relevant to the average size of export shipments and costs of negotiating an advised letter of credit. There are an average of 700,000 export shipments per month from the United States and 85 percent of them, or about 600,000, are under $25,000 in value. The same survey finds that the letters of credit, with a value of from $10,000 to $25,000 for the costs associated with negotiating them—not counting extra costs for amendments, discrepancies, financing, or confirmation fees, ranged from $70 to $340. A mean average might be around $185 with an additional $50 for regions such as the Middle East (except Saudi Arabia) and reduction of $50 for most of Asia.

The result is a cost in the range of 1 percent on an $18,000 shipment. The typical negotiation fee is 1/10 of 1 percent or a minimum of $75.

If you are unfortunate enough to negotiate through one of the higher cost banks, or in the event of necessary amendments, or discrepancies, your costs could escalate quickly to 3 percent. If you are working with a smaller transaction, say $10,000, your costs could go as high as 5 percent. For this reason, you must check your bank charges, avoid amendments and discrepancies, and avoid taking letters of credit for smaller transactions.

Furthermore, letters of credit impose restrictions that you may prefer not to live with, especially when you are dealing with a qualified and reputable buyer. Sometimes a letter of credit can be used to delay payment by an importer who seizes upon every technical discrepancy to defer negotiation. Product and procedure aside, competition and a harmonious relationship with your steady customers or distributors might force you to consider alternatives. Generally, it is easier to get letters of credit in the Pacific Rim area where they are usually offered as a condition of purchase before they are requested by the seller.

The greatest resistance to letters of credit will be found among European buyers who trade among themselves largely without letters of credit. You may offend some buyers in requesting this instrument. Apart from creditworthiness, common reasons for requesting letters of credit are political risk and/or currency incovertibility. You can understand that among the major currencies of the world such as the Deutsche mark, French franc, British pound, and the Japanese yen, just as much for the United States dollar, these reasons for requesting a letter of credit are usually not valid.

As mentioned in prior pages, the proforma invoice is the document that you would issue to the buyer to be used by him to establish the letter of credit. The proforma should contain all of the relevant information required for the buyer to open the L/C in your favor such as quantity, size, product description, costs, terms, and conditions of sale. The buyer may use the proforma to obtain an import license before receipt of delivery of your product. You may use your proforma to obtain an export license, if required. Once again, you as the entrepreneur and businessman will be called upon to exercise common sense and good judgment in deciding on payment terms. Overseas credit risk evaluations are not that dissimilar to those that you employ in your domestic operations. Information may be a little more difficult to obtain, but due diligence will usually produce the results that you are seeking. The letter of credit is an important financing tool in the arsenal of options available to you when selling in international markets. However, it should not be your only option for the obvious reasons that have been discussed throughout this text.

Other Terms of Sale

Other forms of sale include bank drafts, which are drawn down upon presentation of documents. Drafts, as with letters of credit, can provide for partial payments for partial shipments. This is the preferred method of selling and financing if delivery is to occur over an extended period of time. Documents required for partial or complete drawdown of a bank draft are similar, if not identical, to those of a letter of credit.

Depending on your customer, your product, market demand, supply, competitive position, or simply, your sales policy, a portion or all of the value of the sale may be collected up-front by the seller. Obviously, this is the preferred method of financing a sale, but it is a rare occurence, indeed. However, if you are the only game in town, and plan to be in business for a short while, you may insist on this form of payment. As in any business intercourse, you must reserve the option of compromise. International opportunities are long-range, and offer unlimited growth potential for small- to medium-size business throughout the United States. Due to the diverse nature of the global economy and the dynamics of change, you will be required, from time to time, to be creative in your approach to financing your international trade.

Depending on your customer, and your market, and your competitor's policy, you may be required to sell on open account. If so, you must be clear on your invoice as to when the payment begins. If your sales terms are 2/10, net 30, do you mean 30 days payment from date of shipment, date of invoice, or 30 days from date of receipt of goods by the customer in his international location. You may specify payment is due upon receipt of goods with the understanding that ocean shipment may take as long as six weeks from date of loading. It is obvious that the buyer would want to receive, count, and inspect the goods and still have 30 days before payment is due.

You, the exporter, however, would prefer 30 days from date of invoice, but the transit time, customs delays, and document transfers all required for delivery to your customer may well exceed the 30 days. This is a point of negotiation between you and the customer and should have been clear on your initial proforma invoice when you quoted the material.

Your buyer may make requests of you, the seller, with regard to performance. If you are partial shipping parts for assembly, the buyer may want some financial protection to ensure that he ultimately receives 100 percent of the purchased parts. This could involve a performance bond, an escrow account, a letter of credit, a bank guarantee, or witholding a portion of the payment until final delivery and inspection. Again, trade merchant bank activities and services are invaluable in this regard to assist you with foreign and complex financial documentation.

Financial transactions involve written agreements and other documents that require impeccable preparation, review, study, analysis, and execution. Payment for your goods and services is, afterall, the reason for the international business development exercise. Use all the available resources at your disposal such as consultants, bankers, freight forwarders, customs brokers, and others to ensure that this final, all important aspect of the overall overseas transaction is flawless.

The American Bureau of Collections (ABC) is a worldwide, full-service commercial agency headquartered in Buffalo, NY. ABC has been in business for 60 years and has developed expertise in recovering money owed to clients by foreign buyers. The United States Department of Commerce awarded ABC the President's "E" award for its success as an international collector. Consider the services of this group or similar firms if you have sold on open account and collections have become a problem.

10

Government's Role

In the first chapter of this text we briefly discussed the impact of politics on international joint venture formations. The comments were motivated by the president's visit to Poland and Hungary in the summer of 1989. The current administration in Washington is dedicated to providing economic assistance to these and other Eastern European countries if funds can be used to create free market economies. It was not a coincidence that Adam Smith published his book, *The Wealth of Nations*, during the same year that United States independence was declared, 1776, as further evidence that political and economic reform are inseparable. The question becomes, is there a legitimate, acceptable role in the 1990s for the United States government in assisting United States small- to medium-size businesses to participate in free market development in less-developed countries?

Politicians on both sides of the aisle in Congress are searching for an answer to this question that involves the role of free men, free women, free trade, free enterprise, and freedom itself. Democratic socialism and communism, as a political system, created national enterprises that have failed, in catastrophic proportions. Other totalitarian societies, carrying the burden of failed government enterprises, are in trouble around the world. It's incredible, after witnessing events in Eastern Europe, the Soviet Union, Nicaragua, and Panama, that the ANC party in South Africa continues to pursue an open policy advocating communism should it gain political and economic power over the present free-market economy.

In today's world of satellite communications, repressive regimes have encountered great difficulty in shielding benefits of free market economies from its own, oppressed people. The immigration of vast numbers of people into West Germany from East Germany in 1989 alone was an example of the magnetism of political and economic freedom that is drawing people of all cultures, regardless of the front end sacrifice. Freedom is powerful, politically and economically.

America has many challenges in the coming decades. Paramount among these is the expansion of our economy and job creation in the new global economy. In this new economy, technologies, goods, savings, and investments are moving effortlessly across international borders making it extremely difficult for individual countries to control their own economies. A welder in Detroit, Michigan, suddenly finds himself competing, not with another welder in Detroit, but with another welder in Taiwan, Korea, Mexico, or China.

In the beginning of this text we briefly discussed the competitive plight of the United States production services worker in the world economy as labor intensive jobs are transferred abroad. As global defense needs are diminished in favor of world peace initiatives, the industrial military complex will be dramatically reduced. This has already put additional labor intensive jobs at risk. We must, as a nation, look to immediate solutions for this potentially serious economic problem that results from the loss of manufacturing-based jobs if our economy is to remain healthy and strong. Recognizing the complexities of the problem, this book has attempted to encourage small- to medium-size businesses, the major United States exporters, to explore creating international partnerships as one of many strategies in preserving and increasing United States global market share and generate new quality job opportunities at home.

America's support of political and economic reforms in less-developed countries must involve aid and encouragement to governments that permit private enterprises to joint venture with American small- to medium-size businesses. If we can create new, quality jobs in each country through strategic alliances, such as joint ventures, in the private sector, then major free-market development hurdles would have been cleared.

Small- to medium-size businesses, entering new, global markets for the first time, should be armed with multiple marketing strategies to include sales, assembly, and manufacturing. We, as Americans, must continue to develop creative international marketing skills and open our minds to new opportunities. A dynamic, business expansion tool in the future for small- to medium-size business is the international joint venture. This decade presents more international business development possibilities than in the preceding nine decades. Our approach to maximizing these opportunites will depend, as always, on America's commitment. If one of many solutions resides in joint ventures, is there an acceptable and legitimate role for government to assist in these developments?

EXISTING GOVERNMENT PROGRAMS

The United States government is actively involved in supporting American commercial activities overseas. We have discussed many of the United States Department of Commerce programs such as Export Now, which were incorporated to encourage small- to medium-size businesses to enter global markets. Simply exporting from the United States into a very competitive world economy will not provide the long-term answer for America's economic future. Overseas buyers of United States goods and services will ultimately want to participate in some way in the production of these goods and services that their economies consume.

Typical of other government and government-sponsored programs that provide finance and insurance to support small- to medium-size businesses are the Overseas Private Investment Corporation, the Exim Bank, the International Finance Corporation, and the Private Export Funding Corporation. The recipients of funds from these programs must meet financial tests very similar to those imposed by any private commercial lending institution. The business plan submitted with the loan application to these institutions must demonstrate a financial return commensurate with repayment criteria. Financial assistance is almost always in the form of a loan and would fund, and subsequently benefit, the American partner in the joint venture.

A group called the International Executive Service Corps espouse the essence of this subject by saying, the joint venture idea provides many operating advantages for small- to medium-size business to enhance profits and market share in the United States and host country. It has been encouraging to witness a realization of the urgent need for continuing education in international trade and the more recent media attention that has focused on the requisite for public awareness of the importance of the role of the small- to medium-size business in the new global economy.

NEW FREE MARKET ECONOMIES NEED
CREATIVE ASSISTANCE

It is conceded that government education and financial assistance programs are in place to promote, and under certain conditions, finance foreign trade from the United States, but what is needed in the coming decade is a new, fresh long-range strategy for global market expansion for America's small- to medium-size businesses. This undertaking for increasing market share must involve programs that are both commercially sound and politically acceptable. Support of democratic reforms through free market development in less-developed countries using United States foreign aid advances an excellent opportunity to employ creative ideas for international business development. One such idea would advocate the employment of United States foreign aid to fund the start-up contribution of the developing country partner in a joint venture in the host country with his United States business counterpart. Such a program was almost introduced during the trip in 1989 to Poland and Hungary by the president of the United States.

PRIVATE ENTERPRISE FUNDS

The centerpiece of the president's 1989 proposals is the establishment of Private Enterprise Funds in the amounts of $100 million for Poland and $25 million for Hungary. The primary purpose of these funds, as previously mentioned, is to help Poland and Hungary expand their small, but growing private sectors. With subsequent events in December of 1989 leading to free-market economic reforms in Bulgaria, Czechoslovakia, East Germany, and Romania, there is every reason to believe these initiatives will be expanded to assist these emerging new democracies.

According to Mr. Russell Johnson, of the International Trade Administration, of the United States Department of Commerce, the funds will be empowered to disburse hard currency loans or venture capital for approved projects, which may include the establishment of private businesses by Polish and Hungarian entrepreneurs, privatization of existing state firms, technical assistance or training programs in support of Poland and Hungary's private sectors, the funding of projects designed to develop private sector exports, and financial support for joint ventures between Polish and Hungarian firms and American investors. Once established, these funds may expand opportunities for United States companies to benefit from trade and investment with the Polish and Hungarian private sector. However, Mr. Russell added, American companies should keep in mind that the main purpose of the funds is to aid the incipient Polish and Hungarian private sectors, not to directly finance United States exports or investments in these two countries.

Of special interest to the United States business community is the president's proposal that the Overseas Private Investment Corporation (OPIC) be authorized to operate in Poland and Hungary. Following congressional approval, OPIC would be authorized to offer its political risk insurance services and limited financing to United States companies planning investment in Poland and Hungary. It is hoped that these types of programs to aid in the development of free-market economies will extend to other developing countries.

UNITED STATES FOREIGN AID TO DIRECTLY FUND THE LDC JOINT VENTURE PARTNER

The president and secretary of state made a trip to Hungary and Poland in the summer of 1989, and recognized, as all scholars agree, that the new political reforms in Eastern Europe must be accompanied by economic reforms if these new emerging democracies are to survive. The solutions to their survival are not elementary, they are complex, but may be solvable with American intuition and creativeness. The president and the secretary exhibited resourcefulness in proposing that United States aid to Poland, in this case $100 million, be tied to job creation in developing a new free-market economy in Poland. The concept is to be applauded and implementation offers some exciting new possibilities for developing countries around the world in such a manner that new, quality jobs are created and strong economies result. Secretary of State Jim Baker mentioned on his return from Poland and Hungary that a Freedom Foundation may be established for the purpose of initiating this bold new program.

This proposal, unlike existing government and private programs, provides a vehicle for small- to medium-size businesses to enter into joint ventures in developing countries. Such entry would support economic growth in both the United States and in the developing nation. This mix between government assistance and private market development, properly structured and administered, would not interfere with the free market. In fact, it would encourage its expansion.

The notion that United States foreign aid, appropriated by congress for free market development in struggling democracies, could be linked to participation by American small- to medium-size businesses in joint venture relationships in these countries is an idea whose time has come. Rather than rely solely on private capital and countertrade to finance such partnerships, aid could be employed as start-up capital for the overseas partner in joint venture formulations. The recipient of United States aid in the host country would receive some cash and substantial credits in the United States to be used to purchase joint venture requirements such as capital equipment, technology transfers, and training programs. Return of the tax payer dollars to the United States results through purchases of American capital goods and services essential to the start-up and operation of the overseas joint venture.

The criteria for this recommended government assistance program is different from considerations of normal private sector investment. The government assistance program proposed and passed for Poland and Hungary takes the definite form of United States foreign aid. This suggestion of application of foreign aid may be a unique thesis. Under this proposal, aid would be used to fund the developing country partner's share in a joint venture with a counterpart in American industry. Often, the risk of joint venturing in developing nations with privately held capital may be extremely difficult to justify on a spread sheet to owners and/or shareholders. In this proposal, the foreign associate funded with United States foreign aid would have the same financial capability to enter into a joint venture as his newly found American partner. After the joint venture is up and running, it becomes a free market venture for the partners and survives on its own merits.

Mr. Lech Walesa, the new leader in Poland, said in August 1989, while visiting the United States, "We have achieved the first steps of political freedom, and now, America, we desperately need joint ventures to build a free market economy in Poland, or political reforms will not endure." In support of Lech Walesa's request, a freedom foundation, as suggested by this thesis, would work with the private and public sector to determine which industries, services, or products are essential to free-market development in the country being considered for United States foreign aid.

In Poland, there are requirements for food processing plants. The purchase, construction, and operation of these plants offer immediate joint venture opportunities in addition to being future markets for United States farm products. In this instance, the suggested Freedom Foundation could act as a clearing house on behalf of Poland to locate competitive United States companies that could provide the required equipment and services to operate food processing plants in Poland. Once a United States manufacturer or joint venture partner is selected and approved by the Freedom Foundation, foreign aid, primarily in the form of a merchandise credits, is provided to the Polish partner to enable him to fund his appropriate share of the venture. The written agreement between the partners would require that new joint venture purchase plant and equipment, prepay license fees, and fund host-country employee training in the United States. The funds or credits released to the joint venture would be used to meet the requirements of the venture for supplies, equipment, technology, services, and other vital needs.

The United States partner would, of course, be required to fund his contribution as in any commercial activity. What this suggested program would do for the small- to medium-size businesses is provide the capital and credits required for the new developing nation partner to fund his proportionate share of the joint venture with hard currency. Most joint ventures proposed in developing countries never get off the ground due to inadequacy of foreign exchange to fund the participation of the host country's partner. Under this plan, the United States economy would benefit greatly since the majority of this proposed foreign aid will be used in this country to pay for American goods, services, and technology, with the continued advantage of increased market share in the developing country through joint venture operations.

Under this program, a joint enterprise is identified and earmarked as meeting the criteria of the Freedom Foundation. Suitable partners are selected for the venture and agree to an ownership posture of 49 percent American and 51 percent Polish. The agreement is drawn stressing the objectives of the planned enterprise. It is determined that $10 million is required to start the venture. The Freedom Foundation establishes a foreign aid credit of $5.1 million in the name of the new partnership on behalf of the Polish partner. These funds are used to purchase plant and machinery, intellectual property, supporting services, from the United States partner, and to support other needs of the enterprise including his portion of start-up working capital.

The United States partner's undertaking may be know-how, show-how, technology, cash, credits for future contributions, finished goods, special raw materials, ongoing management and engineering support as provided in the agreement. The essential element is that the overseas partner made his start-up capital contribution with the assistance of United States foreign aid. This aid was used to purchase goods and services in America for the benefit of this Polish enterprise. Without foreign aid in support of the Polish partner for free market development, this example joint venture may not have been feasible in the first place.

THE RISK TO THE TAXPAYER

What is the downside risk to the American taxpayer who funds foreign aid? The risk should be very little and the rewards very great. Under this program, the American people would be buying into an expansion of American small- to medium-size businesses through foreign aid that would finance the required contributions of developing-nation joint venture partners. Job creation and economic development in both countries, the United States and Poland in this example, would be enhanced.

THE AMERICAN COMMITMENT IS IN PLACE

The Polish people have the commitment of the president, the secretary of state, and the Congress of the United States. Senator Phil Gramm, coauthor of the Gramm-Rudman Act, wrote in August of 1989, "I believe that an essential element in reducing poverty and developing democracy is the expansion of economic freedom with economic growth. Such a development will take power out of the hands of sometimes corrupt leaders and bureaucrats and unleash the productive spirit of the working people. The basis of our foreign assistance effort should be an attempt to encourage and foster economic growth through free markets and human rights through democratic reforms."

Senator Phil Gramm continues, "We are currently witnessing changes on a revolutionary scale in several communist countries such as Poland and should express our support of freedom's flickering flame. During my tenure in Congress, I have strongly supported efforts to liberalize the Polish economy and improve the lives of the Polish people. I have shared your comments with my colleagues on the Senate Foreign Relations Committee, and you may be sure that I will keep your views foremost in mind as these matters are considered in the United States Senate."

THE PRIVATE/GOVERNMENT MIX IS COMPLEX

What should be the mix between the free-market economy and government assistance as America enters the new global economy? This answer, as presented in earlier paragraphs is much more complex than outlined. The idea of earmarking United States foreign aid to private and private/public enterprises in developing nations to enable them to contribute to joint venture formations could be one of many vital answers for America's economic future. The linkage of foreign aid to job creation, as presented in this context in support of the president's effort in developing countries, should, at minimum, be given serious consideration.

Granted, it will not be an easy task for the Freedom Foundation to match private and public/private developing country interests with private United States interests under this plan, and when accomplished, it may not always be on a level playing field. Much effort will be required to keep the program unbiased and open to all industries in the United States. A written policy must be devised and its guidelines enforced. Competent private-sector business executives should be employed to initiate the programs and monitor the selection of projects both in the host country and in the United States. Retired executives with international experience, preferably in joint venturing, would be ideal to manage and control this program. They should have varied business backgrounds to permit constructive and objective analysis of all possible joint venture opportunities for developing nations that are candidates for United States foreign aid earmarked to developing free economies.

America's public sector, especially the Senate Foreign Relations Committee, and private sector should evaluate creative ideas for possible solutions with a view toward implementation of sound proposals that would assist our economy to maintain a strong, secure, and commanding lead in the global marketplace in decades to follow. More funding of such programs as the Overseas Private Investment Corporation to provide additional guarantees to United States business to invest in developing countries such as Poland is not the total answer. That approach is complex and fails to address the needs of the Polish or any developing nation joint venture partner.

This proposal, to provide foreign aid to the developing country partner for start-up capital, may not be the answer either, but the logic required for its analysis is present in significant proportions. This idea should be considered as an option for government assistance, indirectly, to the United States private sector in support of our competitive position in the new global economy. If adopted and implemented, it would also enhance our political and competitive market position in developing countries, other than Eastern Europe, where it is instigated. It may be difficult for many politicians to support a foreign aid program that is keyed to productivity, but if the purpose of this segment of the United States foreign aid program is to support development of free market economies, then it should have free enterprise characteristics. The program should be related to industry for which there is market demand and real potential for profitability.

This recommendation for aid to affect economic reform in developing countries promotes self-esteem and pride of accomplishment of the overseas partner in the host country. Each partner to the joint venture would be responsible for his individual financial contribution. The aid would fund the start-up responsibility of the overseas joint venture partner. After initiation of the business, the project would stand on free-market principles to survive. The United States participant risks the loss of his investment; the developing country partner risks the loss of his free-market opportunity if the project is not successful. Therefore, this proposal is truly free enterprise in free-market development and carries all of the downside risks of capitalism. It requires that the recipient in the country that is new to free enterprise learn about market forces and business development at the grass roots level. Ordinary foreign aid programs are gratuitous to developing nations without free market ramifications. In the case of Eastern Europe and the Soviet Union, mechanisms to handle foreign aid in the form of cash are not yet in place.

11

The Foreign
Corrupt Practices Act

IT IS APPROPRIATE TO THE SUBJECT MATTER OF THIS TEXT, WRITTEN EXPRESSLY FOR small- to medium-size businesses, to quote directly from Section 78dd–2 of the Foreign Corrupt Trade Practices Act. It is important that you be aware of the following excerpts from the act:

78dd–2. FOREIGN CORRUPT
PRACTICES BY DOMESTIC CONCERNS

(a) It shall be unlawful for any domestic concern, other than an issuer which is subject to section 78dd–1 of this title, or any officer, director, employee, or agent of such domestic concern or any stockholder thereof acting on behalf of such domestic concern, to make use of the mails or any means or instrumentality of interstate commerce corruptly in furtherance of an offer, payment, promise to pay, or authorization of the payment of any money, or offer, gift, promise to give, or authorization of the giving of anything of value to—

   (1) any foreign official for purposes of—

   (A) influencing any act or decision of such foreign official in his official capacity, including a decision to fail to perform his official duties; or

   (B) inducing such foreign official to use his influence with a foreign government or instrumentality thereof to affect or influence any act or decision of such government or instrumentality,

   in order to assist such domestic concern in obtaining or retaining business for or with, or directing business to, any person;

   (2) any foreign political party or official thereof or any candidate for foreign political office for purposes of—

     (A) influencing any act or decision of such party, official, or candidate in its or his official capacity, including a decision to fail to perform its or his official functions; or

     (B) inducing such party, official, or candidate to use its or his influence with a foreign government or instrumentality thereof to affect or influence any act or decision of such government or instrumentality,

in order to assist such domestic concern in obtaining or retaining business for or with, or directing business to, any person; or

   (3) any person, while knowing or having reason to know that all or a portion of such money or thing of value will be offered, given, or promised, directly or indirectly, to any foreign official, to any foreign political party or official thereof, or to any candidate for foreign political office, for purposes of—

     (A) influencing any act or decision of such foreign official, political party, party official, or candidate in his or its official capacity, including a decision to fail to perform his or its official functions; or

     (B) inducing such foreign official, political party, party official, or candidate to use his or its influence with a foreign government or instrumentality thereof to affect or influence any act or decision of such government or instrumentality,

in order to assist such domestic concern in obtaining or retaining business for or with, or directing business to, any person.

The penalties, depending on the course of prosecution, for violating the provisions of the Act, can be quite severe, ranging from fines of not more than $1 million, and in some cases imprisonment for not more than five years. The United States government is adamant in its commitment to enforcing this act. The small- to medium-size business should be aware of its existence and meaning to avoid serious problems down the road when establishing your international business development plan leading into joint ventures. Your new overseas partner could very well be a foreign government.

The most distressing problem has been the vicarious liability incurred under the knowing or having reason to know standard for American executives and companies. It has been difficult to define what an American company should know about the activities of its foreign sales representatives. This was one of the primary reasons for the Omnibus Trade Bill, which modified the FCPA in terms of culpability under this standard. This was done largely by changing that phrase to "knowing" only and then clarifying the definition of "knowing." If knowledge is not proven, then criminal penalties are eliminated. The safest course to follow is the written representative's agreement. If it specifies a sales commission of 10 percent on all sales in his territory, you have defined his remuneration for a specified activity. If you compensate the representative in accordance with the contract, you need not know what he does with his commissions anymore than he is entitled to know what you do with your paycheck. Civil penalties only apply in cases of reckless disregard of risk that third parties might be bribing foreign officials.

PRECAUTIONARY STEPS

There are some precautionary steps that you may consider as follows:

- Do a background search on anyone being considered as a sales representative, consultant, agent, or in general, anyone that may be acting on behalf of your company.
- Include in the representative's contract all activity that you feel may come under scrutiny under the terms of the act. If you can visualize circumstances where legal and appropriate payments would be justified such as getting something out of customs, include that sort of activity in the contract.
- Stipulate, in writing, that any conduct construed to be a bribe under the provisions of the act will constitute a breach of contract rendering the agreement null and void.
- In geographical areas where problems are suspect, ask your sales representatives to submit a yearly statement of good conduct in this regard. You would only need this for your confidential files in the unlikely event it was needed as a result of an investigation.

In terms of prevention, the reason-to-know standard (and even the new knowing standard) is why the article by M. Haskins and R. Holt in *Export Today* recommended dealing with distributors instead of agents under the theory that in most cases money is not paid to distributors, thus reducing the possibilities of vicarious liability. The authors added that the exception would be if the distributor requested an unusually large discount in light of a large sale being negotiated with a government. Also, be alert for exceptional commission requests and payments to third-country banks. At a minimum, maintain good records and know your agents and representatives.

Just what is the difference between a tip, bribe, or commission has puzzled businessmen and travelers for centuries. In case you are ever confronted with an outright bribe, you should know the terminology in various parts of the world. The following table should be useful in pinpointing words that mean extra money for whatever reason.

TERMINOLOGY OF A BRIBE

Baksheesh   (Bak-SHEESH) In Turkey, Egypt, India, and other Eastern countries, a gratuity or gift of alms.

Mordida   (mor-DEE-da) Spanish for bribe. Especially known in Mexico. Literally, "a little bite."

Jeito   (jay-EE-to) Commonly used in Brazil. Signifies "you do me a favor" in the sense of using influence to help. Does not usually involve an actual transfer of money.

Dash   (dash) Used in various parts of Africa. A small monetary gift that is expected when getting anything from a visa to an airplane seat.

Grease   (greese) Also, "facilitating payments." Refers to legal and permitted payments of modest sums to foreign officials for speedy action of their normal duties. Used almost everywhere, including the United States.

Kumshaw   (KUM-shaw)Southeast Asian term for bribe.

PAYOFFS

Ford S. Worthy, in the special Pacific Rim, fall 1989 issue of *Fortune Magazine*, says that a European businessman mentioned to a friend earlier this year that he planned to open an office in Thailand. "Are you crazy?" replied the friend, a Malaysian banker. "Don't you know about all the payoffs that'll be required?" "I know," said the European. "They work."

Worthy continues by saying, a few years ago a well-known United States consumer products company discovered that local manufacturers in Malaysia and in the Philippines were blantantly turning out copies of its most important product, even stamping the company's world-famous logo on the imitation goods. But the American company was loath to turn the matter over to local police. Why? It seemed the only way to motivate the law enforcers to do their job was to slip them a little cash now and then. This the American company would not do.

The surprise here? While such grease may be distasteful, there would have been nothing illegal about it in the eyes of American law. The Foreign Corrupt Practices Act, enacted in 1977 following revelations that many large United States companies had given bribes to foreign officials, is aimed primarily at stamping out efforts by Americans to win business with such payoffs. The law specifically okays payments to officials to facilitate routine government action, everything from processing visas and licenses to providing water, electricity, phone service, police protection, and mail delivery.

During my first visit to Nigeria years ago, the customs inspector asked for dash with both hands held outwardly and together. He wanted money in advance of baggage inspection. Dash was customary in Nigeria. Being eager to comply with procedure, dash was given to the customs officer to minimize problems with baggage clearance. The mistake was in paying before the bags arrived in the claim area. When the luggage finally arrived, the customs official that accepted the original dash was gone, and a different officer was in his place holding out his hands. An additional payment was required to clear customs. The moral of this true story is don't dash until after services are rendered.

When the United States law was passed, Congress hoped other countries would enact similar legislation. Twelve years later, none have. "It hurts us," says an executive of a Fortune 500 company's subsidiary that is trying to build a presence in China.

He complains that foreign competitors often entertain prospective customers far more lavishly than his company would ever judge reasonable under the act. To get around the law, he says, some American companies enlist middlemen to take care of local business practices while Japanese companies take care of such matters by themselves, without paying middlemen.

Straight but savvy companies work hard to understand the guy with his hand out. How does he operate, and what is he really after? Knowing, for instance, that corrupt officials prefer to collect the most money with the least effort, you may find it worthwhile to be difficult. Hong Kong consultant George Baeder recalls a company that asked for 500 letters of explanation after customs officers in one country levied higher fees than called for in the company's government-approved investment plan. In his 1980 book written with Jeffery Race entitled, *Coping with Political Risks in Asia*, Baeder continues by saying, eventually, after 2½ years, the customs agents got the message: they could spend their time more profitably by fleecing victims who didn't ask so many questions.

Worthy concludes with the following. An American businessman cites the case of a European, who, in wrapping up a deal in Indonesia, was asked to deliver a small briefcase full of cash to a local official. The businessman, crimson-faced with shame as he slunk across an outer office full of clerks and secretaries, sighed in relief as he reached the official's private office and unloaded his burden. Whereupon the government functionary matter-of-factly opened the briefcase and took it back to the outer office so that all the clerks and secretaries could collect their shares. To the businessman, it was a crime exposed; to his beneficiaries, it was another day's pay. Yes, business in Asia can be confusing. However much you learn about its ways, Worthy says, don't forget to consult your sense of right and wrong.

In all the years that we operated in the Pacific Rim as manufacturer's representatives, we were able to avoid payoffs as a way of doing business. After the word gets around that your company won't play the payoff game, the requests usually stop.

There is an important distinction that should be mentioned. Sales commissions are a legitimate form of payment for marketing services rendered. Bribes, usually extended for an illegal purpose, are an entirely different matter. The world press frequently gets these two distinct payments confused when writing news-breaking columns about international trade deals on which they are passing judgment.

12

Opportunities in Europe 1992

ERNST & WHINNEY, IN THEIR CORPORATE BROCHURE ENTITLED, *EUROPE 1992: THE Single Market*, September, 1988, present the following understanding of the integrated market. Following the Treaty of Rome in 1957, a customs union was established and significant progress was made in developing a single market, especially in the movement of goods and people. But, a number of administrative, physical, and technical barriers remained to prevent the creation of a true European market.

In 1985, the Commission of the European Community published proposals to create a genuine single European market. Lord Cockfield presented the "White Paper on Completing the Internal Market," a plan that called for 285 regulatory changes leading to a complete elimination of trade barriers and to the free movement of goods, services, capital, and people. After reviewing the 1985 White Paper, all European community governments committed themselves to the single market through a package of treaty reforms known as the Single European Act (SEA). 1992 was set as the target date to complete the internal market. To achieve its goals, the Commission identified three general barriers to be eliminated:

1. Physical barriers (e.g., customs controls and border formalities)
2. Technical barriers (such as different health and safety standards)
3. Fiscal barriers (including differences in the value added tax rates and excise duties)

These barriers are interdependent; for example, eliminating customs controls between member states cannot take place unless other changes are made, including modifications to the value added tax (VAT) mechanisms. Otherwise, market distortions could arise simply for tax reasons.

Creating a single European market will put European standards into effect, superseding national standards. This will be done by harmonizing regulations, standards and controls to the minimum extent necessary for consumer, investor and employee protection. This will then permit mutual recognition by controlling supervisory bodies in each member state of one another's competence, so that goods and services permitted for sale in one community country can then be sold throughout the community.

In the case of financial services, home country control is structured to enable banking, insurance, and investment firms to trade freely throughout the community, subject primarily to control by the authorities in the member state in which they are established. These 1992 changes will affect a wide range of products and services, including such financial services as banking, insurance and securities, and such products as machinery, personal protective equipment, construction products, toys, high-technology products, medical devices, pharmaceuticals, food, drink, and food products. Numerous other products will also be affected.

The single market will also have an impact in several additional areas. Among the more notable changes :

- Publicly owned bodies and governments will eliminate "buy national" policies.
- Telecommunications equipment standards will be harmonized and services opened to competition.
- Government restrictions on capital movements will be removed.
- Transportation and shipping regulations affecting air, sea, and road transport will be relaxed to phase out discrimination.
- Professionals will be able to practice throughout the community through a system of mutual recognition of Higher Education Diplomas.
- Trade mark protection will be available by submitting a single application with a central Community Trade Marks Office and key features of national systems will be harmonized.
- Patent protection will be available for the entire community through a community patent system.

The single European market has wide implications for nonEuropean companies that are already established in, or trading with, the EC, or who will seek to do so in the future. Trade relations with developing nations will continue to be negotiated by the Brussels-based commission. The commission will look increasingly to reciprocal arrangements for European companies in, for example, Japan, Canada, and the United States.

Europe will be unable to take advantage of the full potential of its wealth, size, and human talent while internal barriers remain in place. Although frequently viewed in the popular media as a common market, it remains far from being a single integrated unit. Supporters of a single European market see the initiatives for 1992 as a means of providing a growing unobstructed market of great size, in which market forces, not politics or geography, will determine resource allocation.

Although proponents of a completely open-community economy hope to achieve most of their goals by the end of 1992, some flexibility has been built into the planning process in order to accommodate delays. Nevertheless, integration is moving quickly and most observers feel that significant harmonization will, in fact, be achieved by 1992, particularly because majority voting by member states has replaced the requirement of unanimity (apart from tax changes). At a meeting in Dublin, Ireland, on Saturday April 28, 1990, the European community, until now an economic bloc, committed itself to political union by 1992. Germany and France supported the idea but couldn't define what the shape of this union would take in the future. History is moving so fast in Europe, few at the summit in Dublin doubted that the concept would take on a life of its own. Few want a United States of Europe, but the process set in motion seemed to bring the economic, social, political, and defense policies into greater cohesion. The congress that will make possible political union will begin at the same time as the one on economic and monetary union.

In two other major decisions at this summit, the 12 community nations agreed to take East Germany into membership when it unites with West Germany. They also offered associate memberships to Eastern European nations that adopt democracy and start a move toward free-market economies.

EUROPE 1992 HARMONIZATION STANDARDS

The intention by 1992 is to have 285 regulations implemented to create a single internal market. The following changes represent the major part of the program for 1992.

Standards Testing Certification and Harmonization of Standards for

- Toys
- Simple pressure vessels
- Automobiles, trucks, motorcycles, and their emmissions
- Telecommunications
- Construction products

- Personal protection equipment
- Machine safety
- Measuring instruments
- Medical devices
- Gas appliances
- Agricultural and forestry tractors
- Cosmetics
- Quick frozen foods
- Flavorings
- Food emulsifiers
- Extraction solvents
- Food preservatives
- Infant formula
- Jams
- Modified starches
- Fruit juices
- Food inspection
- Definition of spirited beverages & aromatized wines
- Coffee extracts and chickory extracts
- Food additives
- Materials and articles in contact with food
- Tower cranes (noise)
- Household appliances (noise)
- Tire pressure gauges
- Hydraulic diggers (noise)
- Detergents
- Liquid fertilizers and secondary fertilizers
- Lawn mowers (noise)
- Medical products and medical specialties
- Radio interferences
- Earthmoving equipment
- Lifting and loading equipment

Harmonization of Packing, Labeling, and Processing Requirements

- Ingredients for food and beverages
- Irradiation

- Extraction solvents
- Nutritional labeling
- Classification, packaging, labeling of dangerous preparations
- Food labeling

Harmonization of Regulations for the Health Industry (Including Marketing)

- Medical specialities
- Pharmaceuticals
- Veterinary medicinal products
- High-technology medicines
- Implantable electromedical devices
- Single-use devices
- *In vitro* diagnostics

Changes in Government Procurement Regulations

- Coordination of procedures on the award of public works and supply contracts
- Extension of EC law to telecommunications, utilities, transport
- Services

Harmonization of Regulation of Services

- Banking
- Mutual funds
- Broadcasting
- Tourism
- Road passenger transport
- Railways
- Information services
- Life and nonlife insurance
- Securities
- Maritime transport
- Air transport
- Electronic payment cards

Liberalization of Capital Movements

- Long-term capital, stocks
- Short-term capital

Consumer Protection Regulations

- Misleading definitions of products
- Indication of prices

Harmonization of Laws Regulating Corporate Behavior

- Mergers and Acquisitions
- Trademarks
- Copyrights
- Cross-border mergers
- Accounting operations across borders
- Bankruptcy
- Protection of computer programs
- Transaction taxes
- Company law

Harmonization of Taxation

- Value-added taxes
- Excise taxes on alcohol, tobacco, etc.

Harmonization of Veterinary and Phytosanitary Controls

- Antibiotic residues
- Bovine animals and meat
- Porcine animals and meat
- Plant health
- Fish and fish products
- Live poultry, poultry meat and hatching eggs
- Pesticide residues in fruit and vegetables

Elimination and Simplification of National Transit Documents and Procedures for Intra-EC Trade

- Introduction of a Single Administrative Document (SAD)
- Abolition of customs presentation charges
- Elimination of customs formalities and the introduction of common border posts

Harmonization of Rules Pertaining to the Free Movement of Labor and Professions within the EC

- Mutual recognition of higher educational diplomas
- Comparability of vocational training qualifications
- Specific training in general medical practice
- Training of engineers
- Activities in the field of pharmacy
- Activities related to commercial agents
- Income tax provisions
- Elimination of burdensome requirements related to residential permits

STRATEGIC IMPACT OF 1992

The companies new to European business in 1992 will need to examine each of three principle areas of his company to determine a strategy for entering the single European market.

1. Marketing, which would include customers, distribution, and pricing policies;
2. Production, which would include supplies, product range, and processing technology costs;
3. Infrastructure, which includes organization for human resources, financial resources, and information technology.

The strategic impact also includes an analysis of market forces in these areas: the new freedom of movement of capital, people, goods, and services; the harmonization of standards; broader view of public procurement; and the equality of labor rights. You should rationalize your activities by first looking for a product that can find a specific nitch in the new marketplace. If you do not have such a product, you should consider the option of entering the single European market in joint ventures, mergers, or technology transfers with companies already doing business in Europe. Of course, you can continue to export into Europe through foreign-based representatives, Export Management Companies (EMCs) or Export Trading Companies (ETCs) that maintain a proficiency in importing products and services into the single European market, as long as the market is free and open.

As artificial competitive advantages disappear, National Champion companies, such as Fiat in Italy, will no longer be granted state aid as in the past. And, German brewers, for example, will no longer be able to rely on product purity to keep competition out. Monopoly power will disappear, but major joint ventures will increase between European partners to augment their competitive market position. New harmonized standards will encourage multinational firms in Europe, through economy of scale, to share markets making it more difficult for small- to medium-size businesses to survive market forces, especially in the area of pricing policies.

EUROPE 1992: INCOME AND EMPLOYMENT CHECKLIST

Nation	Per Capita Income	Unemployment Rate
Denmark	12,053	9.2%
West Germany	11,977	7.8%
France	11,776	9.5%
Belgium	11,176	10.6%
Netherlands	10,702	5.8%
Luxembourg	10,500	1.6%
Britain	10,238	6.1%
Italy	9,102	16.6%
Spain	7,616	17.3%
Ireland	7,040	17.5%
Greece	5,759	7.4%
Portugal	4,828	6.2%

*Measured in purchasing power units to remove the effects of different currencies. The market basket represented identical purchases in each country. This checklist clearly shows that Europe 1992's economy is divided between haves and have-not nations. Source: European Communities, embassies

TROUBLING AREAS

The drive to remove trade barriers within the European community by 1992 could have serious implications for the United States and Japan. Trade experts base their fears on current European attitudes and historic evidence about market integration. There were two rulings in the fall of 1988 resulting from work that began years before the convening of the current Brussels meetings that are considering the White Paper's 285 directives. These two rulings involved fork-lift trucks and hormone-free beef.

The requirement being considered for United States business to meet European standards and product certification on European soil may involve costs that make United States products noncompetitive in EEC markets. For example, Hyster has been making and selling fork-lift trucks in Europe since 1952. They felt they knew their market well.

In August of 1988, Hyster learned that the European community's 10,000 bureaucrats working on standards in Brussels had produced a new set of rules for fork-lift trucks. These new rules are part of the European effort to establish common business standards in getting ready for market integration in 1992. To comply, Hyster had to rush to make 15 small design changes in its trucks, modify shipping schedules to Europe, and rely on a West German supplier, since no American vendor met a certain provision of the new EC standard. Hyster managed to make the changes by the January 1, 1989, deadline for continued sales in Europe, but its costs have risen, making it less competitive.

Many United States companies will find similar problems as Europe reregulates itself into an integrated economy. The plan requires 12 member countries to remove all trade barriers by 1992. In adopting these 285 directives, harmonious standards will apply throughout the EEC. As Hyster learned, these new standards will make it more difficult for American companies to do business in the economic community.

The European Economic Community is America's largest trading partner accounting for $145 billion in combined exports and imports, more annually than either Japan or Canada. If you include the output of United States-owned companies in Europe, and the output of European-owned companies in America, the commerce department estimates the size of the market to be $1 trillion.

PRODUCT CERTIFICATION ON EUROPEAN SOIL

Federal trade officials are worried that other rulings under discussion may adversely affect United States interests in the EEC. They also warn that physical presence today in Europe may not be sufficient for United States companies to enjoy the benefits of the integrated market on equal terms with European companies. The 285 directives are spawning volumes of new regulation, among which may be a requirement to certify American products on European soil. This could be a substantial expense, especially for United States exporters without current European facilities.

The United States also complains that the rules are being drawn in Brussels without input from United States companies or government. In essence, the goal of the EEC is to create an internal market, without outside help, to make trade among its 12 members as easy as trade in the 50 United States. America has 230 million people in its market; the EEC has 320 million. Some experts believe that the rules and regulations such as tariffs, quotas, standards, and other, highly visible, direct measures such as competition policy, are designed to build a protectionist wall around Europe to keep out the United States and Japan. Others, however, feel that the EEC will begin to cater more to the American trading bloc that includes Canada, the United States, and Mexico, in an effort to stall a full-scale invasion of Japanese product into the new 1992 market.

ANTITRUST POLICY

It is also important to examine this (Antitrust) competition policy to see how it may be used as a protectionist device to reduce United States and Japanese participation in Fortress Europe. Two sections of the 1957 Treaty of Rome—the organic document of the EEC—address competition issues: Article 85 (which some compare with the Sherman Act) and Article 86. Enforcement of EEC competition law, as well as the making of European competition law policy, falls to the Commission of European Communities, based in Brussels.

EEC antitrust policy is premised on two fundamental goals. First, the commission employs it as a tool to assist in achieving its primary objective—to create a unified European economy. Occupying a decidedly secondary position is the use of antitrust policy to promote competition.

Let's examine what promoting unity and uniformity can do to competition policy. Suppose you are selling a product popular in Italy, but unknown in Belgium. To make the product attractive in Belgium, the manufacturer may want to introduce it at a lesser price than it sells for in Italy, even at a loss leader price. Of course, the manufacturer would impose market restrictions on the Belgium dealers to prevent them from selling back into Italy. But the agreement not to sell outside of Belgium would violate Article 85.

The commission in Brussels would prefer that the product is not sold in Italy than to have it sold at a lower price. That same resistance against lower pricing would prevent a United States firm from using price as a tool to penetrate portions of the EEC where it wasn't doing business. The commission's antitrust policy can have anticompetitive effects.

The Treaty of Rome has been in effect for more than 30 years, but it is only recently, as a result of member states working to complete the internal market by 1992, that the commission has been actively filling in the blanks in its competition policy. They have adopted new regulations and agressively pursued enforcement actions. United States small- to medium-size businesses should start paying more attention to this process. For some, it may come easily, since the commission frequently uses enforcement actions against United States companies to establish new rules.

BLOCK EXEMPTIONS AND FRANCHISES

One new regulation that could harm United States companies is a recently issued block exemption that applies to the franchise industry. *Block exemptions* are declarations by the commission in Brussels that certain types of agreements will be deemed to violate Article 85; they also indicate certain other types of agreement will be in violation.

The EEC's recently adopted block exemption for the franchise industry prohibits a franchiser, says McDonald's, from contracting, as it does in the United States, with a single soft drink company, says Coca Cola, to supply all of its franchises. The advantage to the franchiser is that such a practice enables all outlets from coast-to-coast to be uniform. This is part of their business strategy.

You might think that promoting such a strategy was consistent with the

European commission's goal of integrating its member states into a common market. But such a franchising practice is considered illegal by the EEC. It is only coincidental that companies most likely to supply large European franchisers, of whatever type, are companies whose parent entities are nonEuropean.

Small- to medium-size businesses should also pay attention to other block exemptions that relate to automobile distribution and servicing agreements, specialization agreements among small firms, research and development agreements, and patent licensing agreements. The commission's block exemption relating to patent and know-how licensing will tend to restrict owners of intellectual property much more than United States law. Who is likely to be hurt by such a law? There is clearly more innovation going on in United States and Japanese companies than there is in European firms, so they are likely to be the losers, as are European consumers. After all, it is the consumer who is the ultimate beneficiary of pro-competition rulings.

MERGER CONTROLS

In addition to new block exemption regulations and to enforcement actions, the commission has proposed, and the new EEC's ruling body, the Council of Ministers, is actively considering, a new merger control regulation. That, too, could have profound implications for United States companies trying to acquire European firms and for customers who benefit from the efficiencies mergers tend to produce.

The world's economy is global in scope, and therefore, antitrust laws should be global in scope. This is why representatives from the Federal Trade Commission and the antitrust division of the Justice Department go regularly to Europe and Japan to consult on competition matters. Small- to medium-size American businesses should do likewise, and should pay close attention to Europe as it constructs its internal, integrated market.

Your corporate counsel should keep up to date and remain alert to present and future rulings from Brussels as they pertain to your possible entry into the EEC. This information should lead to a thorough cost and long-term benefits analysis of your decision to enter the common market. The market is vast in size, and merits close examination for entry into your international business development plans. But hurry, because time is about to expire, if you have decided to enter this expansive market.

LOCATING WITHIN THE EEC

Where should you locate your business in the EEC? This is an interesting question since you can choose to establish your business in one or more locations in 12 countries. Mr. John Barnet, in a recent article in the *The Houston Chronicle*, on Sunday, July 9, 1989, reported that Gundle Lining Systems, Inc., a Houston, Texas-based company that makes plastic liners for sanitary waste landfills to prevent contamination of the groundwater, believes it will benefit by having to meet only one set of specifications rather than 12 different sets, said Don Shook, chief financial officer.

"It can only benefit us," he says. Gundle has considered a factory in Europe, but it is too early to say what they'll do about that. Companies aren't the only ones looking at the single European market as an economic opportunity. Countries are using this to lure new business and are actively marketing themselves as a home base. "We see it as a time of great economic opportunity," says John Garner, British consul-general in Houston.

Each country has something to offer your business, and this information is obtainable at embassies, consulates, and their various trade promotional agencies. However, for the purposes of this book, a single country will be examined to provide a sampling of the types of incentives that may await the small- to medium-size United States business in Europe.

Scotland has been the choice of many American businesses, therefore, it was felt Scotland would be an excellent example of what you may expect in locating in Europe. The research information was supplied by the Scottish Development Agency (SDA). Each of the common market countries has such an agency to assist you with location plans and incentive analysis. A comparative study is recommended before your final decision is made.

SDA offers many services to assist you with making a decision as to your plant or service facility location in the EEC.

Financial Assistance

- Regional selective assistance—Nonrepayable grants that reduce the cost of a project up to 30% and are based on initial capital expenditure or the amount of jobs that the project will produce.

- Venture capital—Wide range of direct financial aid including loans at commercial rates, loan guarantees, and equity participation.

- Enterprise zones—Certain areas of Scotland allow exemption on industrial and commercial property, 100% allowances for capital expenditure, along with other breaks.

Property

- Rentfree premises—Premises are available at competitive rates and new tenants may be given a rent-free period of up to two years or occasionally longer.

- Locating premises—Whether leasing or purchasing, SDA can assist companies in finding the appropriate facility depending on the customer's environmental and locational factors.

- Building premises—A facility can be tailor-made to suit a company's requirements and preferences in exclusive and pleasant surroundings in addition to customizing a repayment plan.

Labor

- Training and employment grants—Grants are allowable if the employees are residents of that area and have been registered unemployed for over a certain period of time.
- Employment grants scheme—Once a company has reached capacity and requires new or additional employees, they may receive grants if these new employees are between a certain age and have been registered unemployed for a definite period.

Support Services

- Visits—Organization of visits to Scotland, including tours of practical locations, industrial sites, and premises.
- Introductions—As required, introductions to private-sector financial institutions, potential joint venture partners, customers and suppliers, education and training, research establishments and other companies already doing business in Scotland.
- Advice—Advice on such matters as personnel, training, and procurement along with an industry specialists team.

An article written by Tom Steinert–Threlkeld for the *Dallas Morning News*, that was published on November 18, 1989, in Section F, on page 1, illustrates how the Scottish Development Agency helps make room for high-tech corridor Silicon Glen located a few miles from Glasgow. The Glen has been a focal point of massive inward investment during the 1980s, in the Scottish term. The biggest investor: United States computer and chip companies, trying to find a good launching point for manufacturing assaults on European markets by 1992.

Between 1981 and 1988, United States companies invested $4 billion in the Glen. Most of the biggest names in United States electronics are there in some fashion: workstation-maker Sun Microsystems, Inc., mini-computer leader Digital Equipment Corp., personal computer giant Compaq Computer Corp. from Houston, and distributed-computer-systems pioneer Datapoint Corp. of San Antonio. In fact, United States investment in Scotland began long before Silicon Valley got its name. NCR Corp. set up shop in 1946, International Business Machines Corp., the world's largest computer maker, came in the next decade. Two big chip companies, Motorola, Inc. and National Semiconductor Corp. came to Scotland in the 1960s. The Glen has picked up steam in the past 10 years, propelled by the Scottish Development Agency. Its vision was to create a new economy based on the knowledge and intellectual resources of its people, instead of stripping coal from its valleys or building ships in its ports, said Howard Moody, the agency's marketing director.

For the most part, the drive has not been to create new Scottish technology companies. Rather, the agency is devoted to persuading foreign companies to make major investments in Scotland. To a large degree, that missionary work is succeeding. Some 30 United States companies account for 62 percent of the country's annual electronic revenues. In the last eight years, 57,000 jobs have been created. Computers and peripherals surpass Scotch whisky as Scotland's main export.

To compete with other countries in the EC, the Glen relies on its headstart, its infrastructure of established suppliers, and its educational strength, which may be the biggest advantage. Scotland has eight top notch universities and 70 technical colleges capable of expansion to meet future needs. It has the highest per-capita ratio of college graduates in the EC.

It is in supply industries, such as manufacturing of printed circuit boards, where Scottish companies are widespread. But the Glen has not yet begun to foster the kind of innovative, fast-track companies that are the heart and soul of Silicon Valley. There are no home-grown Hewlett-Packard Co. or Apple Computer, Inc. success stories in the Glen. The best-known regional startup, Rodime PLC, maker of computer disc drives, nearly failed in 1989.

The Scots lack the souls of entrepreneurs, acknowledged Mr. Moody. Instead, they prefer the security of working for existing companies, even if they come from America or Japan. This is why inward investment is sought after and not feared as it is in the United States. "Its an integral part of our economic strategy. We are not shy about going after Japanese or American investment, small, medium, or large corporations," said Mr. Togneri, manager of the SDA's United States desk. He continues, "Yet, new victories for Silicon Glen are coming with increasing difficulty." As European trade barriers begin to fall with the approach of 1992, the number of countries seeking inward investment also proliferates. Even as the battles with the Irish escalate, Scotland must worry about on-the-continent competition from Italy, Spain, and Portugal. As in Scotland, these countries are packaging incentive schemes to persuade overseas businesses to locate inside of their individual borders to bolster their economies within the EEC.

RECOGNIZE THE OPPORTUNITY

Europe by 1992 probably should be in your strategic plans due to the the available opportunity to expand your present market share. Mr. John Barnet, of *The Houston Chronicle* continued in his article by saying, 3D/International's Newhaus sees the single European market as an opportunity for his engineers to practice in various nations without going through different licensing procedures.

"We foresee a great future for the design and construction industries during the 1990's in all the nations of the EEC," he said. "I think the construction boom that we have seen in the United Kingdom these last few years will repeat itself in other countries."

Mr. Barnet continues, they aren't alone in their enthusiasm. "This is the biggest economic chance to come down the pike in 40 to 50 years," said Dave Whipple, corporate vice president of marketing for Iroquois Brands. Iroquois, which moved its corporate headquarters to Houston in 1988 after being purchased by British entrepreneur Malcomb Stockdale, is ready to take advantage of the single European market.

Last year, Iroquois Brands, known mainly as a vitamin and pharmaceutical firm, started to expand its European base with four acquisitions. The company purchased Bio International, Inc., with four operating divisions that include Bio Petroleum Ltd., which operates service stations in the United Kingdom and UPP International, a designer and builder of shredding machines and specialized conveyors.

The company is looking at other merger and acquisition opportunities in Europe. Because of its existing European presence, it is looking for partnerships with local companies in the Houston area that want to do business in Europe, Whipple said. Iroquois also wants to be firmly established in Europe before 1992 to prevent being locked out if the common market nations adopt some protectionist trade measures. "What they are saying now is that you either have business there or are doing business there in a partnership with an established business or maybe you aren't going to be there for awhile after 1992," Whipple said.

OTHER ASSISTANCE

The rules and regulations, being debated by 10,000 bureaucrats in Brussels to govern EEC market standards, are in an embryo, but dynamic state. The small- to medium-size business, through informed counsel, should monitor these daily rulings and consider corporate planning accordingly. If you decide to be physically in Europe by 1992, incentives are available in each of the 12 countries to soften the economic blow of entry. SDA services in Scotland are cited as an example of types of incentives and services that are available in various forms in each of the 12 EEC countries in Europe.

Several United States law firms have established offices in Brussels and other European cities for the sole purpose of monitoring new rules and regulations that emanate from the commission. Many companies, such as Ernst & Whinney and Price Waterhouse have specialized European location services available to assist the small- to medium-size business, either in helping to establish a base in Europe for the first time or advising on the merits of different or additional locations. Current articles on rulings from the commission are published in leading business magazines and journals. New developments are aired on network and cable news media programs. Apart from your corporate counsel and accounting firms, these are the most current sources of information regarding progress and changes in EEC rulings and regulations.

Your internal corporate strategic and tactical planning will determine your interest in locating in the common market before 1992. The message is clear: when it comes to operating in Europe, the rules of the game are changing rapidly. New challenges and opportunities are emerging. To survive and prosper in this environment, companies must understand the new rules, analyze their impact, and develop and implement effective strategies.

KEEP YOUR OPTIONS AT HAND

While the opportunities in East and West Europe are explosive, it would be wise for the small- to medium-size United States business to continue to evaluate the Pacific Rim and developing countries international business development possibilities. These opportunities may more closely identify with your long-term objectives. These areas may offer more joint venture potential as a means to increase market share rather than Europe 1992.

Pricing policies may have a negative impact on the entry of smaller business into Europe 1992. Pricing barriers that have historically protected large enterprises are coming down. Pricing will become more competive as a result of economy of scale, especially in manufacturing and administrative costs of the larger firms. Huge companies that heretofore were protected by artificial controls will be looking for joint ventures and mergers and acquisitions to reduce costs. This merging of multinational groups will put pricing pressures on small- to medium-size businesses. Though entering the EEC with a physical presence may seem to be expedient and intelligent international business development ploy, it may not be suitable or profitable for your company. It requires careful examination and study. Such a step may best be considered if you have a corporate history of overseas business expansion.

Europe 1992 presents an exciting opportunity; just ensure that this market expansion option fits in your long-term, strategic corporate game plan. And, don't overlook promising developing countries as target markets for your overseas business expansion.

13

A New Home
for Joint Ventures

THE PATTERN OF POLITICAL AND ECONOMIC CHANGE IN WARSAW PACT COUNTRIES leading up to the events beginning in Poland and Hungary in the summer of 1989 is identifiable. In the 1930s, two designs for political and economic development of the world emerged: Stalin isolated by his iron curtain in the authoritarian East and the gigantic experiment with open and free markets in the West. After World War II, alliances were formed, NATO in the West, the Warsaw Pact in the East. NATO policy was one of containment, or simply stated, stop the Russians. This policy eventually caused the Russians to look inward at their failed economic policies as they became more dependent on essential imports from the West for such basic commodities as food.

In the mid 1980s, the world experienced the information revolution that led to the knowledge revolution beginning in the 1990s. All of this forced President Gorbachev to look more seriously inward, initiate Glasnost and Perestroika, and permit democratic reforms in Eastern European countries. As the fast-paced events of 1990 move forward, Soviet people march in the streets of Moscow chanting, "Abolish Article 6 of the Constitution to permit multiple political parties. 72 years of communism has gotten us nowhere." Command economics isn't working. During the May Day festival in Moscow in 1990, the Kremlin substituted displays of cultural celebration for traditional military parades as further evidence of radical political transformations in progress.

The United States and its allies must face up to these great opportunities, and the dangers that turmoil in the Communist world poses for capitalistic societies. Communism is in a state of collapse and policy decisions must be taken now in Washington, D.C., as they will affect events in the world for years to follow.

The Soviet Union made a powerful contribution to the Allies in overthrowing Nazism in the World War II at a sacrifice of over 26 million Soviet lives. This gallant undertaking helped cloud over the fundamental superiority of free societies over totalitarian states. Today's dramatic events in Eastern Europe, and now surfacing in the 15 republics in the Soviet Union, reveal the impending collapse of totalitarian communism from its own failures, not by external force of arms. This provides additional proof of the superior dynamism, resilience, and power of free societies to connect economic and political freedoms for the good of its people.

THE WORLD, RICH IN INFORMATION

F. A. Hayek, the Nobel Laurete in Economics in 1974, argued that the world is too rich in information and too widely diffused for centrally planned states to ever satisfy the needs of their people. Political theory is being practiced before the eyes of the whole world and the obvious and noticeable conclusion is that free uncontrolled economic systems are far more effective than state-controlled economies in producing goods and services needed for its people. For a state-controlled system to match a free society, it will need to transform into a clone of that free society. It cannot simply imitate essential and desirable elements.

In Russia, it is said that employment in a cooperative bears a much greater job-loss risk than in state employment. At first blush, one senses that cooperatives could become the birthing place of future capitalists who would be accustomed to understanding risk. With this exposure, they could more easily transform command economics into a free-market economy. Further inquiries reveal that employment in cooperatives is entirely risk free and virtually secure for life in much the same way as in state employment.

Hayek also argued that diversity enables mankind to master more information. World leadership will go to those nations that best assemble and employ knowledge that originates from all over the world. Long-term investment in science, technology, and human capital that results in new knowledge that yields products, processes, new resources and services, and enhanced productivity to provide for economic growth is essential for the United States to maintain its present standard of living.

COMMUNISM, NOT BLIND TO ITS FAILURES

Today, the scientific and business world is global in nature and without borders. In the information age of the 1990s, no nation has a monopoly on new knowledge. The Communists have learned this vital lesson as they find themselves falling further and further behind capitalistic democracies. Events in the Soviet Union and within its Warsaw Pact allies suggests that totalitarian communism has learned this lesson and is ready to accommodate Marxism and Leninism with capitalism.

As early as 1922, Lenin was concerned over the direction that the revolution was taking. He began to challenge some basic ideas of the Bolshevik government. Lenin opposed the control of power in government bureaus. He also feared the Bolshevik enthusiasm for military glory and Russian nationalism. Shortly before his stroke in 1922, he had appointed Joseph Stalin general secretary of the party. Later, Lenin harboured serious doubts about Stalin, who began reaching out for personal power. Just before his third stroke on March 9, 1923, that impaired his speech, Lenin wrote that he had planned to remove Stalin as party secretary. His illness prevented him from replacing Stalin.

Dr. Armond Hammer, Chairman of Occidential Petroleum Corporation, has been a friend and trading partner of the Soviet Union for most of this century. He has remarked that Lenin, just before his death in 1924, said to him personally that communism was not working. Unfortunately, Joseph Stalin, the party secretary, inherited the task of trying to make communism work, and history has recorded the brutality he unleashed in maintaining personal control while forcing the communist system on the people of the Soviet Union and the Warsaw Pact.

Communism is deep rooted in both the Soviet Union and in China, but has very shallow roots in Eastern Europe. Poland and Hungary began the revolution and continually looked over their shoulders, but there were no Russian tanks. Observing this event through television and newspapers that began to trickle into other Eastern European countries, Czechoslovakia, Bulgaria, and Romania, albeit painfully and with great human sacrifice, followed into this new course in history. An imaginative economist, Kenneth Boulding, says ideology goes through three phases: when it is truly believed, when most of the subjects act as though they believe it, and the final phase when nobody believes it, not even the leaders.

In communist ideology, phase one ended with the bloody repression of the Stalin era. The second phase was lived from the end of World War II until the summer of 1989. Phase three is being lived out now in the 1990s. Each nation in Eastern Europe presents problems and opportunities. Each country is distinctly different. You find much capacity in each of its peoples to suffer, to endure, and to sacrifice for freedom's eternal call.

THE AMBIENCE AND THE OPPORTUNITY

The call for political and economic reforms within Eastern Europe is growing with intensity. The call for democracy and free economies is dynamic and changing at dizzying speed. Free enterprise in the west views this movement from state-controlled institutions to a free economy as a market opportunity unparalleled in this decade. With increasing regularity, the call goes out from Poland, East Germany, Hungary, Czechoslovakia, and Bulgaria for western joint-venture partners. It is obvious that vast eastern European markets exist for all goods and services produced in the West. For small- to-medium-size business in the United States, Eastern Europe on the surface appears to be a mecca of opportunity.

While this new market needs and desires everything produced in the west, the region suffers from a vast shortage of hard currency with which to fund its appetites. It may be intelligent for the small- to medium-size business to first determine which Eastern European products have exportable, hard-currency value. Identify these, and you have a vehicle from which to generate convertible currency through countertrade. If you can successfully accomplish this task, you are now ready to export virtually anything into Eastern Europe or begin joint-venture negotiations.

The possibility of joint venturing in Eastern Europe is becoming increasingly more attractive. With each passing day social, political, and economic reforms seem to become more irreversable. As the 1990s begin, however, the jury is still out as to the precise direction that the reforms will take and how the Eastern European leadership will emerge. Democratic socialism and state sponsored industries have failed to provide for the needs of people. In order for true economic reform to work, the free market economy must emerge. Joint ventures with western partners appears to be the most viable vehicle to affect economic reform due to Eastern Europe's shortage of technology and managerial skills.

Hard-currency restraints remain the chief hindrance to bilateral trade expansion in the east. For many joint ventures or partnership opportunities to become a reality for the small- to medium-size business, the General Agreement on Tariff and Trade (GATT) and/or the International Monetary Fund (IMF) will need to address the problem of Eastern European currency valuation. With the possible exception of McDonald's and PepsiCo type examples cited in the countertrade section of this text, the small- to medium- size business must be able to repatriate profits in acceptable hard currencies within a reasonable time after start-up. While countertrade as previously mentioned can be an option for many, entry into Eastern markets is a major financial undertaking and, therefore not feasible for most firms to whom this text is directed.

The needs in Eastern Europe after 40 years of state planning and ineptidue are staggering. If you include the Soviet Union, the market is 400 million people. There is a huge demand for everything. The need for cars, computers, food stuffs, jeans, boots, and staples has been pent up so long that it's explosive. The desire for the basics of life that are unavailable under state-sponsored socialism and witness to political freedoms in the west as captured by the minicam and beamed into televsion sets in the east are the principle reasons for the Eastern European revolution of 1989. They lack purchasing power in terms of hard currency to participate in accumulation of needed goods and services immediately, but this will change in time.

East Germany and Czechoslovakia have been the industrialized base in the east making and using sophisticated tools and machinery for years. If western companies are willing to modernize factories, they will find a great deal of plant capacity. The most promising opportunities, as the decade of the 1990s begins, appear to be in communications, transportation, logistics, and distribution networks. This includes trucks, storage facilities, and sophisticated shops. Chemicals, machine tools, and spare parts production are also emerging opportunities. They also need financial services of all kinds as well as business advice and marketing services, especially in exports. East European countries have traditionally exported only to the Soviet Union. They will need assistance in learning how to market exports to the west. Providing this knowledge may uncover endless commodities that have countertrade potential. These are real opportunities for the United States small- to medium-size business if willing to commit the manpower, education, and time.

PROBLEM AREAS

For over forty years, societies in Eastern Europe have existed and operated under the principles of Marxism. The state has been, and in some cases, remains the caretaker of production and property to include the minds and thoughts of its people. Communism operates on the military-duty board principle in which everyone is instructed in what to do, say, and believe. State decisions are made by the ruling communist party doctrine and followed by the people without question. Before the summer of 1989, those that questioned the state, such as writers or other vocal critics, were classified as dissidents and imprisoned or sent to so-called mental institutions for rehabilitation.

Who are the managers of the state-owned enterprises that have failed to provide life's basic needs for Eastern European societies? What management skills have evolved? Where are the Lee Iacocca's, Henry Ford's, or Ross Perot types that will need to emerge as free-market pioneers in this dramatic conversion of economic principles? What is the present system's understanding of entrepreneurship, private capital, and private property? The communist party faithful that have poorly managed the existing state enterprises using Marxist principles are themselves surrounded by multitudes of bureaucrats, in place for decades. To begin to develop the free economy in Eastern Europe, this infrastructure must be retrained or replaced. You can be certain, they will not readily submit to their own demise and changing of these leopard's spots will be extremely difficult. Training replacement personnel in free enterprise, profit-oriented industries will not happen overnight. Capital, patience, and staying power will be assets for western entrepreneurs.

BARRIERS WILL NEED TO BE OVERCOME

Along with political uncertainty in a revolutionary time, which can be overcome, there have been barriers to direct investment in Eastern Europe, especially in East Germany and Czechoslovakia, that must be dismantled or surmounted. East Germany, soon to be reunited with West Germany, will rapidly be opened to free-market investment. Barriers vary from nation to nation, and many difficulties remain for the overseas joint venture partner in Eastern Europe.

Communist legal systems ban or severely restrict property rights or private investment, restrict rather than protect capital and profits, and lack commercial laws giving investors inadequate recourse in contract disputes. Currencies such as Polish 'zlotys,' Hungarian 'forints,' Czechoslovakian 'korunas,' and East German 'marks' (a currency of the past) are virtually worthless outside of their borders. One bright spot is that Hungary and Poland let investors take their profits out of the country in hard currency and offer substantial tax holidays for inward investors.

INFRASTRUCTURE IS NEEDED

In Eastern Europe, the infrastructure is insufficient to support a free-market economy. In the west, phones are taken for granted. In the east, they are a luxury and in short supply. In East Germany, for example, phone applications are handed down from one generation to the next in wills. Only 17 percent of the households have telephones. Manufacturing facilities are outdated or dilapidated. In the Soviet Union, people often wait years for a new automobile. Under four decades of state-planned production and distribution, managers are unschooled as to marketing, sourcing, pricing, or even basic accounting principles. Even something as simple as a telephone book is nonexistent for all practical purposes.

TRAINING EAST EUROPEAN PERSONNEL

If you joint venture in Eastern Europe, you would be advised to train the host-country personnel in your plant in America. If you train Eastern European personnel in your United States plant facility, they can learn business skills and a greater appreciation of the free enterprise system from your personnel on the job. If you simply transfer the plant to Eastern Europe and train on location, your new employees will be denied the valuable experience of seeing free markets at work. A simple walk through a supermarket or grocery store in the United States furnishes proof of what free markets can achieve. This type of experience is an incentive for Eastern European workers to achieve.

SELLING CAPITALISM

The difference between west and east economic systems was made clear while conducting an engineering seminar through an interpreter in Romania in the 1960's. The subject of the seminar was how to drill for oil and gas using up-to-date technology to optimize efficiency and save time for maximum drilling economics. About halfway through the presentation, the light dawned. The audience was accustomed to democratic-socialism idealogy that ignores costs and promotes inefficiency. Saving days of drilling time to reduce the overall costs of the well was of no interest to this group of engineers. They viewed efficiency and productive technology as a threat to job security. More days and months of operating time adds more days and months of employment. The audience, raised in state-subsidized industries, was not tuned in to free-market economics. This attitude has been ingrained in state-run enterprises in Eastern Europe for over forty-one years.

OVERCOMING PARTY FAVORS

Party favors have traditionally been handed out to the party faithful. This is ingrained in the system of communist party control. It is well known that the hierarchy of management of state enterprises usurp state resources. The discoveries of the material excesses of Erich Honecker in East Germany in the fall of 1989 illustrates this point. The system may be communist in ideology, but party leaders in socialist or communist regimes have been known to enjoy wealth at the expense of the state on a scale that would make some western industrialists envious. This will not be easily overcome as new, free-market competitive business philosophies are developed for implementation of new reforms.

THE BEGINNING OF CHANGE

In December of 1989, the new Polish government began to implement broad steps to move from a state-owned and regulated economy to the free-market system. State subsidies to enterprises, which have been the backbone of the communist system, will be withdrawn. Industries will become profitable or go out of business. Wages will have to be frozen. High inflation and unemployment as nonprofitable businesses close during the transition must be tolerated if Poland is to achieve IMF recognition for internationalizing its currency, which could take two to six years. Foreign investors will have to be patient before profits can be repatriated. The transition period will take time and hardships will abate slowly. At least, in a free-market economy as opposed to state repression, there should be a light, not an oncoming train, at the end of the tunnel.

It is this type of dedication and sweeping reform that will be necessary to attract the investor from the west. Eastern Europe is very open but they don't know how to produce with quality. In a typical joint venture, the eastern partner would put in the location, labor, and know-how in their system, and the western partner puts in technology and management skills. Despite many obstacles, yet unknown, Eastern Europe represents a great long-term promise for American firms. The market is large. The pent-up desire for goods is obvious. The new, dynamic moves of Eastern Europeans toward economic and political freedom is an exciting time in our world. Conversion from wartime to consumer goods production is a welcome turning point in history in the United States after forty years of the Cold War. These political moves and peace initiatives that began in the 1980s open new markets and opportunities for the small- to medium-size business.

There will be more opportunities for the American entrepreneur in the new, global borderless economy in the next ten years than in the previous ninety years. The SAM strategy leading into partnering or joint venturing must be employed to optimize these opportunities in this new world order. Ethnic and culture requirements of trading partners must be considered and respected in the transfer of goods and services. This will include contributions by all parties to the transaction of specified labor, natural resources, services, or management skills. Polish consumer goods must have Polish content. United States technology and management skills must be compensated. The joint venture and licensing agreement is the principle vehicle for future development of economic partnerships between the East and the West.

SIX STORIES OF EASTERN EUROPE JOINT VENTURES

In the April/May 1990 issue of *The International Economy* magazine, six tales of caution and promise are illustrated by executives in medium-to-larger sized United States corporations. The article is prefaced by Webster's New World Dictionary definition of the word venture as:

ven • ture (ven′cher) *n.* {<ME. aventure: see adventure} **1.** a risky undertaking; esp., a business enterprise in which there is a danger of loss as well as a chance for profit. **2.** something on which a risk is taken. **3.** chance; fortune: now only in at a venture, by mere chance —*vt.* **-tured, -tur • ing 1.** to risk; hazard **2.** to take the risk of; brave **3.** to express (an opinion, etc.) at the risk of being criticized, etc. —*vi.* to do or go at some risk —**ven′tur • er** *n.*

This is an accurate term for United States businesses who move in and take advantage of the new opportunities created by the dramatic changes in the Soviet Union and Eastern Europe. Here are some first hand accounts of such venturing abroad.

Mathew E. Gilfix, Director, Strategy & Business Development, Honeywell Inc., Minneapolis, Minnesota:

"The negotiating process in the East Bloc offers a whole range of challenges beyond the norm. Think of your counterparts as European—they feel very strongly about that. Keep in mind that at least one version of what you consider comprehensive legal agreements is written in a Slavic language—with no definite articles. Carefully define and balance the potential business risks and benefits. If possible, control the investment on a step-by-step basis.

"Despite the excitement of East–West dealings, remember that this is a business, not a cultural exchange program. Address all important issues during initial negotiations including operating principles and policies, performance measurement, management selection and compensation, limitation of risk and liability, protection of technology and know-how, and resolution of disputes.

"Finally, think of contracts as prenuptial agreements. When everything is going well, they are irrelevant. When there are problems, be realistic, patient, and don't take anything for granted.

"It is with pride that we, at Honeywell, now look back upon being branded as 'naive, romantic capitalists' for suggesting a government hearing that opening East–West trade channels would possibly contribute to world peace.

"At this point, the entire East Bloc represents a small percentage of Honeywell's European business; however, what is important is its strategic role in the longer-term framework we need to sustain, despite the current Wall Street pressure on short-term performance. These emerging East European markets represent an important and profitable building block in a potentially unified Europe."

Charles E. Hugel, Chairman, Asea Brown Boveri, Inc., Stamford, Connecticut:

"For a joint venture to succeed in the Soviet Union, both partners have to recognize that they have very different objectives. Western companies want to boost local sales for their products and services while the Soviets are determined that joint ventures export enough to at least be self-sufficient in hard-currency. So while we focus on selling locally and eventually repatriating profits, the Soviets are trying to safeguard their hard-currency reserves. This conflict dominates every discussion and negotiation between Western firms and the Soviets. And, although capitalism may be new to the Soviets, negotiation is not. In fact, marathon negotiating is the rule. One must be prepared to invest a great deal of time and expense in the project before its actual formation.

"Western firms can accommodate the differing objectives of the two parties by avoiding short financial horizons. This is particularly true for United States firms which are well known for their emphasis on quick returns. The Soviets now face a long period of trial and error as they try to establish appropriate organizational structures and lines of authority. The Soviets also need to improve their infrastructure. Their communications systems, whether telephone, fax, or mail, are woefully inadequate. They also need to build more roads, airports, office buildings, residential apartments, resort areas—in fact, more of just about everything in the civil sector. Strengthening this sector would benefit the Soviet people.

"The Soviets do understand the problem. Their difficulty is how to go about overhauling an infrastructure that is 20 to 30 years out of date. But I believe these barriers will be overcome. Given more time and experience with Western business practices such as contract negotiation, cost accounting, market pricing, the Soviets will learn the rules of the game. Their next step will be to play the game and play to win for the benefit of their own society and for the Western companies that help them."

Michelle Siren, Manager, East European Services Group, Price Waterhouse, London:

"As many Western businessmen have discovered, negotiating joint ventures in the Soviet Union, as well as in Eastern Europe, is neither for the faint heart nor shallow of pocket. This is partially attributable to matters beyond anyone's control. Consistency is a major problem. One *Fortune* 500 United States company has not only made its introductory presentation to as many different Soviet officials as it has had negotiating sessions over the last three years, but it has seen entire Soviet ministries come and go during this period. Of course, any progress made at one negotiating session was inevitably lost waiting for the next session.

"Western assumptions create a different set of problems. One major manufacturer of foodstuffs wanted to produce cereal for local consumption in an out-lying republic. Substantial sums of money and time were spent investigating the source and quality of manufacturing inputs needed to produce a product that would satisfy company standards. Everything went relatively smoothly until the Soviet partner learned that his Western partner intended that their product be consumed with milk. Supplies of fresh milk being rare in this particular republic, the joint venture suddenly found itself without a market.

"Other companies have been astonished by the extent to which all levels of government get involved in the process of negotiating these ventures, right down to the local councils who have demanded that the Western partners provide social support to the community by building schools, sports centers, and even sidewalks in some cases. Money for these activities are set aside in operational funds established for the joint venture, which are not always as optional as they sound. Sometimes the concept of 'special funds' with dedicated purposes is too foreign for a company that is accustomed to 'retained earnings' and 'profit.'

"A matter not to be overlooked is that the Soviets are not in a hurry to sell the family silver to the West, no matter how impatient they may appear. Apart from all else, Soviets like to negotiate and are to be respected as masters of the game."

Edward Cohen, Co-Director, Tabard Farm, Washington, DC:

"Kartoshka Trust, the joint venture between the Russian farm cooperative, Zybino, and Tabard Farm, the United States partner, has been formed to establish a farm-based food processing facility, the first product of which will be kettle-cooked potato chips.

"Zybino, both a dairy-cattle breeding station and potato farm, is about 130 kilometers south of Moscow in the Tula Region. With about 1000 inhabitants, the cooperative has renegotiated its status with the Soviet government to both permit the farm to do business on the open economy and make joint ventures with foreign concerns.

"While the government produces a variety of potato chips in one of its factories, the Soviet Union does not have any product similar to that produced by Tabard Farm. Considering the abundance of potatoes and sunflower oil in the Soviet Union, it seems logical to both parties to use these resources for the mass market consumption demands paid in rubles and also hard-currency markets.

"Negotiations are continuing between Zybino and Tabard Farm, and more developments are expected in the next few months. Critical areas include lack of Soviet experience in commerce and sales and a lack of packaging potential."

Clifton W. Clarke, Manager, International Trade and Policy, Digital Equipment Corporation, Maynard, Massachusetts:

"In January of 1989, a task force of Digital senior managers traveled to the capital cities of Budapest, Prague, and Warsaw. Our objective was to appraise conditions in these markets. Hungary emerged as the prime candidate for our first direct involvement in Eastern Europe; two prominent local partners worked with us in a joint venture to sell and service Digital products in Hungary.

"Perhaps the greatest challenge in Hungary—and throughout Eastern Europe—is managing risk and uncertainty of change. Most managements dealing internationally have developed the skills and expertise needed to function within the limits of a market economy. In Hungary, however, the atmosphere is very different. Hungary today is neither fish nor fowl, and the task is to develop a plan that assumes what conditions will be over a period of time. In light of the interplay of social, economic, and political change in Hungary, one must take the long view, yet be attentive to risk in the short term.

"Being aware of the style and conditioning of management that took place in Hungary over the past 45 years—to be sensitive to the difference in orientation of those with whom you are dealing—is also important. Attitudes formed within a centrally planned system will change slowly over time. Though eager to change, these people need to learn how to be entrepreneurial. I have been most impressed by the consistency of the course followed by various ministries of the Hungarian government. In light of the political ebb and flow throughout our negotiations, as even now, they have been able to stay the course and reach out to western companies to bring in capital and technology in a stable manner. I also came to respect the shared vision of the Hungarian people, both in and out of government. While reforms and change grind on, there is a common desire for a market-oriented economy and a reorientation towards the West that supersedes difficulties."

Thurston Sails, Inc., Bristol, Rhode Island:

One company that manufactures a product not usually associated with the Soviet Union is already established there. Thurston Sails, Inc. of Bristol, RI, with the help of Eric Fisher, head of American Partners, signed a joint venture agreement with a cooperative in Odessa, Aquamarine, formed "Aquatron" to produce high-quality boat sails.

Almost immediately, problems arose. The cooperative had difficulty obtaining a bank guarantee which was required before Thurston Sails would ship any of the equipment that was needed. To facilitate the granting of the guarantee, a local branch of Zhilsotsbank became a partner. And to ensure a reliable location for the manufacturing facility, the Children's Sport School of Odessa was invited into the joint venture.

Getting the necessary goods into the Soviet Union also proved to be problematic. Fisher, calling the delays "inexcusable," said that $30,000 worth of modern sewing machines, the Dacron and the state-of-the-art computer plotter were held up by customs from several days to up to three weeks.

The other major problem was the lack of raw materials and sail cloth, in particular. "The goods they have been working with are just garbage," said Steve Thurston, president of Thurston Sails, Inc. As such, all the Dacron has to be imported, costing the venture approximately 120 rubles ($187) per square meter. With this high price, the venture cannot sell the finished product for the low prices expected in a state-subsidized economy.

With all the difficulties experienced, Thurston is still positive about his commitment to the venture. He found the work force extremely competent and hard working, saying that "the quality of the sails they make will be up to Western standards within six months." In the end, Thurston and Fisher believe the potential rewards are great. "Right now we are the only game in town," Thurston said. "Other companies in other cities are looking at our venture to see how it flies. The whole thing has the possibility of mushrooming." Then again, he went on to say, "If Russia decides to close the doors, we're screwed."

THE SEED ACT OF 1989

The Support for East European Democracy (SEED) Act of 1989 (H.R.) 3402 was passed by Congress on November 17 and signed by the president on November 28, 1989. The act authorizes United States 240 million to support the Polish-American Enterprise fund, of which United States $45 million has been appropriated for FY–1990. (The Act also establishes a similar Hungarian—American Enterprise Fund. It is anticipated that Funds for other reforming Eastern European countries will occur as events continue to unfold in Eastern Europe in the 1990s). Title II, Section 201 of the act defines the purposes of the Enterprise funds for Poland and Hungary as to promote:

(1) development of the Polish and Hungarian private sectors, including small businesses, the agricultural sector, and joint ventures with United States and host country participants, and

(2) policies and practices conducive to private sector development in Poland and Hungary, through loans, grants, equity investments, feasibility studies, technical assistance, training, insurance, guarantees, and other measures.

The Polish–American Enterprise Fund will be established by the Agency for International Development (AID), which plans to set it up as a nongovernmental organization directed by a private board of directors. AID expects to establish the fund by early February of 1990, and have it ready to accept applications for projects by March of 1990. Further details of the fund can be obtained from:

OFFICE OF PRIVATE SECTOR DEVELOPMENT
Asia and Near East Bureau
Room 6443
Agency for International Development
320 21st Street NW
Washington, DC 20523
(202) 647–3759

Another good source of information regarding creation of Polish–American joint ventures would be the Polish–United States Economic Council. It is administered by the United States Chamber of Commerce and the Polish Chamber of International Trade. Information on available assistance from the Chamber of Commerce can be obtained from:

DIRECTOR, EAST-WEST TRADE
International Division
United States Chamber of Commerce
1615 H Street, NW
Washington, DC 20062
Tel. (202) 463–5482
Fax: (202) 463–3114
Telex: RCA 248302 CCUS UR

COMMENTS ON EASTERN EUROPE

Mr. Zbigniew Brezezinski, one of the first experts to accurately forecast the dramatic changes in Europe, from his article entitled, "Galloping Past Conventional Wisdom," in the April/May 1990 issue of *The International Economy* comments as follows:

On Eastern Europe: "Poland is the catalyst and spearhead. It is the only country right now which is simultaneously implementing the institutionalization of comprehensive political reforms and of a massive, ambitious, risky, time-urgent effort to move toward a free market economy."

On the Soviet Union: "The Soviet Union is going to be confronted by prolonged crisis which I would not define as transition but rather as an historic crisis. [It] is what I call prolonged democratizing chaos."

On Opportunities for the United States: "I am quite surprised by how relatively slowly United States business is to pick up on this opportunity. I think this opportunity in some ways is comparable to what international business faced 20 years ago in Spain and Portugal."

On Gorbachev: "Is he a good guy or bad guy? He has dismantled the Soviet Empire, he has destroyed Soviet creditability as a great power, he has unleashed democratizing forces that are generating more paralyzing conflict in the Soviet Union, and he has placed on the agenda the possible dissolution of the Soviet Union, all in the name of an objective that we approve of, namely democratization. That is not a bad record."

TRADE WITH THE SOVIETS

President Mikhail Gorbachev, of the Soviet Union, in a speech recently delivered to a group of businessmen in San Francisco encouraged them to immediately take advantage of the economic development opportunities in his country. He further stressed that companies that act now will find greater opportunity than those that follow when risk is greatly reduced. Knowledgeable international marketeers generally agree that opening trade options with the Soviet Union should focus on four primary activities as follows:

- First, and the most difficult at present due to the softness of Soviet currency in western markets, is the direct sale of products and services into the Soviet Union in exchange for hard currency.

- The second, and the most publicized, is th form a joint venture with Soviet partners for the production of commodities and services with these primary objectives; firstly, to export product to generate hard currency, and secondly, to sell into the local economy for domestic consumption. Current joint venture law requires the overseas partner to recover his initial investment and future distribution of earnings from the hard currency proceeds derived through exports.

- The third method of trade or market entry calls for a direct United States dollar investment in the Soviet Union in anticipation of developing strong market share that produces substantial earnings in rubles. The hedge is in the expectation that the ruble will eventually be convertible for hard currency to permit return on the initial investment and provide for repatriation of future earnings.

• The fourth method, frequently criticized as being too complex an undertaking except for major industrial marketeers, is countertrade. This involves quid-pro-quo or the exchange of something of value for something else of value that can then be sold in global markets for hard currency.

It was possible to recently visit in the Soviet Union as a guest of two research institutes manufacturing products for Soviet Industrial consumption in a specific market nitch. They were concerned with how to market their technology, products, and services in the new global economy. The free-market concept being introduced in the Soviet Union will require these types of government entities to fund their own destiny with hard currency, which at present, can only be generated from sales into world markets. It suddenly became apparent that an opportunity and a fifth method to trade with the Soviet Union may be readily available to the small international entrepreneur. Such a method would involve two distinct, but necessary steps as follows:

1. First, you would identify products produced by Soviet industry that would be saleable in international markets for hard currency. This would involve entrepreneural instinct and in-depth research. The task is to locate a product and/or service that meets world market standards of quality, performance, reliability, service and is price competitive.

If you are satisfied with your discovery, negotiate and sign a letter of intent (or Protocol) with the appropriate authority with principles of agreement that can become the basis of an exclusive manufacturer's representative contract to sell the product or service in selected world markets. We were able to reach agreement and sign exclusive contracts on the second visit in the Soviet Union.

Write an international business and marketing plan that can be used as the guideline to determine if you can sell these products and/or services in global markets. You need to target countries that have hard currency and determine the amount of product testing required to establish free market credibility and acceptance. Establish a credit and inventory policy that will be flexible enough for initial market entry. The task in this first step will be to develop a network of indigenous representatives and/or distributors in countries that you have targeted for sales of Soviet product for hard currency. This network establishment may also involve strategic alliances to improve market share. Once the marketing plan is complete, work from the initial protocol to negotiate a formal manufacturer's representative contract for the territories that are mutually agreed.

2. After you have established a network that is producing foreign exchange from sales of exported Soviet product, your new task is to reverse roles and become a manufacturer's representative for companies in the United States that desire to market into the Soviet Union in exchange for hard currency. Selling much needed commodities and services provides for internal economic devel-

opment in the Soviet Union and will contribute to the satisfaction of their growing appetite for western consumer goods produced in free markets.

In the new, global borderless economy, country of origin becomes far less important than availability, price, quality, service, and performance in a consumer democracy. Toyotas are purchased more for these attributes than for their origin. Often, joint venture negotiations become difficult when overseas partners are more concerned with expansion into Soviet markets than in exports for foreign exchange. This proposed opportunity for the small entrepreneur is focused on achieving first things first and in understanding the Soviet perception of their priorities.

This proposed method of trade with the Soviets is based on free-market principles. Seminars were conducted on this trip to explain international business development from the free market vantage point. These sessions were useful in promoting a mutual understanding of how Soviet products could be marketed in the global markets including discussions about commercial considerations required in an effective manufacturer's representative contract. Their questions about sales commissions, profits, gross, net, and revenue sharing schemes are intelligent and reflect a strong desire to learn about the free market and selling overseas from practical considerations.

This fifth proposal is countertrade, but with a marked difference in procedure. The first step is to locate product that can be exported. Protocols evidence the beginning of formal agreements. Export sales are concluded by the marketing network for hard currency. Representing Western firms who desire to sell in the Soviet Union can be more easily accomplished when hard currency is accessible.

It is obvious in the PepsiCo example known to most international traders that their transaction was profitable due to quid-pro-quo. The PepsiCo approach was to exchange their proprietary product for specific Soviet products deemed to be saleable for hard currency. This fifth proposal suggests the exchange of Soviet product for discretionary hard currency income that may be used for purchases of products the Soviet Union requires from Western markets.

Your charge, if you accept the challenge to trade with the Soviet Union, should begin by making friends on arrival, establishing relationships, recognizing opportunities, accommodating perceptions, addressing the vital needs of both parties, yes, making toasts at dinner to the achievements of the day. You conclude each visit with a formal signing of a protocol. Finally, when you arrive at a mutual agreement, contracts are formally signed. This method of trade with the Soviets underscores the value of a selling technique used in venturing abroad that first recognizes the principal need of your client, and with enthusiasm provides the commodity or service to satisfy that need. This trading opportunity, recognizes the fundamental need in the Soviet Union for foreign exchange.

Pricing for the Free Market—Enen Strategy

The most perplexing problem in the Soviet Union is how to accurately determine product costs while making the transition to a free market economy. The Soviet Union is undergoing economic reforms under the policy of Perestroika. These reforms will someday lead to entry of the Soviet Union into GATT and the IMF and the ruble will be freely exchanged in global markets. Until such time as a free monetary policy is adopted, economic reform will cause difficulty in establishing meaningful exchange rates between the Soviet ruble and global hard currencies.

The area of most concern with exchange rates for Soviet enterprises is in the competitive pricing of Soviet goods for exports into the world economy. We recently felt there was an opportunity to pioneer an international marketing strategy that allows reform to a free market economy by permitting Soviet goods to be competitively priced while the government deals with the exchange rate over the next few years.

At the heart of the free market is the consumer's choice. The price of anything in free markets is what someone will pay. In short, the market determines the price. The two powerful forces at work in the free market economy are the consumer and the competitor. Consideration of both aspects of the free market economy must be at the forefront of all global marketing decisions.

The problem for our venture is to create substantial sales of Soviet products in the global marketplace to generate hard currency. Initially, this venture must have certain advantages over and above the competition that include product availability (inventory), favorable pricing, some credit, and field service equal to that of the competition. We proposed that our Soviet associates consider the following points:

1. The Soviet Union is in a period of economic reform and conversion to a free market economy.

2. Soviet exchange rates are dynamic and cause serious problems for Soviet enterprises in pricing competitively for free world markets.

3. A creative, new bold solution is required to address this problem during the transition to a free market economy.

4. The Soviet enterprises that solve these difficult transitional problems will play a major role in the reform of the Soviet economy.

A Possible Solution

Rather than be burdened in the initial phases of market entry with exchange rates and pricing fluctuations, our venture will abide by the rules of the free market. The boldness of this proposal is in letting the market determine the price rather than trying to work through the exchange rate problems as they currently exist. At some future date, when the Soviet ruble is freely exchangeable in world markets, the venture could revert back to manufactured cost. At present, however, the task to generate hard currency and introduce reform is most urgent. Urgent matters call for bold and innovative steps. Here is the solution:

1. The venture determines market prices, which clearly indicate what the consumer will pay for product.

2. These prices are used as a guideline for offering Soviet products in world markets. Initially, Soviet prices may have to be somewhat lower than market price "to open and enter" a new market.

3. The sales commission, if any, paid to manufacturers' representatives, is deducted from the sales price of the product.

4. The remainder, in hard currency, would be distributed by a mutually agreed formula to reimburse manufacturing and marketing costs.

5. The comfort factor, audit or control of pricing, is ensured by up-to-date world pricing information as published by competitors in a given industry.

The adoption of such a policy to provide for the transition into a free market economy is courageous for the Soviet partner. It requires the discarding of the idea of starting from manufactured costs in rubles and working through the government's exchange rates. It favors early free market entry to earn hard currency through a competitive global marketing strategy and a workable sales pricing policy.

14

The 1990s Challenge

AFTER WORLD WAR II, THE UNITED STATES WAS THE DOMINANT PRODUCER OF GOODS and services in the world. American manufacturers assumed that the world would unquestionably consume what we as a nation produced. If products or services were acceptable in the United States then certainly they could be marketed overseas. In the 1950s and 1960s, the Yankee Trader earned the title Ugly American in international markets. We acted as gladiators to the world, rather than as students in search of supplying global needs. While this reputation was being earned, the Japanese were researching world markets to determine what consumers needed and wanted to purchase in the way of goods and services. Also, during this same period, the quality of American goods dropped in comparison with Japanese and European standards.

In the late 1970s and 1980s, United States manufacturers corrected the quality problem, but past experiences were not easily forgiven by world consumers. In this same period, the trade deficit, added to a chronic budget deficit, increased the need for overseas borrowing and the United States converted from a creditor nation to the world's largest debtor nation. At the same time, considerable investment income flowed out of the United States, and income from overseas investments declined. Strengthening of manufacturing capability to ensure growth and expansion of America's economy is the 1990s challenge for smaller business. Opportunities in Eastern Europe, Europe 1992, the Middle East, Mexico, Canada, the Pacific Rim and other countries are virtually unlimited. United States technology and know-how is needed in developed and undeveloped countries to ensure growth of economic and political freedoms. Small-to medium-size businesses must explore these frontiers for market expansion if quality jobs are to be created in the United States as we approach the 21st century. The threat of nuclear war has subsided, but new and competitive commercial battles are yet to be fought. Joint venturing and sharing with overseas partners for mutual benefit should be America's international business development strategy for the 1990s.

CHANGES IN AMERICA ARE NEEDED TO ENHANCE COMPETITIVENESS

Competing in the globalized, borderless economy in this decade of the 1990s presents serious challenges to United States businesses. This is the age of information technologies and modern communication. Minds must be opened to new strategies required to compete in world markets. Old antiquated ideas and organization must be discarded in favor of changes that permit a more competitive effort.

LONG-TERM THINKING AND STRATEGY MUST PREVAIL

The focus on short-term profits in America permits global competitors to enter low-end markets. The Japanese used this strategy to introduce the Japanese automobile to United States markets. After consumer acceptance, margins were adjusted to compensate for market entry cost. The strategy was long-term and the net result in market share underscores the value of patience and planning in international trade. Our Wall Street mentality, in addition to focusing on quarterly profits, must be flexible enough to also provide capital for long-term planning and strategic marketing considerations, and for ample research and development investments to keep America ahead in frontier technology. When such advances occur, they must be transformed into commercial victories. There must be an organizational commitment from the top of the organization to adopt long-range objectives for overseas trade to recognize opportunity and nurture effective, profitable joint ventures.

GOVERNMENT MUST COOPERATE WITH INDUSTRY

Cooperation between government and industry in the United States is minimal and is thought by many to be adversarial. In Japan, there is a spirit of cooperation between industry and government which has contributed greatly to commercial expansion the past 40 years. The Tax Reform Act of 1986 stripped American investors of incentives and dried up much speculative capital in the United States previously reserved for entrepreneurs. The formidable Japanese competitor has the distinct advantage of low-cost capital when compared to his United States counterpart.

CONTROLLING GOVERNMENT COMPETITION FOR GROWTH CAPITAL

The savings and loan crisis of 1989 and ensuing federal regulations has resulted in drying up commercial venture capital loans from United States banks. If you combine this situation with liquidity shortages caused by competition for funds absorbed by the federal deficit, the United States government is actually competing with businesses for overseas market expansion capital. Tax policy in America also contributes to short-term thinking. Incentives must be restored if America is to maintain competitiveness. Innovative, sensible, low-cost, but effective government programs and tax benefits should be implemented by the United States Congress on Capitol Hill to encourage the small- to medium-size business to enter global markets.

NURTURE HUMAN RESOURCES

Neglect of human resources by failure to develop our intellectual assets is a serious problem in the United States. American universities are the envy of the world, but lower education in the United States is in disarray. Educational standards must be elevated and these new measurements of learning achievement must be universal. Teachers must be fairly and adequately compensated and respected for their contribution to education. The Japanese and Europeans are far ahead of the United States in this area. If we are to maintain American standards of living for our workers, education must be significantly improved for all United States labor in order for us to be competitive in the global village.

INITIATE SAM STRATEGY AND PARTNER TO WIN

The SAM, sale-assemble-manufacture, strategy should be employed as necessary to maintain or increase market share. If you are new to the global economy, you should learn international trading skills by initially selling overseas from your United States base of operations. If you are selling internationally now, you should consider assembly as the next logical step in your long-term business development strategy. If you are just beginning to export product, look for the opportunity to increase market share by introducing local content into your product before your are forced to make that decision through some regulation or policy change in the host country. The assembly operation usually follows joint venture formulation in the host country. Manufacturing should also be in your marketing strategy, keeping in mind that key components may be retained and made in your United States plant and shipped to the joint venture. Levels of technology transfer should be relegated to the sophistication and adsorption capability of the marketplace, and above all, be market driven.

THE FUTURE IS IN YOUR HANDS

The future of the economy of the United States of America rests on the shoulders of small- to medium-size businesses and their abilities to continue to recognize and capitalize on new and expanding opportunities in the global economy. A major strategy and opportunity to increase market share dramatically is the international joint venture with overseas trading partners for mutual benefit to include creating jobs and profits in both countries. If these words have awakened a new sense of opportunity and urgency for new marketing strategy for the 1990s, then it has been well worth the effort and time to produce. Hopefully, you will also benefit from the many personal experiences presented in this book.

The door has closed on the 1980s and a new decade emerges. Exciting and abundant opportunities exist for the smaller business, more now than at anytime in the history of America. Perestroika also exists in America in the 1990s; a time for rethinking and restructuring our approach to marketing in the new, borderless global economy. We have much to offer nations in need of assistance in developing their natural resources in free-market economies to improve their standard of living. In meeting their needs, a rare opportunity exists for United States companies to enjoy the benefits of increasing market share by venturing abroad. The entrepreneur who recognizes opportunity and acts in the 1990s will benefit in many different ways. These will include appreciation of equity participation in overseas enterprises, elevated earnings from higher levels of productivity in your domestic operation, job creation in both the host countries and the United States, new product development driven by meeting diversified needs in the global marketplace, and the personal satisfaction that in a time of tranquility among world powers you are contributing to the permanent world peace through global partnering and international commerce.

America is very much in business, but sometimes it takes an event like Pearl Harbor to stir America's ability to compete and win. Many manufacturing jobs are being lost to Americans on an almost, unnoticeable slip-sliding, slow moving pace. Everyday there are additional announcements made about layoffs. As defense spending is futher reduced, and the cry for entitlement spending increases, more jobs will be lost unless we, as a nation, respond to the global challenge. Foreign competition is fierce. The backbone of America's economy, the small- to medium-size business, must venture abroad in the 1990s to be competitive. The 1980s were seen as the decade of self-indulgence and self-gratification.

Many Americans assume that high standards of living, social programs, wealth, and industrialized nation status is a birth right. Historically, that may have been somewhat true. Today, America's wealth and status as a world power must be earned on a very competitive international playing field. This new and final decade of the 20th century must be the decade of partnering to win. The

Getty philosophy for risk taking in oilwell drilling must now be applied to business strategy for entering expanding international markets. Enter into partnerships abroad for market retention and/or expansion. Establish joint ventures overseas to vastly improve market share and thereby stimulate activity and growth of your United States based manufacturing. This strategy, international business expansion via joint ventures, will create multitudes of jobs at home and ensure a rising standard of living for all Americans for generations to follow.

Appendix A

Sample Sales Representation and Distributorship Contract

August 4, 1990

XYZ Corporation, Inc.
25 Business Expansion Avenue
Good News, USA

Distributors (PTE), Ltd.
Seaside Drive
Singapore

SALES REPRESENTATION AND DISTRIBUTION AGREEMENT

Gentlemen:

This letter, when signed by you and returned to us, shall constitute the Agreement between us governing your appointment as our Exclusive Sales Representative and Stocking Distributor in Singapore, Malaysia, Indonesia, and Brunie, which hereinafter shall be called the "Territory."

We appoint you our Exclusive Sales Representative and Distributor for the sale within the Territory of those products covered by this Agreement, subject to the terms and conditions set forth in this letter. By your signature, you accept the appointment and agree to all of the terms hereof.

1. The "Products" covered by this Agreement are all those products appearing in the catalog that is enclosed herewith and such catalogs as we shall send to you in the future and identify as being subject to the Agreement.

2. "Promotion of Sales." You agree to visit regularly with all prospective purchasers in the Territory, and to plan a program to establish and maintain an effective sales and distribution system. You also agree that during the term of this Agreement you will not act for any other principal, in any capacity, whose products compete with XYZ Corporation, Inc., unless previously agreed upon in writing.

3. "Authority to Purchase." You are authorized to purchase merchandise covered by this Agreement for your own account at prices and terms set forth in the price list 1990 in effect from time to time, a copy of our current price list being enclosed herewith. All orders for Products purchased by you are subject to acceptance or rejection by us at the above address.

4. "Purchase of Products." You will neither be entitled to, nor will you be paid any commission on sales we make to you as a distributor pursuant to the terms of Paragraph 3, above. Your remuneration in consideration for your purchases shall be reflected in your Exclusive Distributor's Discount.

5. "Authority to Sell." You are further authorized to solicit orders from commercial buyers (other than yourself) in your Territory for Products covered by this Agreement at prices and terms which at the time are in effect. All orders are subject to acceptance or rejection at the above address.

6. "Commissions." Will be paid on orders solicited by you accordingly to the terms of Paragraph 5 above for Products shipped by us during the term of this Agreement to purchasers in your Territory and accepted and paid for by the purchasers. The commission for such sales shall be the difference between the price list 1990 in effect at the time and the actual sales price set by you. Commissions due and payable will accrue to your account with us upon receipt of each purchase order from your Territory. Commissions will be paid to you immediately upon receipt of payment from the purchaser.

7. "Terms and Conditions." All sales to you shall be subject to the terms and conditions set forth on the price lists sent to you from time to time. All prices will be in effect at time of shipment and are subject to change at any time.

8. "Direct Inquiries." It is agreed that we shall advise you of all direct inquiries received by us from pruchasers in your Territory and consult with you on the pricing of each inquiry to establish your accrued commission should a sale be

consumated. If you are unavailable for consultation, pricing to accommodate a minimum commission rate of ten percent (10%) shall be quoted to purchasers in your Territory in each circumstance.

9. "Use of Catalogs and Advertising Material." It is understood that you will not use our catalogs or other written advertising material without our written consent.

10. "Expenses." It is understood that we shall not be responsible for any expenses that you may incur in the performance of this contract. It is also understood that you will not be responsible for any expenditures incurred by us in the performance of this contract.

11. "Trademarks." You bind yourself not to register, use, or permit the use in your name or by or on behalf of any person, company or firms of a trademark, trade dress, brands, labels, labeling, designs or other indicia of ownership resembling those which are used on goods sold by us or any of our suppliers, nor to associate the same directly or indirectly to any business with which you are associated or to any articles manufactured or distributed in any form whatsoever other than the Products. These obligations shall survive the termination or expiration of this Agreement.

12. "Independent Contractor." You shall be an independent contractor and shall not enter into or assume any obligations on our behalf, nor shall you make any guarantees, warranties, or representations of the Products on our behalf.

13. "Specific Performance." You shall send a written report of your organization's activity that you have performed in the Territory on our account on a monthly basis in written form. This report shall include market data, competitor sales, if any, volume of business that you have outstanding in quotations, probable result, new personnel changes in your organization or with purchasers, if any, and in general, the state of the market as it pertains to our business. In return, you will receive a monthly update on events occurring within our company that will have an effect on your market area, your potential sales, and specific inquiries from potential purchasers in your Territory. Also, we agree to visit your Territory with you on an annual basis as a minimum and more frequently as we determine is warranted by increasing business activity in the Territory.

14. "Terms of the Agreement." This Agreement, when signed by you and returned to us, shall become effective as of the date of this letter and shall remain effective for a period of time of one year, and shall be automatically renewed for similar periods of one year unless either party fails to perform under the terms of this Agreement, or either party, prior to 90 days of expiration, serves written

notice to the other party informing him of his desire not to renew the contract. If this Agreement is so terminated by either party the other party shall not be entitled to damages or compensation of any nature, regardless of any expenditures or loss of future profit incurred by either party. Also, in such case, you agree to return to us all samples, catalogs, price lists, and other material belonging to us, within 30 days.

15. "Inventory." Should this Agreement be terminated in accordance with Paragraph 14, we will repurchase all inventory at the actual price that you paid for the Product, but less any freight or handling costs incurred by you in obtaining the Product.

16. "Previous Agreements." This Agreement supercedes any and all previous Agreements between us and there are no understandings or Agreements relative to this contract not fully expressed herein. No changes shall be made in this contract except by written amendment signed by you and an authorized executive of XYZ Corporation, Inc.

17. "Applicable Law." The rights and duties of the parties to this Agreement shall be governed by the laws of the State of Delaware, United States of America.

It is our sincere hope that this letter clearly sets forth our mutual understanding, and we look forward to your acceptance by signing the attached copy and returning it to us.

Cordially yours,

By: _____
Director, International Marketing

Accepted and Agreed:
Company: _____
By: _____
Title: _____
Date: _____

Appendix B
A Guide to Contacts and Publications

GOVERNMENT

Agency for International Development (AID)
Washington, D.C. 20523–1414
202–647–1850

Publications
- *AID Importer List* (catalogs importers interested in bringing United States products to select AID-recipient countries). Free.
- *Export Opportunities with the Agency for International Development.* Free.
- *Facts about AID* (describes AID's foreign aid program). Free.

UNITED STATES DEPARTMENT OF COMMERCE
Publications Room 1617-D
Washington, D.C. 20230
202–377–5494

Publications
- *Market Share Reports* (statistics on foreign import demand from National Technical Information Service), $11 (call 703–487–4600).
- *How to Get the Most From Overseas Exhibitions* (offers guidelines and procedures). Free.

U.S. & FOREIGN COMMERCIAL SERVICE, INTERNATIONAL TRADE
ADMINISTRATION
Room H2116
Department of Commerce
Washington, D.C. 20230
800–343–4300, Operator 940

Publications

- *US&FCS Counseling Kit* (contains information on Matchmaker trade missions, commercial news, catalog and video catalog exhibitions). Free. Available from your district office.
- Catalog exhibition program is a way to test international markets. United States exporters give the US&FCS information on their companies and US&FCS takes it around to 10 to 15 markets in a given region. US&FCS brings business leads back to United States exporters. Cost: $150–$250.

EXPORT-IMPORT BANK OF THE UNITED STATES
811 Vermont Avenue, N.W.
Washington, D.C. 20571
202–566–8990
Toll-free: 800–424–5201

OVERSEAS PRIVATE INVESTMENT CORPORATION
1615 M Street, N.W.
Washington, D.C. 20527
202–457–7010
Toll-free: 800–424–6742

Publications

- *OPIC Programs for Contractors and Exporters* (lists programs for United States companies doing business in developing countries).

U.S. SMALL BUSINESS ADMINISTRATION
Office of International Trade
1441 L Street, N.W., Suite 501A
Washington, D.C. 20416
202–653–7794

Publications

- *International Trade Assistance SBA Fact Sheet No. 42* (information on SBA's programs for the small business exporter). Free.
- *The Exporter's Guide to Federal Resources for Small Business,* $4.50.
- *The World is Your Market.* Free. Call local SBA district office for copy.

U.S. GOVERNMENT PRINTING
Superintendent of Documents
Washington, D.C. 20402
202–783–3238

Publications

- *A Basic Guide To Exporting*, $8.50.
- *Business America* magazine (lists upcoming international trade shows, articles on exporting). $49 annually.
- *Commerce Business Daily* (lists government procurement opportunities). $261 annually.
- *EC 1992: Growth Markets, Export Opportunities in Europe*, $4.75.

U.S. DEPARTMENT OF AGRICULTURE
Information Division, Room 5920 South Building
Foreign Agricultural Service
Washington, D.C. 20250–1000
202–447–7937

Publications

- *AgExporter* (a monthly magazine), $11 annually.
- *Electronic Reports* (on-line service includes foreign trade opportunities available through the USDA's CID systems), $75 monthly minimum, $12 hour connect charge, 95 cents per 100 lines of information. Call: 202–447–5505
- *U.S. Export Sales.* Free.
- *How to Get Information on U.S. Agricultural Trade.* Free.

ASSOCIATIONS

AMERICAN ASSOCIATION OF EXPORTERS & IMPORTERS
11 W. 42nd Street, 30th Floor
New York, N.Y. 10036
212–944–2230

Publications
Telephone or write for Listing

CHAMBER OF COMMERCE OF THE UNITED STATES
Publications Fulfillment
1615 H Street, N.W.
Washington, D.C. 20062
202–659–6000

Publications
- *Small Business Resource Guide* (a comprehensive guide to government agencies, trade associations and private organizations). $4.95 includes postage.
- *How to Expand Your Market Through Exporting, pub. No. 2004.* Free.

THE SMALL BUSINESS FOUNDATION OF AMERICA
20 Park Plaza, Suite 438
Boston, Mass. 02116
617–350–5096

Publications
- *Exportise* (a how-to guide to exporting for small business owners). $49.50.

PERIODICALS

- *Computerworld* (weekly magazine published in more than 40 countries for computer professionals).

P.O. Box 2044
Marion, Ohio 43306
800–669–1002
Annual subscription: $48

- *Export Today* (9 issue magazine offering practical advice, specific export questions answered by experts).

733 15th St. NW, Suite 1100
Washington, D.C. 20005
202–737–1060
Introductory subscription: $49

- *The Exporter* (monthly magazine dealing with distribution, finance, systems and regulatory problems for exporters).

6 West 37th Street
New York, N.Y. 10018
212–563–2772, fax 212–563–2798
Annual subscription: $144

- *Global Trade* (monthly follows news on international transportation, finance, and commercial services).

NORTH AMERICAN PUBLISHING
410 North Broad Street
Philadelphia, Penn. 19108
215–238–5300
Annual subscription: $45

- *International Trade Reporter—Current Records* (weekly newsletter on trade, changing regulations, import/export expansion opportunities and tariffs).

BUREAU OF NATIONAL AFFAIRS
9435 Key West Avenue
Rockdale, MD 20850
Toll-free: 800–372–1033
301–258–1033
Annual subscription: $768

- *Venture Japan* (quarterly journal focuses on helping United States firms do business with Japan).

ASIA PACIFIC COMMUNICATIONS
7 Park Avenue, Suite 5G
New York, N.Y. 10016
212–447–1267
Introductory subscription: $54

References

1. Axell, Roger E.: *Do's and Taboos Around the World.* Compiled by the Parker Pen Company, New York: John Wiley & Sons, Inc., 1986; 109, 157.

2. MacLaren, Terrence F.: *Eckstrom's Licensing in Foreign and Domestic Operations.* New York: Clark Boardman Company, Ltd., 1989; Sec. 1.03 [2]: 1–10, 11.

3. Ibid, Sec. 2.03 [2], 2–7, 8.

4. Ibid, Sec. 4.01 [4], 4–24, 25.

5. Ibid, Sec. 4.02 [1], 4–33.

Index